"At last! Enlightenment about entr___
and not just what it is, but also w___
—ELISA MORGAN, *president emer___*

Cleaning
House

A MOM'S 12-MONTH EXPERIMENT
to Rid Her Hom___
YOUTH E___

Kay Wills Wyma

Foreword by Michael Gurian

Praise for
Cleaning House

"At last! Enlightenment about entitlement in our kids—and not just what it is, but also what to *do* about it."

> —ELISA MORGAN, author of *She Did What She Could,* president
> emerita of MOPS International, and publisher of *FullFill*

"Parents, take note: Kay Wills Wyma's experiment could change your life, especially if your kids suffer from 'me first!' syndrome. If you want your children to be more responsible, more self-assured, and more empathetic, *Cleaning House* is for you."

> —JIM DALY, president of Focus on the Family

"*Cleaning House* is both a beautifully told story and a practical guide to parenting in today's complex world."

> —MICHAEL GURIAN, best-selling author of *The Wonder of Boys*
> and *The Wonder of Girls*

"*Cleaning House* will be one of the most influential parenting books of our generation. When it comes to directing parents how to raise fabulous kids, Kay Wills Wyma nails it."

> —MEG MEEKER, MD, author of the national bestseller
> *Strong Fathers, Strong Daughters*

"*Cleaning House* offers the perfect solution for parents who want to free their children from the entitlement trap. Hilarious stories, amazing creativity, and a huge dose of grace make this book difficult to put down! Kay Wills Wyma paves the way and offers tools to help our families experience the satisfaction and confidence that comes through meaningful work."

> —SANDRA STANLEY, North Point Ministries

"In *Cleaning House,* Kay Wills Wyma has crafted a book that hits home on many levels. It's a case study for any parent who wants to change the entitlement culture among their kids. But at a deeper level, it hits each of us who long to live our daily lives in a way that pleases God."

> —RONALD L. HARRIS, senior vice president of the National
> Religious Broadcasters

"Here's a book designed to help parents get their kids a one-way ticket to reality about responsibility, but it would be great to get voters to read it and apply these simple but brilliant principles to members of Congress!"

—Mike Huckabee, former Arkansas governor and host
of Fox TV's *Huckabee* and radio's *Mike Huckabee Show*

"*Cleaning House* delivers practical advice, helpful encouragement, and laugh-out-loud moments for weary parents who want to lovingly change the hearts and future of their overly indulged children."

—Chuck Bentley, CEO of Crown Financial Ministries
and author of *The Root of Riches*

"For parents who are weary of the Me generation, [this book] provides a practical roadmap...to bring your children from entitlement to empowerment.... As a parent, grandparent, and school principal, I believe this book will become a favorite of parents and one they will reference frequently."

—Jody Capehart, co-author of *Bonding with Your Teens
Through Boundaries*

"In an age of youth entitlement, this is a must-read for moms who desire to raise godly kids with servant hearts!"

—Joe White, president of Kanakuk Kamps

"This book inspires hope, despair, and then more hope: hope that we *can* get our kids to do more chores, then despair that no, maybe only Kay can do it (she had a book contract!), then hope again—because Kay shows us, step by baby step, how to make it happen, in the real world, with real kids."

—Lenore Skenazy, author of the book and blog *Free-Range Kids*

"With unique creativity and wry humor, this sensible, determined mom herds her five distinctly different offspring into an acute lifestyle change; namely, learning to master the inevitable demands of life.... With 'a spoonful of sugar,' *Cleaning House* cools the dangerous 'me first' fever weakening our American culture."

—Dr. Howard G. Hendricks, distinguished professor emeritus of
leadership and Christian education, Dallas Theological Seminary,
and Jeanne Hendricks, speaker and author of *A Mother's Legacy*

Cleaning House

A Mom's 12-Month Experiment
to Rid Her Home of
Youth Entitlement

Kay Wills Wyma

Foreword by Michael Gurian

WaterBrook
Press

CLEANING HOUSE
PUBLISHED BY WATERBROOK PRESS
12265 Oracle Boulevard, Suite 200
Colorado Springs, Colorado 80921

Details in some anecdotes and stories have been changed to protect the identities of the persons
involved.

ISBN 978-0-307-73067-1
ISBN 978-0-307-73068-8 (electronic)

Cover design by Kristopher K. Orr; photography by Joel Strayer

Library of Congress Cataloging-in-Publication Data
Wyma, Kay Wills.
  Cleaning house : a mom's twelve-month experiment to rid her home of youth entitlement /
Kay Wills Wyma. — 1st ed.
      p. cm.
  Includes bibliographical references.
    ISBN 978-0-307-73067-1 — ISBN 978-0-307-73068-8 (electronic)
  1. Child rearing. 2. Parenting. 3. Pampered child syndrome. 4. Entitlement attitudes.
5. Responsibility in children. 6. Chores. I. Title.
  HQ769.W955 2012|
  649'.1—dc23

                                        2012002034

Printed in the United States of America
2012

10 9 8 7 6 5

SPECIAL SALES
Most WaterBrook Multnomah books are available at special quantity discounts when purchased
in bulk by corporations, organizations, and special-interest groups. Custom imprinting or
excerpting can also be done to fit special needs. For information, please e-mail SpecialMarkets@
WaterBrookMultnomah.com or call 1-800-603-7051.

This book is dedicated to my husband and kids, who not only put up with and participate in all my harebrained ideas, endure my singing responses to their questions, and tolerate my often-embarrassing yet well-intended actions in front of their friends but also genuinely support their wife and mom with the closest thing to unconditional love this side of heaven.

I am forever grateful.

CONTENTS

Foreword by Michael Gurian

America's children are in danger of remaining children all their lives. We live in the first era of human history in which consecutive generations of boys and girls are encouraged to remain children for as long as possible. They are encouraged to do so by a social system that worries over their fragility more than it challenges their inherent strength. The pendulum has swung over the last decades from the greatest generation to the entitled generation.

Kay Wills Wyma woke up to this situation in her own home, and that awakening set her on a wonderful adventure. Kay says, "I came to realize that not one of my five children knew how to do their own laundry. Not one could clean a bathroom—I mean, really clean it. Not one could cook, serve, and clean up after a full dinner. I wasn't sure my eight-year-old could even cut his waffles." Kay realized she was not raising her children to be successful adults but instead was letting them remain children forever. She, like so many of us, was hovering, over-praising, giving up her authority, and actually making her children's lives more difficult in the future by making their lives easier now.

Kay Wyma's *Cleaning House* joins with Amy Chua's *Battle Hymn of the Tiger Mother* and Pamela Druckerman's *Bringing Up Bébé* in asking all of us to rethink how we parent. Chua opened our eyes to a Chinese-American way of parenting, one that might seem harsh to some, but speaks loudly to the sacred task of raising children in full cognition of their inherent strength. Druckerman, taking a different slant, opened our eyes to a French way of parenting, one that might seem relatively passive to some people, but one that also nurtures children's inherent strengths. Kay Wills Wyma joins these mothers in saying, "Let's parent our kids as if they are inherently strong, not inherently weak." This is an immense gift to give us, and Kay's book, at once passionate and practical, is a gift to every parent.

As a parent myself, I have often felt the temptation to "do for" and constantly "give to" my children. I have had to constantly remind myself that each boy and girl in our care is asking us to challenge them to *their strongest, most loving potential*. This challenge is a challenge toward purpose and life service, so it can't be met by parents doing for and only giving to kids. Kids must do for the world and family; they must give to the world and family. Every chore a boy accomplishes is a gift of purpose and an act of service. Every problem a girl solves herself is a strength builder. Every moment one of our children reflects, *I wonder why my parents made me do that,* is a moment in which they are learning how to love and be loved.

Enjoy this book and its journey. I hope it will fill your heart and mind with even more passion for purposeful parenting than you had before you read it. Wyma is a wonderful storyteller and a powerful, wise mother.

—Michael Gurian
New York Times best-selling author
of *The Wonder of Boys* and *The Wonder of Girls*

The Epiphany

D riving down Preston Road, I was dutifully transporting children to school with my then-fourteen-year-old son sitting shotgun, when I learned how this kid defines the American Dream. As is typical of this particular area in Dallas, we were surrounded by opulence: on our left was a Lexus, on our right a Porsche, and directly in front a silver Maserati.

"Mom." Abandoning his pose of boredom, my son perked up. "Which one of those do you think I'd look best in? I think the Porsche... Yeah. That's what car I'm going to get when I'm sixteen."

Fighting back nausea, I looked at him. "What planet are you on? And how do you think you will pay for one of those cars?" A question I knew had no answer, since his primary activity involves a screen and remote control.

Who is raising this kid? I thought. *Is materialism and money all he thinks about? Where have all my words of wisdom gone? The hours of volunteer service, the countless lectures on being content with what you have, and all the brilliant soliloquies I've delivered on the fact that "stuff" will never really satisfy you—has none of that penetrated his brain?*

After dropping him off, I passed through the last school zone on my way home and dialed my sister-in-law, who is also one of my best friends. Not only did I need to vent my frustration, I needed reassurance that I wasn't crazy and that there is a light at the end of this self-centered teenager tunnel. She delivered on the former but couldn't help much with the latter because she has a few slackers of her own. After we exchanged similar stories, I had a sobering epiphany.

"I think I'm raising little socialists," I said, "the serve-me kind that are numb to the benefits of ingenuity and hard work, the kind that don't just need to be taken care of—they expect it."

And why not? That's what I have apparently been raising them to expect. In that moment and in the days that followed, I came to realize that not one of my five children knew how to do their own laundry. Not one could clean a bathroom—I mean, really clean it. Not one could cook, serve, and clean up after a full dinner. I wasn't sure my eight-year-old could even cut his waffles.

Ugh!

To be fair, my children can do a lot of amazing things. They are genuinely great kids. But they'd been getting a sweet free ride, especially in their home life. With me stepping in and doing for them—rarely, if ever, putting genuine responsibilities on their plate—they didn't have a chance to realize their potential.

As I've since discovered in conversations with other parents, ours was not an isolated case. Raising independent kids is countercultural these days. Instead of teaching our children to view themselves as capable, we step in to do everything for them. We start when they're still young, using safety as our lame excuse ("She'll fall if I don't hover"), then we continue "protecting" them ("If I don't help him get As, how will he get into college?"). We pave a smooth pathway, compulsively clearing away each pebble of disappointment or difficulty before it can impede their progress. By the time they reach adolescence, they're so used to being taken care of that they have no idea they're missing out on discovering what they can do or who they can be.

I was reminded again of how low I'd set the bar of expectations after my eighth grader, the one who plans on driving a Porsche at age sixteen, brought home an assignment from his English teacher to prepare a declamation. The task: select a speech or essay—something quotable and interesting—commit five minutes of it to memory, then recite it in front of the class. Seemed straightforward enough.

And yet, following in his mother's footsteps, my child procrastinated to the point that his teacher finally chose a passage for him. I tried, with little success, to smother my laughter when I learned that my "what's the least I can do to get by?" teenager would be memorizing and reciting Teddy Roosevelt's 1899 address to the Hamilton Club in Chicago—an address entitled "The Strenuous Life."

I kid you not.

Here's a brief portion of what TR said:

> In speaking to you, men of the greatest city of the West, men of
> the State which gave to the country Lincoln and Grant, men who
> preëminently and distinctly embody all that is most American in
> the American character, *I wish to preach, not the doctrine of ignoble*
> *ease, but the doctrine of the strenuous life, the life of toil and effort,*
> *of labor and strife; to preach that highest form of success which comes,*
> *not to the man who desires mere easy peace, but to the man who does*
> *not shrink from danger, from hardship, or from bitter toil, and who*
> *out of these wins the splendid ultimate triumph.*
>
> A life of slothful ease, a life of that peace which springs merely
> from lack either of desire or of power to strive after great things, is
> as little worthy of a nation as of an individual. I ask only that what
> every self-respecting American demands from himself and from
> his sons shall be demanded of the American nation as a whole.[1]

Oh, there is much more. And it's all incredibly convicting. TR would climb out of his grave, metaphorical big stick in hand and all thoughts of speaking softly abandoned, if he knew what we have done to the country that he and so many other determined leaders worked diligently to shape. And I'm embarrassed to say that my kids would probably opt for "mere easy peace." They'd most certainly shrink from "hardship" and "bitter toil."

What Message Are We Sending Our Kids?

Incidents like these and countless others brought to my attention a malady that had infected my home. Youth entitlement seems to have reached epidemic proportions in both my family and society as a whole—and I was appalled to realize that I, like many of today's well-meaning parents, am a primary carrier of the germ.

With the greatest of intentions and in the name of love, we have developed a tendency to hover, race in to save, protect from failure, arrange for success, manipulate, overprotect, and enable our kids. Freeing their schedules for sports, school, and increasingly important time with friends, we strive to make our children's lives easier or to make success a sure thing by doing it all for them. We shower them with accolades, proclaiming how wonderful they are—yet we rarely give them the opportunity to confirm the substance of that praise. All our efforts send the clear, though unspoken and unintended, message "I'll do it for you because you can't" or "No sense in your trying because I can do it better and faster."

Those messages are really the *opposite* of what I want my kids to hear from me. I want them to hear the truth—that with hard work, perseverance, and discipline, they *can* do anything they put their minds and muscles to.

This realization convinced me of the need to redefine my parenting approach. Instead of communicating "I love you, so let me make life easy for you," I decided that my message needed to be something more along these lines: "I love you. I believe in you. I know what you're capable of. So I'm going to make you work."

I'm not sure where this entitlement thing originated. I don't remember my parents doing my homework for me or checking every answer before school the next day. They really only helped when I was legitimately stuck and asked for assistance. I don't remember them running in to protest when a teacher gave me a bad grade, warranted or not. I sure don't remember my folks leaping hurdles to get me on the right team at the right school with the right teacher. For the most part, they let the chips fall where they might and expected us kids to adapt and aim for success as best we could. I don't remember getting by with a messy room anchored by my unmade bed. (Okay, so our housekeeper, Beatrice Howard—Bea to me—not my parents, checked our rooms. But she made the chain of command crystal clear: my dad, my mom, and then her. She wasn't there to work for us. She worked for my parents. She was our boss.) We did work Saturday mornings, though, sweeping the garage, mowing the yard, washing the cars, cleaning windows, and such. Our efforts were inspected for quality, because "If a job's worth doing, it's worth doing well," as my dad (over)emphasized.

Yet in today's society the primary role of parents seems to be racing in to "help" their kids. We manipulate circumstances to clear a pathway for our children to reach the top and be the best. We might even complete their homework ourselves, just to be sure it's done right. At the very least we check it all.

We impart the message that achievement is paramount. Then we do everything in our power to ensure their success—by sticking ourselves smack-dab in the middle. The result? A group of kids now labeled as "Gen Me," because they behave as if the world revolves around them. Some experts even use the term *narcissistic.* Is their behavior worthy of a clinical diagnosis? Maybe or maybe not. But evidence clearly suggests we now have a group of overserved kids who are struggling on the other side of education to find their place in life.

A few years ago, a *Newsweek* article described this group with the brief story of Felicite:

> Since leaving college Felicite has changed jobs more than once a year. The 26-year-old Parisian—who didn't want her full name used in case it was seen by her current employers—tends to switch for "excitement" rather than money. Indeed, whenever her latest job doesn't pay enough for her to rent an apartment, she simply

moves back into her parents' home in the suburbs. Her latest plan: to quit her position in advertising for humanitarian work overseas. "I'm still young!" she says. "I just want to have fun in my job."

Felicite is emblematic of a growing trend. Around the developed world, more and more twentysomethings are staying home with their moms and dads so they can pursue their interests instead of worrying about secure jobs that will pay off mortgages."[2]

Around the same time the *Los Angeles Times* reported on a San Diego State University study that pointed to a rising trend of egocentrism:

All the effort to boost children's self-esteem may have backfired and produced a generation of college students who are more narcissistic than their Gen X predecessors....

Some of the increase in narcissistic attitudes was probably caused by the self-esteem programs that many elementary schools adopted 20 years ago, the study suggests. It notes that nursery schools began to have children sing songs that proclaim: "I am special, I am special. Look at me."[3]

More recently, Emily Bennington, a career expert and coauthor of *Effective Immediately: How to Fit In, Stand Out, and Move Up at Your First Real Job,* wrote an article for the *Huffington Post* in which she described the behaviors she and her colleagues have observed in recent college graduates, the more disturbing of which is kids needing their parents to be present during postcollege job interviews. "Naturally," she noted, "it's easy to blame the students in these situations ('they're too entitled'), but the bigger problem is us. We—as parents—are so eager to shelter our kids and keep them safe from any possible harm that we fail to realize that this in itself is harming them."[4]

Although the parents I know fully intend to prepare their kids to succeed in life, stories like these and an abundance of other real-life examples demonstrate that we undermine our own goals when we race in to ensure our kids' success and happiness. Our "helping" strategy sounds good until we find ourselves immersed in a society of overindulged, underprepared adults who sorely lack a solid work ethic.

REVERSING COURSE

Whatever happened to teaching, directing, and modeling rather than doing everything for our children?

Remember taking driver's ed? I learned how to drive in Wichita Falls, Texas, at the local driver's education school. After enduring hour upon hour of boring lectures, students moved to the hands-on portion of the class: actual driving. Our instructor pulled up to the curb, hoisted the gigantic Student Driver sign onto the roof of the car, then climbed into the passenger's side, which was equipped with an extra brake pedal. Off we went. On those countless white-knuckle rides, our instructor rarely employed the safety brake as he calmly guided each nervous driver onto a freeway, into a parallel parking spot, and through our small downtown—all while enduring ridiculous teenage humor, jeers, eye rolls, snickers, and under-our-breath comments. The old guy patiently taught us how to navigate a car by ourselves. Why? Because he knew that one day soon he would be sharing the road with us...as oncoming traffic.

Thanks to his approach, by the time I took my driver's test, I could do it all and do it well. Would I have eventually learned how to drive if, during our driving sessions, he'd been doing it for me? Probably. But it would have been much harder. Because I was allowed to do it myself—and occasionally fail, or at least hop a curb or two—with a capable instructor by my side, I gained significant confidence and valuable experience.

Yet as a parent, I'm constantly surprised by an inexplicable desire to take the driver's seat for my kids. A desire to basically do everything for them. I can barely stop myself from stepping in, even though I know my meddling doesn't help them in the long run. Maybe it's my need to control it all, to get things done quickly and efficiently, and to maintain order. Whether it's ordering for them at Chick-fil-A, making their beds, all but brushing their teeth, I'm surprised at the lengths to which I've gone to make life easy for my kids.

When I catch myself muttering under my breath, "I told them to pick this up," and then proceeding not only to pick up pajamas, towels, and shoes but also to organize their closet while I'm at it, I'm solidifying my children's expectation that someone will always be around to do their work for them. I also make it harder for them to put things away, since I've basically stolen the chance for them to organize their closets based on their own logic. When I step in, not only am I doing the work, but I'm inviting the countless whines of "Where are my kneepads?" It's the same with cooking or sweeping or mopping or bush trimming. I'm not sure any of these things have ever crossed their minds as tasks they might need to know how to do.

None of us want needy kids. We want them to be equipped to conquer the world rather than waiting for it to serve them.

So I decided my brood's free ride was about to come to an abrupt end.

A MOM ON A MISSION

Before getting too far along, let me introduce myself. My name is Kay Wyma. I'm a recovering enabler, procrastinator, controller, manipulator, and so much more.

Primarily, though, I'm wife to Jon and mother to five kids who have begged me to disguise their identities because, as everyone knows, close association with parents can be fatal to one's social life. Plus, these issues aren't about a certain set of kids. We're all dealing with youth entitlement—in our own homes, at schools, or in the workplace. Here's the cast of kid characters at my house:

- *Boxster,* age fourteen, hopes one day to drive the car that inspired his nickname. He fully embraces the typical characteristics of the teen years. His siblings drive him crazy, and he consistently prefers food prepared outside our home. Yet the kid's character rivals that of most adults. He is unabashedly loyal and puts forth amazing effort when compelled. But compelled he must be if we expect him to break free from teen apathy.

- *Snopes,* age twelve, is our fact checker, a no-nonsense gal who keeps track of what's going on and is quick to point out inconsistencies, especially any involving a mom who might be traveling a mile or two over the speed limit. Since the day she was born, she has been blessing those with whom she comes into contact—except, on occasion (usually in the morning), her siblings.

- *Barton,* age ten, is a quiet, responsible kid who's on top of everything. She earned her nickname because, like Clara, founder of the Red Cross, this child epitomizes volunteer service. Like all tween girls, she has her less-than-lovely moments, but more often than not, she is my go-to girl, even when I don't know I have a need.

- *Fury,* age eight, shows a stubborn resistance to change, much like a corralled stallion determined to shake loose any weight on its back. But when the kid buys into the task at hand and chooses to use that tenacity for good, watch out. He is a hard worker who gets the job done and done well (once we get beyond the protests).

- *Jack,* age three, is too young to care whether or not he has an alias, poor kid. His name could be Poppins, because like Mary, he's "practically perfect in every way." So we're spoiling him a bit—while hoping our efforts won't land him in the rotten category. Perfection aside, he does have one small, often annoying habit he's been feeding: he's known by many as the Future Hoarder of America.

Welcome to my world.

It's a world where my name changes multiple times a day. For large portions of the day, I go by James, as in "Drive me to school, James." "My stomach needs a Slurpee. Take me to 7-Eleven, James." "I have a pressing engagement at the soccer fields. Drive on, James."

At other times I'm Flo ("Yo, Flo, I ordered chocolate-chip pancakes—not Eggo waffles!"); Alice (the Bradys' trusty house-management expert—all right, maid); RoboCop (no description necessary); Nacho Libre (why are teen boys compelled to communicate via wrestling and bug slugging?); and Matt (as in Welcome).

I'm a regular gal. No PhD, no counseling degree, no company letterhead. I'm a mom. A mom whose home has somehow become the epicenter of entitlement, a place where children have grown accustomed to being served instead of serving. Where kids whine instead of work.

As I've already explained, I first realized my problem while talking with my sister-in-law after the mind-numbing "I think I'd look best in a Porsche" conversation. This realization was reinforced as I later walked upstairs to see four disheveled beds surrounded by excessive levels of kid crud and clutter. I returned downstairs and instructed one of my dear precious ones, Fury, to head to his room and make his bed.

"Why should I make my bed?" came the response. "That's *your* job."

My reaction was swift.

"What? That's my job? Where do you get off thinking that's *my* job? *I'm your mother.* You don't tell me what I do. And by the way, I do a lot more than make your bed! Lots. Oh, and I may not be able to help you with your algebra, or add and subtract multiple numbers, or remember grammar rules, or…well, that's beside the point. Just so you know, though, I used to do complicated math stuff. Yeah, when I worked in an office, I did deals. *Big* deals. *Huge* deals!"

Okay, so I didn't say any of that, but I wanted to. Truth is, I had no response. I was caught off-guard, shocked and in disbelief that the child could actually think that.

Clearly things were amiss. Action was required.

Enter the "Experiment."

One fine February day, I decided that my kids had a few things to learn about life. Things that are key to productive and independent living. To that end, I developed a list of duties I wanted my children to master before leaving our nest. Then we launched into the Experiment: a twelve-month endeavor to teach our kids how to be productive in our

Top Twelve Things a Kid Should Know Before Flying the Wyma Coop

1. how to make a bed and maintain an orderly room
2. how to cook and clean a kitchen
3. how to do yard work
4. how to clean a bathroom
5. how to get a job…outside our home
6. how to do laundry
7. how to do handyman jobs
8. how to host a party
9. how to work together
10. how to run errands
11. how to put others first through service
12. how to act mannerly

home. Each month I introduced a task to help equip them to reach their full potential. I gave them responsibilities, such as making their beds, doing the laundry, cooking meals, and other jobs designed to help them learn how to do life.

Given my own issues as a recovering procrastinator, implementing this strategy has been a challenge. Don't be fooled by any semblance of organization. In fact, I'm a founding member of the Women's Auxiliary for the Organizationally Impaired. Just thinking about the Experiment initially made me want to crawl in bed and pull the covers over my head. (Of course, I haven't showered without interruption in fourteen years; why I thought I could have a moment of silence alone in my bed is beyond me.)

But I can't ignore the serious consequences of allowing youth entitlement to continue unchecked. These kids are part of the generation that will be leading the world in a few short years. Not only that, but they—all of us, in fact—were created to work. It's been around since the beginning of time, an integral part of man's existence, a privilege before we made it toil. (See Genesis 2–3.)

So I set out with trepidation but sincerely hoped we all—especially me—could complete the Experiment and do our part toward replacing the "I'm here to be served" attitude with a "Look what I can do through hard work" mantra. Along the way I learned that success is not just motivating them to work; it has a great deal to do with stopping myself from doing it all, remembering to get my hands off, and being okay with their hands-on learning.

The following pages detail my yearlong effort to transfer responsibilities from my shoulders to theirs. I've tried to document the good, the bad, and the ugly moments of my attempt to lead my kids toward responsibility and independence, capability and confidence. We have yet to arrive in the land of the fully equipped, but at least we're headed in the right direction.

Just the other day, I needed to handle a phone call. I'm not sure why, but failing to notice the time, I returned a call at 5:45 p.m., the bewitching hour, no matter the age of your kids. As if on cue, the three-year-old fired up the whine, which quickly escalated to a demanding scream. Stuck at the stove stirring a stubborn banana cream pie filling, I emphatically motioned and mouthed to the nearest sibling (Barton), "Please take care of Jack. I need to finish this call." Wrinkle-browed, she thought about balking, but true to character she jumped right in.

Several minutes later, still in the midst of the phone call and still stirring the filling, which refused to thicken, I heard screaming upstairs. Then a very loud "Oh noooo!"

At this point I faced a choice. I could end the phone call, quit stirring my concoction, and actually be a responsible mother. Or I could stay the course and finish my pie. I, of course, opted for the latter.

With sweat now literally dripping off the elbow of my stirring arm, from having stood over that stove for close to forty-five minutes, I noticed Barton standing next to me, scribbling on a piece of paper. When done, she lifted it for me to see. With spelling and grammar skills parked upstairs at the scene of the accident, she had written, "Jack went Pee on the flor upstairs."

Nice.

Since I've established my obsession with my pie and phone call, you may not be surprised that I didn't immediately head upstairs to clean that mess. I looked at the able-bodied child next to me and remembered that she'd been introduced to Lysol months ago as part of Task 4.

"Would you pleeease clean it up," I mouthed, knowing full well pee outside a toilet bowl is a big request.

In a whisper, she begged, "Mommm. Noooo!"

Boxster stood close by, gawking and laughing at the entire scene because it involved a bodily function. I turned to him.

"Will you go clean it up? Come on… You can do it. I'll make it worth your while."

"No way! I wouldn't do it for fifty grand."

"Don't worry about it," I muttered. "I'll just clean it later."

Both kids slipped away, and I began to wrap up my call, confessing all that had transpired. Before I could finish, however, Barton returned, scribbling another message. When she held up the paper, I saw that, under the frantic initial note, she had written, "I cleened Jacks Pee ☺." (No doubt stunned by the experience, her spelling and grammar skills were still upstairs.)

What could I do but smile...for so many reasons. That she would reach beyond her comfort zone and clean a disgusting mess, change the kid's clothes, and place the dirty clothes in the washer warmed my heart. She did a job she didn't think she could handle. She went beyond what I asked.

Moments like this, when my kids and I both get a chance to see how capable they really are, assure me that the Experiment wasn't just a hare-brained idea. Crossing hurdles like these prepares her (all the kids, really) for much more challenging situations in the future.

WE'RE ALL IN THIS TOGETHER

One thing I've learned is that the journey of life goes more smoothly when you're traveling *with* someone. Roads traveled alone tend to lead to disaster and sometimes despair.

I've also learned it's a good idea to tap older and wiser resources. So, as we began the Experiment, I volunteered a few veterans to travel with me as I chronicled our adventure on my blog. These seasoned souls come from different backgrounds and experiences, but all share the common bond of survival and were more than willing to offer tips and tactics learned from their own travels. I call them my Ironing Board because they helped me smooth out the wrinkles—not the facial ones caused by parenting stress (although I'm sure I could use some help there), but the uneven patches in our family life that left me feeling rumpled and creased.

In addition to my Ironing Board, guest bloggers offered great insight and helpful hints on navigating our road. I also extended an open invitation on my blog to anyone brave enough (or desperate, or in need of comic relief) to come along for the ride and share ideas, innovations, and insights. Friends from all over the world, from all walks of life, have told me they have the same parenting issues with their kids, in India, Australia, Great Britain, and even impoverished western Africa.

Just the other day I was chatting with my sweet friend Clara. She comes twice a week to help me with Jack so he can avoid living his life in a carpool line. Believe it or not, all my kids napped at home in their own beds when they were little. I wanted Jack to have the same opportunity, so I whittled my school carpool responsibilities to a minimum except for the days Clara helps me. I shared with her my ideas on our Experiment and how the kids would be assuming some of the chores around the house. Being a mother of four, she commiserated. She told me that she'd been so frustrated with the mess in her teenage son's room that she had taken his door off the hinges. She then told me that her eighteen-year-old doesn't see any reason to get a driver's license. Why should he? Everyone else can drive him.

The only way to conquer youth entitlement is one house at a time. What a privilege we have to celebrate all that these kids have to offer and to help them realize their potential by bringing on the work. It's incredibly exciting to consider the abundant possibilities just around the corner for a generation empowered by parents and other adults who believe in them, support them by teaching real-life skills, and then pile on the responsibility. Think about the ramifications of unleashing this tech-savvy crew on global economic issues, seemingly incurable diseases, and age-old political conflict.

So here's to seeing what can happen when we tell our kids, "I believe in you, and I'm going to prove it by putting you to work."

Let the empowering Experiment begin.

Operation Clutter Control

Starting Simple: Beds and Clutter

> Cleaning your house while your kids are still
> growing is like shoveling the walk before it
> stops snowing.
>
> —PHYLLIS DILLER

I've never been accused of being a perfectionist or a neat freak. In fact, as mentioned earlier, I'm somewhat organizationally challenged. I tend toward a guiding philosophy of: What's the point in putting things away when you're just going to have to get them all out again?

Hmm... I think I've heard my kids say the same thing.

In my career-girl days, more than one boss eyed my desk, suspicious that anything productive could transpire among the piles of paper. But by that point, my organizational-impairment issues were already deeply woven into the somewhat knotted fabric of my character, as my college roommate could attest.

Poor thing had no idea what she'd signed on for when she agreed to live with me. In an effort to make new friends, we had both gone blind potluck in our freshman dorm at Baylor University. We met over the phone. Then, as girls do, we giddily agreed on matching bedspreads and various sundries, and hugged the day we moved in.

It didn't take long for Susan to realize that even though I might be an agreeable roommate—fun, spontaneous, laid-back—I was a bit of a slob. Cluttery, one might say. Sure, like the good girl my momma (and our housekeeper, Bea) taught me to be, I would make my bed (most days), but I would leave every article of clothing plus some other stuff on it or thrown to the floor beside it. To transform my makeshift wardrobe into a bed each night, I'd just shove the piles aside and snuggle up under my cozy hill of clothes, ready to wear whatever might be on top to class the next day.

By contrast, Susan was organized, a borderline Type A. But once she collided with my whatever-goes attitude, she soon crossed over to the dark side of creative clutter.

When friends in my dorm brought their visiting parents to our room, I initially thought that the photos they snapped were scrapbook additions to memorialize their daughters' campus life experience, that their oohs and aahs expressed admiration for our adorable furnishings.

I was wrong.

Our room had become a destination location for freshman girls, a showcase of clutter should their folks be inclined to chide them for a disorderly room. Mind you, Susan and I weren't dirty…just carefree and casual about putting things away. But on the inside, like most reasonable people, we both craved order. Every so often we'd get a taste of it.

If my mom happened to be in town for a visit, she would stop by and declutter our room while I was at class. Neatly hanging pants and dresses in my closet. Folding, ironing, putting shirts and shorts in drawers. Pairing and placing shoes on the space-saving over-the-closet-door racks. She worked wonders like a fairy godmother waving her magic wand. (Might this be the origin of my enabling issues?!) For about a day, Susan and I would revel in the clothes-free floor and beds, making each other well-intentioned promises to maintain order.

In the years since, I've addressed many (though certainly not all) of my organizational challenges. Still, I can empathize with my own brood of clutter-happy kids. I can appreciate those unmade beds. I get the "Why put it away? I'm just going to wear it tomorrow" attitude. I care about cleanliness but, like them, not so much about clutter.

But my empathy doesn't change the reality that, with seven bodies in our house, keeping the clutter under control is an absolute must. So, for years I've been scurrying behind my family, picking up and putting away as if clutter patrol is my job. I'm quick to gather the shorts abandoned on the floor right where they were taken off, to put away the towel that left a damp spot on the carpet where it was thrown the night before, to make the beds in hope that tidy rooms will provide productive work environments when their occupants sit down to study, even to flush toilets when that simple action proved too much for my children to remember.

In truth, however, my real responsibility as their mother is to teach, not to handle tasks for them. I need to help these kids tackle their tendency toward untidiness before it becomes a permanent fixture in their lives.

Determined that necessary life lessons will be learned, I decide to stifle my laissez-faire flair and strategize the best way to instigate order, introduce work, and inspire commitment—a real, life-altering commitment. In short, a *habit*.

Habit [hab-it]

noun

1. an acquired pattern of behavior that has become almost involuntary as a result of frequent repetition: *the habit of making one's bed as soon as you get up every day.*
2. customary practice or use: *picking up after oneself is a habit in some homes.*
3. a particular practice, custom, or usage: *the habit of doing chores, whether or not one thinks they are boring or someone else's responsibility.*[1]

Home Habits

Why do bad habits so easily sneak their way into our lives, while good habits take so much more work? Studies suggest it takes twenty-one days to make a permanent mental shift and form a positive habit.[2] But experience suggests it takes up to a few months in our house. Maybe longer. Suffice it to say, our empowerment makeover may take a while to sink in.

That said, the idea of introducing only one primary goal or task each month makes it all seem doable. I've decided to start with the bedrooms, throwing in bathroom clutter for good measure. (We'll save Tilex for another month.) The goal for this month is to form a tidiness habit. Basically, I just want stuff off the floor and beds made—*every day*.

It's crazy that even though I know we need to change (and making beds doesn't seem like that big a deal), when faced with actually running the gauntlet I've designed for us, I'm dreading this more than the kids are. Apparently, I like change just about as much as they do. Doubts start to creep in. Will this ridiculous Experiment even work? Is it a waste of time and energy? What if I lose heart halfway through? What kind of an example will that set for my kids? Yet, fueled by frustration, I'm determined to move ahead.

I think I've established that I'm not a parenting expert. Feeling a tad at a loss for how to start, I conclude it might be helpful to know the steps involved in forming a good habit. Here's what I learned from wikiHow.[3] (Okay, so it's not some Oprah-endorsed, best-selling, self-help guru, but this isn't rocket science.)

Step 1: Know What You Want
Got it: I want my overindulged kids to make their beds and lose the clutter.

Step 2: Make a List of the Benefits of the New Habit

- It will teach them responsibility.
- It will make them better citizens.
- It will build their self-esteem.
- I won't have to do it myself or look at it anymore!

That last one is the most compelling benefit, from my perspective. Those unmade beds not only testify to a "serve me" attitude but also are an incredibly annoying, ever-present reminder of how lame I've been at enforcing chores.

Step 3: Commit to the Habit

I'm on it! Hoping determination will win out over my tendencies to procrastinate and to forget the follow-through.

Step 4: Set Your Own Goals, and Reward Yourself

Since the plan is to nurture a habit in the kids, I'll be setting the goals on their behalf, as well as finding a way to reward them.

My friend Lauren shared her strategy, which we'll be implementing. A mother of three, she decided to incentivize her teenage girls by putting a jar filled with thirty one-dollar bills in their rooms at the start of a month. Each day she checks to see if the beds are made and the stuff is put away. If rooms don't pass inspection, she takes a dollar out of the jar. At the end of the month, the girls keep whatever cashola is left in the jar.

With five kids that's a lot of money each month. But we don't provide an allowance. We've tried, but I kept forgetting and often found myself "borrowing" from their meager stash. It became a tiresome, never-ending discussion of them being "owed," so I stopped. And since I'm often buying them things like Frappuccinos, I Heart Yogurt, Slurpees, and other goodies, this approach would shift the responsibility for such nonessentials to their wallets. Perhaps those less inclined to clean their rooms will be inspired by their plunder-partaking siblings.

Step 5: Start Slowly

Sounds reasonable. Better to start with just their rooms rather than hitting them with all the changes at once, military-school style. The laundry will have to stay on *my* to-do list—for now.

The Ironing Board

Ann Bentley is a mother of four boys ages nine to twenty-seven, grandmother of one, and host mother to a sixteen-year-old Vietnamese exchange student. Married thirty-one years to her college sweetheart, Chuck. A hopelessly addicted reader/learner/seeker of wisdom.

Sue Bohlin loves to both teach women and laugh, and if those two can be combined, all the better. She is happily married to Dr. Ray Bohlin, president of Probe Ministries, and together, they have two grown sons.

Jody Capehart is happily married to Paul, who is in his fortieth year of playing french horn in the Dallas Symphony Orchestra. They have three grown children and five grandchildren. Jody's passion is for her family.

Julie Fairchild is a mother to four mostly grown kiddos and a husband who's a child at heart. In her spare time, she and a friend run Lovell-Fairchild Communications, a publicity and grass-roots marketing agency that specializes in projects with organic faith.

Kathleen Fischer, mother of three, is a registered nurse with a master's degree who is passionate about teens. She speaks and writes on the challenging subject of parents successfully navigating teen waters.

Step 6: Go for Consistency Rather Than Performance

I'm not sure what that's going to look like, but it's probably worth thinking about. I guess for us, it's about consistency over perfection. I'm not asking much. Their beds *should* be made every day. The clutter, though,

Jane Jarrell is a mother, wife, accomplished speaker, and author on hospitality and parenting. She uses wit, charm, and personal stories to teach women practical ideas and creative solutions for life.

Dottie Jones is first a wife, then a mother, and as time permits, an author and speaker. She is the cofounder of both Life Ministries and Ministering to Moms. Dottie happily shares her wisdom and insight through teaching and mentoring.

Ruth Meek, mother of four and mentor to many, is a highly sought-after speaker (and soon-to-be author) on simplifying Christmas, the benefits of silence, and intimacy with husbands.

Lucina Thompson is a friend, wife, mother of two, and a true lover of God's Word. Lucina teaches a women's Bible study at Watermark Community Church. She is passionate about her kids and her extended community in poverty-stricken regions of Africa.

Sue Wills is a mother of four (including me), grandmother of fifteen, and hostess extraordinaire. She has never met a stranger and is a constant target for wisdom-seeking women.

Peggy Zadina, mother of two grown girls and grandmother of one precious girl, has been married to the same man for nearly forty years. This interior designer loves golf, bridge, and encouraging others in their family relationships.

will be a challenge, especially considering the fact that the kids share rooms. I want bedroom and bathroom floors clear but will accept reasonable items on desks and counters. No piling allowed. One person's clutter will most definitely be another's issue. *Eek*...I can already hear the blaming.

Consistency just isn't my strong suit. But I want to stay at this even when day twenty-one rolls around and we're still struggling with the new habits.

Step 7: Consult a Friend

Whatever you do, don't go it alone, for sure! I'll have my Ironing Board of reliable experts as well as a cohort of sympathetic friends to rely on.

Step 8: Even After the Goal Is Hit, Keep It Up

Absolutely. We're trying to build skills for life, so my hope is that the habit will stick and we'll see a permanent change. I'm not looking for perfection, though. My goal here is to get the kids to start taking care of their spaces and quit thinking they exist to be served.

The Pitch

With *habit* defined and strategized, it was time to initiate the assault on apathy. Dottie Jones, one of the wise and well-traveled mothers from whom I've sought direction, gave me some great advice: always begin any major overhaul with a family meeting. This advice was easy to embrace because I had seen it modeled by my father; he always held family meetings to discuss matters affecting us. So we did.

And unlike other family meetings—the dreaded, old-fashioned lectures from Dad on behavior modification—this meeting actually involved the kids' participation in defining issues and possible solutions. Personally, I would much rather be included in a decision impacting me than be expected to simply embrace an edict bellowed in my direction.

In the meeting, we discussed the plan. Every kid gets a jar with money. If a particular kid's room is a mess or the bed is unmade (or both) when I check each morning, one dollar disappears from the jar. Seems reasonable and straightforward, right? Here are a few of their responses:

- "What are you and Clara going to do if we are doing all the work?" *Appreciate the concern, but Clara (my friend who helps out twice a week) and I will be quite all right.*
- "Do the bigger kids get more than thirty dollars in their jar?" *Hmm...no. It seems to me a bed is a bed no matter your size.*
- "What if I just forget and then remember right when I get in the car for school?" *Sorry. You snooze, you lose.*

I'm sensing a "mean mom" comment headed my way from at least one of the kids. But honestly, we all know (including them) that it's lame to pretend any of this is taxing. Even so, I've really got to be on the ball here and make sure I follow through. Otherwise, the chaos of clutter will continue to reign.

ONE SMALL STEP TOWARD PERSONAL ACCOUNTABILITY

After our family meeting, we went to The Container Store, where each child chose a clear box or jar. Back at home, the kids personalized them, then I filled them with fifteen dollar bills and fifteen dollar coins (just for variety...and because those gold dollar coins are so cool), and set them on their dressers. I also explained to them that no dollars could be used until the month was up, though we may later change to an "end of the week" time frame. Deferred gratification is a good thing.

I got a jar for myself too. Hey, I could use thirty bucks at the end of the month for a little self-indulgence. Yes, they get to check my bed, and I'm throwing in daily exercise for good measure. Gotta love accountability!

On the news the other night, an interviewee exclaimed, "Where does government end and personal responsibility begin?"

I muttered to Jon, "It has to start at home first."

The more I think about it, the more I'm convinced the failure to take personal responsibility is an endemic issue for our culture. As our kids age, the youth entitlement problem leads to a needy society, incapable of critical thinking; incapable of making decisions; incapable of problem solving, creating, deducing, finding cures. Being overserved leads to atrophy of personal initiative. No wonder our kids opt out rather than dive into responsibility-laden opportunities.

Let's face it, only a precious few are born with the internal drive to achieve. The overwhelming majority produce that drive only when their existence or well-being depends on it—or when they come to believe that one of the innate purposes of being human is to accomplish something of worth. We really aren't helping our kids when we race in to help. Sure, by doing things for them, we accomplish the task of the moment and make their lives easy. But in doing so, we deny them the character-building op-

Expert Advice: Personal Responsibility

From Chuck Bentley, chief executive officer of Crown Financial Ministries and father of four, comes this nugget of wisdom:

> Lesson 101 for children is personal responsibility; without this they are helpless to accomplish their God given purpose. The cornerstone of personal responsibility is the character trait of Work. To teach your children to work, to produce, to accept responsibility for results, to bear the burden of completing a task that meets expectations is the foundation for their maturity into adults.[4]

portunities that come only through encountering resistance. In the long run, our well-intentioned assistance weakens both their bodies and their spirits.

What was it that Neil Armstrong said as he stepped out of a spacecraft (which, have we forgotten, was created by human ingenuity when challenged by the call to put man on the moon)?

"That's one small step for a man, one giant leap for mankind."

Well, in our house, a month of making beds and clutter removal is one small step that I hope will morph into great leaps and bounds for these kids as they grow into productive citizens.

I know. It's a bit dramatic, but a recovering enabler needs one big idea to cling to, something that will help me focus on the hoped-for greater good of our Experiment and somehow remember to follow through.

Mixed Results

Over a week into Task 1 of the Experiment, and the rooms are looking good! Consistency has entered the building. Floors can be seen. Beds are being made, though our definition of "made" may differ wildly from yours. None are smooth and tight enough to bounce a quarter, but covers up is just fine with me. I'm even hearing comments such as, "You were right, Mom. I think my friends would feel a lot better with our room like this."

Whoa.

I didn't think that kid was even listening when I pontificated months ago about how rude it is to invite your friends into a virtual pigsty. At that time eyes were rolled and moans were groaned that everyone's room looks like this. So I had opted for the course of least resistance, determining that my child could reap the rewards of a messy room reputation—all the while knowing deep down that, like my mother, I'd eventually clean it up myself.

Now, after basking in the beauty of the "you were right" comment, I admitted to myself that what I'd expected to be a nightmare—making the kids do menial labor and checking their work—hasn't been so bad after all. Best of all, they are getting a taste of how good it feels to be orderly. Such firsthand rewards are even more encouraging than a dollar in the dresser jar.

Still, keeping rooms clean can be a bit of a challenge around here since everyone has a roommate. Poor Jack shares our bedroom; he still sleeps in our walk-in closet! So not only are these kids decluttering their own messes, but they are also navigating the tricky waters of dealing with their siblings' stuff. I've heard the "It was her underwear, not mine!" whine more than once.

Mean Mom response: "Work it out."

I'm well aware that this could lead to World War III. Or they just might figure out how to

1. serve others—and we all know that serving your family is the toughest order around;
2. creatively find a solution to use one another's strengths (one of my girls actually loves organizing and cleaning, while the other enjoys making the place look cute); or
3. just do the work, even if it isn't your stuff, because—guess what?—life isn't fair.

As I suspected at the outset, this transition has been easier for the girls than for the boys. The girls get the idea that cleaning up the clutter means putting *all* the stuff away. My boys have been edging around the letter of the law with no interest in the spirit of its intent.

- Pajama pants on the bathroom counter: "What's the big deal? They weren't on the floor."
- Toothbrush and toothpaste left out by the sink: "Why does it need to go in a drawer? I'm just going to have to get it out tonight."

- Wet towel on the floor: "That's where I put it." (Is he for real? Does he actually think the floor constitutes "put away"!)
- Pajama boxers draped over the tub: "Those aren't dirty. I'm wearing them again tonight." (Oh wait, that's not one of the kids, that's Jon—the husband. An entirely different issue.)

I suspect some people might find it slightly pathetic that I'm so excited about my kids making their beds. I get that. We should have had this down at age four. Oh yeah, we did do it when they were four. When did we stop? Did I just forget? Was it after three kids that I gave in? Four? I don't remember. But somewhere along the way, tidiness flew out the window...and some kid slammed it shut. But I can't look back, only forward. The past is the past, but the future always holds hope. I understand that the teen years seem the absolute worst time to introduce increased expectations. But if we're successful in this phase, imagine what they can do when the funk has lifted! And despite the occasional pushback, we really are making progress.

My least favorite part of our Experiment so far is my new role as the Enforcer. In our quest for tidiness and clutter control, I dutifully make my rounds checking the kids' rooms. Upon poking my head into the boys' room, I discover a mess of sheets, blankets, and pillows. We've got a violation here.

"Well, today you lost a dollar," I tell the teenager when I get downstairs.

"What are you talking about?"

"Your bed wasn't made."

"Yes, it was."

"No, it wasn't." (I feel myself getting sucked into his vortex of juvenile stubbornness.)

"It was made."

"I don't know what your definition of 'made' might be, but your bed was not, by anyone's standard."

"Still"—now he takes a subtle talk-to-the-hand tone—"don't know what you're talking about."

Annoyed, I shoot back, "What are *you* talking about? The bed was *not* made, and your clothes are on the floor."

"No, they weren't."

I fight the urge to scream. As anyone with a teen knows, we could go upstairs and look at the unmade bed together, and he would still claim that it was made.

While he adamantly defends his room's tidiness, the toddler decides he wants his milk in a blue cup instead of the perfectly fine and already filled green one. He proceeds to insist on the blue cup, increasing in volume and determination to the point of writhing on the ground, wailing the words, *"Bluuueeee cuuuupppp!"*

Having traveled the toddler road before, I respond calmly, "Your milk is just fine in that cup right there."

"Noooo. I waaaannt bluuueee-hoo-hoo." Sob, sob, sob.

Great. Stereo action. A toddler in one ear, a teen in the other.

Ignoring them both, I roll my eyes and settle in, waiting for the "Calgon, take me away" moment to end. Once they both realize that I'm not budging, their stubbornness subsides. The toddler reaches for the green cup, and the teen admits the truth—not that he's wrong, just that the bed wasn't made.

Jon's reaction when I laughed about my experience later that day: "Well, I hope you took the dollar."

I did. But when I first saw the bed unmade, I had to fight the urge to make it. *He just forgot. He has such a good heart. I'm sure he meant to make it; he has a lot on his mind.* Reality was all too apparent: the covers and pillows clearly lay right where he had wriggled out of them that morning. Still, inexplicably, I searched for a way to allow his bed to pass inspection, a reason to give him grace, just this once. As I turned from the bed to check the bathroom, I saw his clothes piled on the floor in a corner by the window.

I forced myself to take the dollar.

We're All in This Together

I had a wake-up call about a year ago at Cotillion (a social etiquette and dancing program) when the leaders asked the group, "Who made their beds this morning?" When only 5 percent of the hands went up, I realized we are not serving our kids by letting them get by with the least they can do. My eleven- and thirteen-year-olds needed me to set high standards and expectations.

At the moment, we are on a point system for things each child desires. A long-term point system for my son who craves the iPod touch that *everybody else* has and for my daughter, clothes (she loves clothes as I love chocolate). I tally the daily points, which they get for the usual stuff—bed made, room clean, clothing put away, and so on—but also for excelling in school and activities, getting along with their sibling, and being positive. The tough part is they get double the points taken away for not doing the above things. This combination of positive and negative feedback has worked better for us than anything else we had tried. We have also done this system for short-term rewards (iTunes gift cards, and so on).

So here's a cheer for all of us moms trying to do the right thing. For we all know it's easier to do it ourselves than make the kids do it. But who said the easiest path is the best one?

—Kristy

THE DANGERS OF APPLAUSE
WITHOUT ACCOUNTABILITY

It really isn't about making the beds. It's about equipping and empowering our kids.

My husband, Jon, and I had very different childhoods. He grew up in the impoverished mountains of Bolivia, a child of missionaries. I grew up on the affluent side of a west Texas town, child of a banker. Jon had very little free time on his hands. He spent any of those golden free moments outdoors, usually kicking a soccer ball. I had lots of free time, though without all the electronic distractions of today. I watched TV, listened to music as I lounged by the pool, and played hours and hours of tennis. His first car: a Toyota Tercel, acquired at the age of twenty-one. Mine: a BMW 320i, given to me at age sixteen. (Yes, I'm one of *those*.)

So you get the picture. As a necessity, Jon was intimately acquainted with hard work. Expectations were placed on him at an early age to be a man, to work hard, to take responsibility.

Though financially comfortable, my home life also emphasized the value of work. We had a maid, and household chores didn't take a dominant role in my everyday life, but my folks still required their kids to work hard. We were expected to make As on our report cards, to give 100 percent to each task, and to avoid idle time. I was even required to make my bed.

The standards set by our parents taught Jon and me that whatever was expected of us, we could do.

So what if I was the only girl I knew mowing the yard? My dad didn't see this job (or many jobs) as gender specific. Clearly I, like my brothers, had the capacity to fill the self-propelled Toro with gas, fire it up, and create geometric patterns of neatly clipped rows of grass.

My dad hammered home a couple of other principles every time he had a chance: the aforementioned, "If a job is worth doing, it's worth doing well" and "You can do anything you set your mind to." I hear myself saying the same things to my kids, but I came to realize I haven't been equipping them to embrace those truths.

Although good intentions pave my road of enabling—I want my children to be happy and their lives to be free of what I might deem unnecessary pain—my actions result in degradation rather than empowerment.

Once, when Snopes asked for help on a fifth-grade English paper, I couldn't stop myself from progressively increasing my involvement. I tried to guide her in coming up with descriptive language, but it took too long. I didn't have time to weather stammering and searching for words. Screaming siblings were vying for my attention. So rather than stand behind her, let her type (as slow as that might be), encourage her to struggle through word choices, and make her correct the errors, I literally pushed her aside and took over the helm in front of the computer. I corrected every grammatical error, filled in missing details, and added creativity to pull the reader into her story. Her report on *Redwall* emerged from its cocoon a beautiful butterfly, a far cry from the hairy caterpillar she had shown me moments earlier.

When she came home from school with the paper that not only sported a huge "97" in glaring red marker (firework marks exploding around the number) but also a note from the teacher on how proud she was of the terrific effort, Snopes looked embarrassed, not proud. It wasn't her work being praised, and she knew it.

I could do nothing more than apologize as I stared in those sad golden eyes. At that moment she could have been the poster child for why we parents should equip rather than enable. I couldn't believe I had fallen into the entitlement trap, even though my longstanding policy has been not to help the kids with their homework because I genuinely want them to pass or fail on their own.

When I step in, fix problems, and do those little household chores (or homework!), I send the message that they *can't* do it themselves. And if they can't do the small things, how will they ever attempt the big

...ings? So much for my "you're so great" kudos when they're rarely backed by actions to prove I believe it. Actions that include transferring sole-proprietor ownership of work to the kids.

When I started the Experiment, I thought my issue centered only on entitlement. Now I recognize that the enemy is not only entitlement but the accompanying low self-esteem, the result of my *implied* message that they aren't capable. Ouch. The entitlement attitude, seemingly a sign of self-importance and arrogance, actually conceals a cavern of insecurity. You may wonder how they can be insecure since they've bought into the belief that "the world revolves around you." Apparently, much of our children's self-esteem has been built on a faulty foundation.

In a recent article for the *Atlantic*, Lori Gottlieb interviewed Jean Twenge, a professor of psychology at San Diego State University and the coauthor of *The Narcissism Epidemic*. Asked about the ever-rising rate of depression among young people despite elevated views of themselves, Twenge responded: "Narcissists are happy when they're younger, because they're the center of the universe." She further explained:

> Their parents act like their servants, shuttling them to any activity they choose and catering to their every desire. Parents are constantly telling their children how special and talented they are. This gives them an inflated view of their specialness compared to other human beings. Instead of feeling good about themselves, they feel better than everyone else.

Twenge went on to describe how those ego-boosting efforts of parents result in greater problems as their kids reach adulthood.

> People who feel like they're unusually special end up alienating those around them. They don't know how to work on teams as well or deal with limits. They get into the workplace and expect to be stimulated all the time, because their worlds were so struc-

tured with activities. They don't like being told by a boss that their work might need improvement, and they feel insecure if they don't get a constant stream of praise. They grew up in a culture where everyone gets a trophy just for participating, which is ludicrous and makes no sense when you apply it to actual sports games or work performance. Who would watch an NBA game with no winners or losers? Should everyone get paid the same amount, or get promoted, when some people have superior performance? They grew up in a bubble, so they get out into the real world and they start to feel lost and helpless. Kids who always have problems solved for them believe that they don't know how to solve problems. And they're right—they don't.[5]

Just so you know, I'm one of those moms that other moms whisper about at the park. I have never hovered around the play equipment. I explain to my kids the dangerous spots, the places to avoid, and then let them play. When my toddler climbed up age-inappropriate equipment and stood at the edge of an eight-foot drop (the kind designed for older kids to reach out to grab a nearby pole and slide down), I rarely ran to his rescue. I figured that if he's foolish enough to step off, he will learn to never do it again. Call me crazy, but I know that if I stand at the edge with my arms up and catch them *every* time they step off, they will expect me to be there *every* time. With five kids, I can't always be there. I need them to be able to assess and live within reasonable and safe boundaries. And to this day, not one of them has stepped off.

So here's the question I'm asking myself: Why am I standing with my arms up to catch my kids before they even get a chance to fail at work? Instead of encouraging independence and an ability to assess a situation with an eye to what needs doing, I've taught them to be utterly dependent on me. But if I put my playground philosophy into action, empowering them to do the work themselves and experience success in small ways at home and at school, they will receive the message that they really can do whatever they put their minds to and—potentially—monumentally affect the world in the process.

But before tackling the world, we'll need to whip the beds into shape. Today is sheet-washing day. Of course, I forgot to say anything about it yesterday. (It's that recovery thing. To my issues with enabling, procrastinating, and controlling, we can add remembering.) So I kind of threw the kids a curve ball this morning when I woke them up and asked them to take the sheets *off* their beds instead of making them. They had no idea what I was talking about because (enabler alert!) to date someone has always done it for them.

In a sleepy stupor, "You want us to what?"

"Take the sheets off your bed. Only the sheets, not the blankets."

"Why?"

Okay, do they not even realize that someone takes the sheets off and washes them? Do they think that some genie blinks and clean sheets suddenly appear on their beds?

I had to help the girls, all the while trying to convince them that stripping the bed is actually easier than making it. I moved on to the boys' room.

"Today we wash the sheets," I droned. "So don't make your bed, just take the sheets off."

We're All in This Together

When I asked my thirteen-year-old son to make his bed and clean up his room, he was quick to respond with, "Mom, you are a stay-at-home mom, and that's your job. That's what stay-at-home moms do."

I've got lots of work ahead of me!

—Julie

"Okay."

To my utter shock, the teen didn't balk—at all. He literally hopped up and took the sheets off. No questions. No complaints. Who *is* this guy?

As I walked out of the room baffled, I realized the only possible explanation for his ability to strip a bed.

He must have learned it at camp.

A Measure of Success

Tonight, I mentioned to a couple of the kids that their clothes were on the bathroom floor. I was quickly silenced with a reminder that their rooms don't get checked until the morning. Details, details. Then one of them came into my room to point out—yes, you guessed it—a little clutter action of my own. I wish I was joking. No pedicure for me this month.

But that small loss is definitely outweighed by what we've gained this month. I can now navigate their rooms in the dark without stepping on land mines of toys. You might wonder why I would be rummaging through their rooms in the dark. Well, because I am an enabler. I actually wake them up every morning. Yes, I have only just realized that I don't even encourage the use of that modern invention, the alarm clock. No, I want them to begin each and every day being served.

I'm even their Snooze bar. "Just five more minutes—please?"

"Sure, honey, I'll come back up." *Come on, Kay.*

Along with safer navigation in the dark, the cleaner rooms have resulted in the kids discovering that they can *use* their rooms. Fury actually pulled toys out of the closet and played on the uncluttered floor with his friend the other day. I caught Boxster doing his homework on his very own uncluttered desk. I found the girls reading peacefully *on* their made beds. Who knew their rooms could be a destination vacation? Okay, the vacation part is for me. It's so nice to have them someplace besides under my feet. Why didn't I start this years ago?

Admittedly, Task 1 set the bar so low it was almost impossible for any of us to fail. But the bar was set, and we cleared it. Well, most of us cleared it. Some of the older ones needed occasional reminding (yes, I include myself in that category!), but their rooms are clearly neater. And they like it. It feels good, in more ways than one.

WHAT THEY LEARNED THIS MONTH

- Clearing clutter leaves more time and space to focus on friends, homework, and fun...and actually feels good.
- A little daily effort yields visible results. It also makes you want to do more.
- Personal responsibility isn't all that painful.

WHAT I LEARNED THIS MONTH

- A child will jump only as high as the bar is set. But he will jump. He just needs the bar to be set until the day he can do that for himself too.
- Their resistance to taking on more work isn't nearly as strong as I expected.
- I had no idea the number of areas in which my enabling tendency prevails.

Kitchen Patrol

*Discovering the Joys of Cooking—Along with
Menu Planning, Shopping, and Washing Dishes*

> As a child my family's menu consisted of two
> choices: take it or leave it.
>
> —BUDDY HACKETT

W hat did we do *this* time?" moans the teenager.

Strange reaction to our preplanned, Dottie Jones–prescribed family meeting, take two.

Coming off a fun and friend-filled weekend, I'd been looking forward to a talking "with" instead of talking "at" strategy session. Last month we did more telling than asking at the family meeting. Now that we have the first task under our belt, I anticipated this meeting might be exciting and full of fun ideas originating from the kids. (A mom can hope.) But Boxster's response wasn't encouraging. His tone suggested a history of Abu Ghraib–esque torture sessions. As if we're *ever* hard on them. The fact of the matter is, we rarely have meetings. So instead of gently explaining the purpose, coddling his tender feelings, Jon and I opted for one of our favorite teen-tantrum strategies: ignore it.

"First of all," Jon forges ahead, "great job on the beds and bathrooms.

We've been very impressed by your efforts and action without having to be reminded. Too often, anyway."

The smiles can almost be heard.

"Now," I jump in, "we're ready for our Month of Meals. This doesn't mean you get to stop with your rooms. Kitchen duty will be added to the daily dollar."

Cheers from one side of the room, moans from the other. No surprise from whom.

Jon lets me explain the premise: Monday through Thursday, the kids will be responsible for the evening meal. This includes shopping, preparing, and cleaning up before and after dinner. Then, together, we fill in the details.

"That's the 'what.' The 'who' is you. Y'all get to decide the when, where, and how."

More cheers...and "pleeease noooo" moans.

The perfect time to introduce my new mantra: "'Remember, work isn't always fun. It's something we all have to do."

Instead of sharing the work each day, the approach I encourage, they decide to individually handle *all* responsibilities for a day. Next, they stake claim on their days. The youngest worker sits like a deer in the headlights, trying to figure out what cooking means while everyone else clamors for the best day. Poor kid gets Monday. This is the child who for breakfast will eat only an Eggo Nutri-Grain whole-wheat waffle with the edges removed—cut into perfect squares that aren't crunchy, because if a piece is the least bit crispy, it's inedible. Have I mentioned I'm an enabler? I promise to help young Fury, but he still has to cook and clean. Here's our lineup:

- Monday: Fury
- Tuesday: Snopes
- Wednesday: Barton
- Thursday: Boxster, who has already informed us that he
  will be buying our dinner at Wendy's

His proclamation brings up an interesting point. So we decide, together, that if someone wants to eat out, the House, meaning Jon and I, will subsidize ten dollars for such purchase—basically a frugal estimate of the amount it might cost to eat at home. The chef (who is also the host) will make up the difference from his or her savings.

"Ten dollars!" the takeout teen protests. "It should be more like twenty-five!"

He has a point, but with places like Costco and Sam's Club, we get our meat at discounted prices. Factor in the reality that none of us are heavy eaters, and we're a pretty cheap date. I'm sure the day will come when my boys are eating us out of house and home, but right now our entire family can split one rotisserie chicken or three pieces of fish or one pot of chili, with enough left over to complete a meal the next day. We can even eat out for less than twenty-five dollars, with some major sharing and water-for-drinks action going on. I know it seems low, but we stick with ten dollars.

June Cleaver Doesn't Live Here

Honestly, I'm not looking forward to our Month of Meals at all. Dread might better describe my attitude. But I've set the standard, and now we all have to live by it. Sometimes being the grownup is such a drag. The whole cooking task sounds like a lot of work: taking the kids to the store, helping them plan meals, teaching them how to turn on the stove, guiding them through recipes…the list goes on. I love entertaining, but the kitchen and I have only a functional relationship at best, which makes me wonder if I'm best suited to be teaching these kids the ins and outs of culinary skills. Could this be yet another excuse as to why I *do* rather than *teach*? Do I think they need an expert in order to learn?

No, it's not about perfection, and it's not a competition; it's about living life well.

As I've spoken with other parents, it's become clear that mealtimes aren't the center of family life in the same way they used to be. Regularly dining at the table together, grocery shopping, cooking, and even cleaning up seem to be things of the past. For those who live in rural areas, not only are such events work-as-usual, but growing and harvesting may also play a role in mealtime. However, with busy schedules demanding our attention, the vast majority of us city dwellers tend to treat the family meal as a peripheral item that can be easily replaced by more pressing activities. We frequently opt for the convenience of fast food, many times consumed in the car, rather than savoring home-cooked meals eaten at our own tables and seasoned with conversation about the day.

This was definitely the case in my childhood family, especially after I hit adolescence. All of us were athletes, and our varied practice times didn't coordinate well with family dinners. My mom spent her afternoons racing from school to the tennis center to the municipal golf course to the aquatic center to home, then back to pick us up. Even if she had made us walk or ride our bikes rather than provide transportation, our practice times varied. So, home cooking got the boot early on. Irritated by this, my dad enforced a mandatory Thursday family dinner. He wanted us to eat together in the dining room with place mats, real silverware, crystal glasses, and even lit candles. He also required a home-cooked meal and forced conversation. "Forced" in that each of us had to share something that was going on in our lives.

We kids acted as if Thursday dinner was a life sentence to Alcatraz. We whined and moaned about the unfairness of it all, then dramatically succumbed to Dad's outrageous requirement. (Hmm. I guess we know where my kids inherited their love for theatrics.)

To this day, though, Thursday meals are among my most treasured childhood memories. My siblings and I laugh about my mother's hamloaf (yes, there is such a thing), our countless fights over rolls, the way we would secretly throw food at one another, or how we'd excuse ourselves from the table to toss whatever "inedible" item we'd hidden in our napkins. I'm so thankful my dad made us clear our schedules to be together. The unintentional bonding that occurred in those few weekly minutes had a lifelong impact on our relationships.

My mom never made us shop or cook, but we were required to clean up after the meal. That shared experience, too, yielded a bounty of memories. We all recall how a sister was consistently called away from her duties by a well-timed weekly phone call, thus delegating her chore to a sibling. And how a brother, while "washing" dishes, would combine all the gross scraps and leftover drinks into a cup, then offer five dollars to anyone who would drink it.

In retrospect, I only wish our required family activities also had included some basics in food preparation, beyond baking cookies. Early on, even in college, I missed not knowing how to function in a kitchen. The only things I could cook were chicken enchiladas, quesadillas, cereal (okay, so that's a stretch, but it was a staple), cakes, and cookies. That was about the extent of my recipe repertoire when I got married.

I'll never forget standing at the entrance of our local grocery store the week I came home from my honeymoon. "How could anyone live thirty years without ever truly shopping at a grocery store?" you might ask. Well, a young professional content with Cheerios, fruit, and dairy products can find everything on her shopping list by walking the perimeter of the store or simply stopping by a gas-station convenience store.

So as a new bride, compelled by the need to cook for my husband and armed with a sense of duty, I wandered up and down the aisles, filling my basket with everything I thought to be a necessity. Strapped for cash, I carried a wad of coupons clipped from the newspaper (another new experience for me) and bought countless items I would never use, mostly because I didn't know *how* to use them.

For weeks that turned into months, I struggled in the kitchen, consumed with guilt and embarrassment over my pathetic meal offerings. Relieved that someone had given us a waffle maker as a wedding gift—

one kitchen appliance I knew how to use—I served my poor husband
waffles three nights a week. If only I was exaggerating. Sweet Jon never
said a word until one night when I came crying to him in desperation.

"I can't handle this anymore!" I sobbed.

"Handle what?" He was oblivious to my struggle.

"This cooking thing! I'm terrible at it. You have to be sick of waffles.
I can't make them anymore. And I for sure can't eat them anymore!"

"I don't care if you cook."

What? He doesn't care? My mind reeled. *Isn't that what a wife is supposed to do?* Apparently not in his world. This information blew to pieces
all the preconceived ideas I had gleaned from *Leave It to Beaver, The Andy
Griffith Show,* and *The Brady Bunch.* (Okay, so we know that Alice did
most of the cooking, thus supporting my sister's claim that most problems in life are actually staffing issues.)

Jon really, truly didn't care. And believe it or not, his contented attitude freed me to learn how to cook and shop. Which I did. I took a few
classes, learned about kitchen staples, and began to add recipes to my
limited repertoire. I wish I had recognized earlier what sports, activities,
and busy schedules stole from me. And while I believe many extracurricular activities can serve positive purposes, I'm determined not to let
those good things rob my family of even more valuable ones. Great and
empowering lessons come from pitching in around the home, especially
in the kitchen. Wonderful conversations can be had while stirring a cus-
tard or washing dishes.

However, as we prepare to bulk up culinary muscles, I'm careful to
keep my expectations reasonable. I want the kids to know that there is
more to life than chicken fingers, to respect but not be afraid of the oven
and stove, to learn how spices and seasonings affect smells and tastes—
and perhaps ultimately to fall in love with cooking. I want them to press
through the anxiety and stress of placing their creation in front of an in-
evitably critical audience. And when the repast doesn't earn rave reviews
from all the mealtime judges, I want them to learn that their worth should

never be tied to success or failure. I hope that, rather than feeling inhibited by a lack of ability, the kids will learn to identify their limitations, then figure out how to overcome them. I hope they relish the satisfaction of doing something they never knew they could. Then, as they serve their meals (as dry and tasteless as some are bound to be), I hope they can find joy in the act itself. I want them to find fulfillment in serving others so they'll be compelled to seek additional opportunities to do so.

Maybe my goals seem a bit grandiose for kitchen patrol, but such potential is inherent in all our daily tasks. Life-fortifying opportunities dangle right before our eyes each and every day. This month I hope to see the kids successfully grab hold of them with their oven mitts.

Groceries 101

Fury, our Monday Meal Man, wants the family to have dessert tonight. The kid is no dummy; a little something sweet always makes the rest of the meal taste better! At the same time, we try to encourage (often to no avail) healthy eating, so I set a limit of one dessert per week. Each child will have the chance to make and serve dessert once during the month. I'm using this one to incentivize a dubious kid.

My dread of surrendering my kitchen to the kids initially proved to be well founded. Despite excitement about cooking whatever he wanted, Monday Meal Man lost his enthusiasm upon realizing that we had to go to the grocery store to buy his ingredients.

"What? Why would *I* have to go to the store? It takes *forever*!"

I know. He's got quite a flair for the dramatic. And should we ask the obvious question: Where does he think the food comes from?

"Welcome to my world, kid. If you want brownies"—his plan for dessert—"get in the car."

After his mini-tantrum, followed by a consequence—I wasn't in the mood for an attitude—Fury reluctantly made his way to the car. Picture Tim Conway doing his old man shuffle across the floor while Carol

Burnett as Mrs. Wiggins, filing nails and smacking gum, rolls her eyes. Moaning and groaning with every step, if they could be called steps, he blubbed, "No-ho-ho-ho-ho," increasing emphasis and volume with each "ho."

His mood lifted as we entered the store and ran into one of our neighbors. Mike shook Fury's hand and encouraged him by pointing to the bagged groceries he had just purchased and noting that they would soon be turned into dinner, cooked by him. Fury smiled sheepishly, and a little kick entered his step. As we started off in search of butter for the brownies, I explained to him the layout of a grocery store, realizing I have never taken the time to teach the kids anything about shopping.

"Okay, so if you need something cold, you'll find these items around the edges of the store. Frozen stuff is usually in the center. Produce on one side."

"What's produce?"

Hmm. Of course he has no idea of the meaning of produce. "It's stuff that's grown, like fruit, vegetables, lettuce, tomatoes…the fresh ones."

As we made our way to the butter and he realized the grocery store offers more than drudgery, his attitude further improved. Once I threw in a little math game, he became almost giddy.

"Can you find the butter?" I asked as we faced a refrigerated wall filled with cheese, creamer, and other dairy sundries.

"No."

"Keep looking. I see four different kinds." The kid loves games, no matter how lame.

"Where?"

"Look for small boxes that say 'butter.'"

"Like that 'Sweet Cream' thing?"

"Yes."

"Why are there so many?"

Ah, another good question. "Well, some have salt. Some don't. Some are national brands. Some are generic. Some organic. They also cost different amounts of money. You tell me which one is the best deal and how much money we can save buying the one on sale."

I could almost see him salivating. Yes, we're geeks.

After he found the perfect butter, we talked about why the same product can cost more or less when made by different manufacturers. We looked for the items he needed, bought something for his sister, weighed fruit, and squeezed tomatoes. We had a blast.

At the checkout counter, I watched Fury load his goods onto the belt. The glum complainer had morphed into a young man eager to help. I realized that some of the cheer could be chalked up to the newness of the activity, and I knew it wouldn't be this way all the time. Even so, as he chatted it up with supernice-checker-guy Chad, I was kicking myself. How many opportunities had I missed on the countless visits to the

We're All in This Together

I try to set everyone's task to where I think their individual strengths lie. Therefore the eight-year-old puts away the low-lying pieces of what comes out of the dishwasher, and the teenagers put away the higher-located items. Likewise, the nine-year-old chooses and prepares our fruit for dinner, the younger teen makes our vegetable, and the older teen fixes dessert or prepares part of an entrée or handles any cooking that is tedious or requires sharp-knife skills. Everyone helps pick out meals, goes to the grocery store, and puts away groceries once we are home. Of course, this is not set in stone: the third-grade boy is awesome at making green bean bundles wrapped in bacon, and the fourth grader likes garnishing, like fanning a strawberry.

—Dallas mom

grocery store? More often than not, I'd found ways to avoid even taking them into the store, focusing on the immediate benefit of a quick get-in-get-out grab over the long-term rewards of a learning opportunity. I have as much to learn from this task as they do.

Shopping completed, the kid and I headed back to the house. Gone was my slow-walking sourpuss; welcome home, superhelpful kitchen boy. He cleared the table, gathered ingredients, eagerly listened, followed instructions, emptied the dishwasher, then loaded it with the stuff left waiting in the sink. I'm not kidding! The girls hovered, itching for an opportunity to get involved. But it was his call. Fury cooked a simple menu of chicken, rice, and black beans, set the table (with his sisters' help), and served his food. Not one person complained about our meal. We ate, chatted, and truly enjoyed our time together. Then he cleaned it all up. I helped him wash the dishes, but barely. He genuinely wanted to do it all, and he was so proud of himself.

I don't know if the rest of our Month of Meals will be anything like the first, but what a way to start!

THE RECIPE FOR RESPONSIBILITY

Early on, I realized that even though the role of Enforcer doesn't come naturally to my laid-back personality, I couldn't let it bother me that the kids didn't *want* to work; the fact was, they needed to work. And now that I've entered the enabler-recovery program, I've seen their potential spring to life when I crack the whip. Okay, maybe a combination of whip cracking and getting out of the way.

Even this morning as I dutifully made my rounds to check beds and bathrooms, I fully expected to find something out of order. I haven't reminded the kids in weeks, and I sometimes forget to check. But no. The only thing I saw out of place was a pair of pajamas on the floor, beside a beautifully made bed. I left the dollar in the jar and picked up the offender's pj's. The sight of all those pillows neatly placed on his bed was so gratifying that I just couldn't take the buck.

Then this afternoon, my ten-year-old bustled around the kitchen, setting the table, washing the dishes, preparing a beautiful dinner for us. And where was I? Sitting on the couch. Working on some things I needed to get done. Yes. I need to let that sink in. Sitting on the couch. During the day. While the sun was up. And to top it all off, she literally hummed happily, as if on cloud nine while she worked.

The point is, I'm fairly certain that not only have I set the bar low, but I have settled for so much less than they have to offer—in every arena. A school administrator recently told a friend of mine that all the stuff that kids have these days isn't what's spoiling them; it's their moms. Moms who hover. Moms who step in to fix problems. Moms who coddle. Moms who do not allow their children to suffer the natural consequences of their actions. No wonder a twenty-five-year-old can be found still living at his parents' home.

How does society view this, one might ask? Apparently we're all for it. This is what our leadership in Washington said to a cheering crowd of graduating college seniors: "If this reform becomes law.... To all the young people here today, starting this year if you don't have insurance, all new plans will allow you to stay on your parents' plan until you are 26 years old."[1]

Yikes.

Not that I have any intention of pontificating on political affairs, but isn't this exactly the mentality fueling our problems? The entitlement card that postpones independence, caters to fears of failure, provides parachutes, avoids reality. Great message to send the future leaders of America: Keep relying on your parents. Avoid life for just a few more years.

Forget Washington. I'm just trying to rewrite the message in my own home. Getting the kids to expand their capabilities in the bedrooms, bathrooms, and kitchen might seem trivial, but the ultimate objective—

equipping and empowering my kids to function at their highest potential and contribute to their family, community, and world—is anything but. Our kids want us to challenge them to do more, particularly once they experience firsthand how much better it feels to be productive rather than to be catered to.

Just take a look at the kid who made our dinner tonight. She's clearly encouraged by her venture into new territories of responsibility.

Barton woke up this morning brimming with anticipation for to-night's meal. She planned her menu several days ago: her favorite breaded pan-fried tilapia, sautéed corn, mashed potatoes, and a beautiful fruit platter. (Soon, we'll tackle the beyond carbs menu options. But until we get the hang of it, they can cook essentially whatever they want as long as freshly grown ingredients grace the plate in some form or fashion.)

A bit uncertain about all the steps involved, Barton asked me to stand by and help her. We had such a wonderful time chatting as we shucked the fresh corn, struggled through removing husks and hairs, and then learned the safe way to cut the kernels off the stalks and into a but-tered skillet.

She took painstaking care to ensure that she created a meal that would satisfy everyone. It was especially sweet watching her season the corn. This kid loves salt and ground pepper. But she considered her brother and sister who hate pepper. Rather than spice it up to her liking, she turned to me and said, "I'll just put in a little salt. Then anyone who wants can add more if they need. I'll leave the pepper out." Her thought-fulness confirmed that this task was accomplishing so much more than I had hoped. It was taking a kid out of her comfort zone. Putting her hands, literally, on potentially dangerous and formerly off-limits utensils, giving her a huge dose of self-worth, and—for me, the pièce de résis-tance—planting her eyes on serving others. In this single dinner prepara-tion experience, my daughter went from focusing on whether our dinner would suit her taste to considering others' needs ahead of her own.

Not all her siblings initially shared her excitement, but some of it has rubbed off on them. An unexpected windfall from our project has been contagious good attitudes. When the kids witness one of their siblings genuinely enjoying the results of his or her labor, the reluctant participants more eagerly embrace their own tasks.

THE DRIVE-THROUGH BLUES

Barton's cooking coup provided an unmistakable contrast to another less-than-appetizing experience this week.

As agreed in our family meeting, the kids could choose either to cook their meals or purchase takeout, if they preferred. At the outset, I loved this idea. I envisioned them experiencing the agony of choosing an eating establishment agreeable to seven opinionated palettes. Oh, the moments we've sat in our driveway at a stalemate, trying to identify an affordable restaurant option that wouldn't provoke objections from one or more family members. So the opportunity for a kid to experience firsthand the difficulty of pleasing a crowd seemed like a winner for sure: take the measly amount of money we would spend at home, apply it to the cost, add your own money, then feed the unappreciative masses—and learn that it costs more to eat out.

Boxster tapped in for this option. Not only did he not like the idea of cooking, he's at that age where he finds repugnant even a hint of someone telling him what to do. Add in the fact that his younger siblings were excited about cooking, and the deal was sealed.

"What are you going to make for dinner?" I asked when I picked him up from school.

"Remember? I'm not cooking."

"Oh yeah. Okay… Where are you *buying* dinner?"

A twinkle gleamed in his eye. Actually, just that glimpse of whimsy was worth the whole Experiment. I miss those carefree moments of joy, now usually suppressed by teen coolness. "Remember, I'm buying Wendy's for everyone."

Proud of his choice, which he was certain would please everyone, he came to get me around five thirty so I could drive him to pick up his meal. He knew kitchen duties were included in his evening as chef, but none of that diminished his eagerness to prove a point, which seemed to be that anything prepared outside our home surpasses all meals he's ever endured at the hand of the resident cook. This would be the night that he could harvest his converts. Then maybe *every* meal could be from an eating establishment outside our home.

We pulled into the Wendy's drive-through. I made him crawl into the backseat and order out the window. Awkward? Maybe. But I had my principles too. As he placed the order, I was delighted to discover that he had actually thought about what everyone likes to eat. Who knew he ever paid attention to the others' interests, desires, or meal choices? Not that they were difficult, but still…

"I need three orders of the kid chicken nuggets," Boxster yelled at the drive-through speaker.

"What's your side?" barked the attendant.

"Uh…"

"Fries or fruit?"

"Oh. Fries, for sure."

"What to drink?"

"All Dr Peppers."

"Okay. Anything else?"

"Yes. A hamburger meal—plain. With fries and a Dr Pepper."

"What size?"

"Um…small?"

"Anything else?"

"Oh yeah. One more chicken nugget meal with fries…and a juice box." (He had momentarily forgotten Jack, whose last-in-line role often leads to his being overlooked. Jon and I, preferring something at home, had opted out of his fast-food run.)

"That all?"

"Yes," he said. Then, "Thank you." (I liked that last part, for sure.)

"That will be twenty dollars and fourteen cents."

I wondered if he'd expected that amount. I handed him the promised ten dollars, he added his eleven, and off we drove with a bag of goodies. I could almost feel his excitement.

Too bad he wasn't met with the same excitement at home.

"Hey, everyone," he yelled as we came through the door. "Dinner is served!"

No one moved.

"Hey! I have Wendy's!" The anticipated cheers just weren't happening.

One of his diners moseyed in. "Eww. I don't like Wendy's."

"Oh, I do." Snopes, always the sensitive one, had noticed her brother's smile starting to turn down at the edges. She elbowed Fury to stop complaining.

Then Barton wandered in. "Yee-uck. What's that smell?"

"Fine!" Boxster imploded. "I try to do something *nice,* and you all just *complain*!"

I felt so bad for him. The strange thing was, these kids actually love Wendy's. I'm not sure what in the world was going on with the genuine disgust that evening.

Then came the worst part of the whole show: a dejected Boxster sat down to his own "plain" burger, only to find it loaded with mayonnaise, mustard, onions, lettuce, and tomato. He couldn't believe his eyes or his luck. I felt so sorry for him I whisked it up, put him in the car, and drove right back to Wendy's. How dare they mess up my kid's order! Especially after he paid with his own money! I briefly wondered if this meant I'd fallen off the enabler-recovery wagon. Then I decided to capitalize on yet another teaching opportunity: how to return an order gone wrong and get what you paid for.

I let Boxster continue to buy meals for his next two turns, before I realized my strategy was backfiring. Not only did he run through his cash

(I was hoping for a good lesson here), he heard a message neither of us anticipated—the message that he *can't* cook. He would never admit it, of course, but he felt terrible watching everyone else earn kudos for their efforts. The other kids have fumbled through their creations, sometimes hitting a home run, sometimes serving a concoction that we all politely tolerated. Whatever the case, they've invested themselves in the task and so, thrilled by their own accomplishment, they proudly watch as the family consumes their efforts.

On Boxster's night, however, he basically endures the meal. He wants everyone to acknowledge the fact he spent his money on them. Much to his disappointment, no one cares about his purchased meals. Or at least no one is as excited as he expects them to be. Clearly, hard work does benefit the laborer. The easy way out—in this case, buying a meal— means missing out on any sense of personal accomplishment.

We're All in This Together

I absolutely *love* www.e-mealz.com. A site recommended by Dave Ramsey, the measly five dollars per month fee equates to my using a dollar-fifty coupon per week at the store to make it a freebie in my mind.

The menus for the seven nights are well organized, contain a shopping list—even down to the numbered meal, so if you only pick one meal off the menu that week, it is an easy step to shop. Perfect for the kids to pick and choose and do their part!

I have found all the meals to be pretty easy. It really makes the kids see how they can make more than mac and cheese!

—Lanita

So, yes, he feels our pain for all those times we pony up for a meal out and our costly efforts go unappreciated. But he's also feeling a bit more pain and in a different way than I anticipated.

When you come up against such walls as a parent, you can only back up and start over.

Next week Boxster will cook a meal whether he wants to or not. He might fight me—on the outside. But I know that deep inside, he will be relieved to finally be able to commiserate with the other cooks and take some pride in whatever he creates. Plus, I know that my ace-in-the-hole girls will, without prompting, heap the praise no matter what the menu holds. I can't wait.

Could I Get Some Cheese with That Whine?

As Fury peeked into our refrigerator, considering his own menu for the evening, he had no idea what ingredients might be necessary to create his pending "B for D" masterpiece. Our little chef wanted some pancake action, a surefire home run. Plus he had always wanted to flip the flapjacks. It just looked like so much fun. And how hard could it be?

Thankfully, we had the necessary staples. Buttermilk, flour, eggs, butter, baking powder and soda, plus a little salt for good measure and some mini chocolate chips for the few sweet-toothed in our crowd. Fury had already used his dessert card on week one, but he's no dummy. A little creative crowd-pleasing effort goes a long way.

We pulled together the ingredients, and in he dove.

I should have known when the third egg exploded into the bowl of buttermilk to join its two splattered companions that pancakes and a progressively grumpy eight-year-old were not a good combination. The harder he tried, the more disastrous the outcome—and the crabbier his mood.

He moaned louder as flour poofed everywhere when he tried to stir the batter. Nothing was going smoothly. After spooning the batter onto a hot griddle, his flipping attempts resulted in folded over blobs and cries of frustration. His whining ended with me cooking the rest of his dinner. Granted, he flipped a few more pancakes and stirred the scrambled eggs. But when the going got tough, he quit. And being a newbie at this, I let him give up. At the end of the day, I just didn't have it in me to cheerlead the kid to success. I guess we both have room for improvement.

Despite the cooking disaster, the family did sit together and enjoy "his" meal. Fury may not have made everything, but his siblings heralded the delicious dinner that agreed with every picky palette at the table.

Once I finally sat down at the table to eat, I informed Chef Fury that dishwasher duty remained on the checklist—unloading *and* loading. In previous weeks, he couldn't wait to get his hands on the silverware caddy. Today all he could do was moan. The fact of the matter is, he didn't want to do anything. He wanted *me* to do it for him.

"Why are you sooooo mad at me?" he cried.

"What are you talking about? I'm not mad at you."

"Yes, you are. Why else would you be making me do the dishwasher *again*?"

Again? Is he talking about last week? Wow, I really am a slave driver. Ooohh…helping with the dishes more than once in a month. That *is* unreasonable.

"Listen, tonight is your night." I determined to avoid the mistake I'd made earlier by letting him weasel out of cooking. "If you don't do your job, you'll have to pay me to do it."

"That's not fair!" Stomp. "Not fair." Stomp. "Not fair." Moan.

"It's your choice."

Nothing was being asked of him that he couldn't do. Plus, I'm always there to help—probably too often and too much. It really boiled down to the fact that he only wanted work based on *his* terms.

Isn't that how we all want it to be?

He disappeared after the meal, reappearing now and then to see if I meant what I'd said about his dishwasher responsibility. I reminded him twice and left the kitchen messy for about an hour. After that, I assumed my natural position next to the sink, unloading the dishwasher, then rinsing and loading the evening's dishes. I cleaned the table and countertops, swept the floor, put everything away.

As I tucked him into bed, I quietly went to his box and paid myself. Not enough for my desperately needed pedicure, but enough for him to miss it. I added his five dollars to the two dollars I collected from the kids who left clothes on the floor that morning. The newness is wearing off, hard work is being felt, perseverance is entering the picture.

For some, a glass of wine would be in order. For me, it's my Keurig coffee maker that comes to the rescue. Nothing like a piping hot, fresh-brewed cup of coffee for a quick escape. Thank you, Van Houtte decaffeinated dark extra bold. You help me put it all into perspective.

We're All in This Together

With our other three kids out of the house, I let my teen play for a while, then decided to commence overdue training in chores. Here, verbatim, is our conversation:

Me (cheerfully): Okay, time to do the dishes.

Matthew (genuinely confused): Dishes? What do you *do* to dishes?

Me: We wash them.

Matthew: But I'm a *boy*!

Oh my word. We are worse off than I thought. Just so you know, we *did* wash the dishes together—and had a good conversation while doing so.

—Leslie

Is the Pain Worth the Gain?

Up to this point in the Experiment, our efforts have proven worthwhile—at least in my opinion. Certain comments might suggest the kids aren't yet ready to thank me for making them work:

- "This is a lot harder than I thought it would be."
- "When I go to Henry's house, his *mom* cooks."
- "We're the *only* kids that have to do this."
- "What do you mean 'unload the dishwasher'? That's a girl's job."
- "Hey, their family is doing the work thing too!"

I love that last one, said matter-of-factly about a friend, almost with relief. As in "Phew! Our mother *isn't* crazy or supermean! Someone else has to do this weird work thing too."

I've noticed they are a little more tired than normal, but they're also proud of what they've accomplished, especially on the food front. The biggest surprise for me? They are now doing the tasks I've nagged about for years ("take your dish to the sink," "unload the dishwasher," "cut your *own* pizza")—without the annoying moans and groans. You know the ones. Audible sighs aggressively released to make a point that they are doing something they should not be required to do. Yes, I've heard them complain to their friends about how horrible all the work around our house has become. But the absence of genuine disdain is noticeable, and a hint of pride is bubbling just below the surface

Consistent with any work situation, success and failure have shared the spotlight this month. The kids who worked reaped the rewards, the greatest of which was improved self-esteem. The meals haven't been without bumps, but confidence expanded as a result of not quitting even when a third stab at homemade pizza continued to taste "interesting." The muscles of determination grew stronger through repeated efforts even when panned by the resident food critic(s).

Poor Snopes bore the brunt of "this is gross" under-the-breath comments when she served pasta with butter and parmesan cheese four times. She weathered the negative remarks, though, staying the course despite slightly hurt feelings. Isn't that an experience we want for all our kids: persevering through tough situations in a safe environment?

In the name of perseverance, I forced Boxster to cook rather than buy when his turn rolled around. When he pushed back, I stood my ground but offered to help so he wouldn't feel overwhelmed. He cooked the entrée, and I did the rest. Despite digging in his heels at the mention of his cooking, he rose to the task and prepared some mean tacos. He feigned agony at the dinner table, but I could tell he was proud of the delicious meal.

By contrast, what seemed logical from the world's standard proved a colossal failure on every level. Yes, buying meals and eating on the run save time and accomplish the basic purpose of feeding and fueling hungry bodies. But paying someone else to do the work meant missing out on the accompanying rewards—a reminder to me as much as anyone that time-saving, convenient luxuries that smooth the road of life aren't always the best answer.

Our Month of Meals task didn't deserve the dread I wasted on it. Creative flair abounded in food presentation and surprisingly nice table settings. I've learned more about my kids' ingenuity as I've watched them put together menus. And the results, for the most part, have been tasty— even when served on paper plates by those eager to simplify the cleanup. (Believe me, in a family of seven, they still have plenty of dishes to wash even when opting for paper plates and plastic utensils.)

One of the month's more memorable scenes occurred on Monday. Fury, who had morphed into Able Assembler when he whipped up his soup for the evening meal, was dutifully clearing the table afterward. I saw the little guy longingly watch as his sisters ran out to jump on the trampoline.

Then I heard, "Can I help you clean the dishes?"

What! Who said that?

Could it be? Yes, it was. Boxster, from the kindness of his heart (oh, it's in there), offered to help his often annoying little brother—with absolutely nothing in it for him. The teenager cleared the table and helped fill the dishwasher so our junior cook could enjoy the rest of his evening outside, gleefully bouncing with his sisters.

I didn't say a word.

I just savored, and continue to savor, the moment.

WHAT THEY LEARNED THIS MONTH

- All the kids have learned how to navigate the grocery store and how much food costs. I can still picture the shock on Snopes's face when she saw the hundred-dollar-plus tab for a small cart of goods.
- Meals are more than food on the table.
- Dishes are not girls' work.

WHAT I LEARNED THIS MONTH

- Some of my well-meaning lessons don't work as one might expect. I would never have guessed that allowing one of the kids to purchase meals for the family would be self-defeating.
- I didn't realize just how much I've shackled these kids by racing in and doing for them. On autopilot, I've shopped, cooked, and so much more, failing to see the countless opportunities to teach them about life and build self-esteem by helping them do what most of their friends have never considered doing.
- We tend to all sit together and linger at the dinner table to talk when they cook.
- My amazing kids have a creative flair for cooking. Watch out Iron Chef!

Grounding Time

*Planting, Weeding, and Getting Acquainted
with the Great Outdoors*

> A perfect summer day is when the sun is
> shining, the breeze is blowing, the birds are
> singing, and the lawn mower is broken.
>
> —JAMES DENT

I'm approaching April with as much initial uncertainty as I brought to March's Month of Meals. Our challenge in these next few weeks is to help these kids learn some basics about maintaining and caring for the *outside* of the house, an ambitious endeavor given that I have very little green in my thumb.

Yesterday offered a glimpse into how badly we need some education on "ground" rules.

While jumping on the trampoline, Fury clearly broke some well-established bouncing rules. The kid has a fascination with cause and effect, especially when it involves his little brother. He has been warned and disciplined for rolling balls under Jack's feet to see what happens when his brother lands on them, and he's also been cautioned against double-bouncing the little guy—a *huge* offense. Fury was caught in the act of violating the first rule by his father, who not only had just walked in the door early from work but also found yet another opportunity to say to me, "Do you *ever* watch these kids?" (Why is it always in the moment that I'm not watching that their father catches them in an infraction?)

Knowing that a serious consequence was about to be dished out, the young offender mummy-walked upstairs, moaning at every scoot, to receive the inevitable punishment. Dad, however, took pity on the poor kid and opted for a new consequence: "Go outside and pick, by the root, twenty weeds."

The relieved kid dutifully headed out the back door, followed by his father, to complete the task. After several minutes of watching the child become agitated as he wandered the yard aimlessly, Dad walked over and asked the obvious question, "What is wrong with you?"

"I can't doooooo this!" groaned the exasperated kid. "I *caaaan't.*" Sob, sob, sob.

"Hey. Chill. Can't do what?"

"Pick weeds." Blub, blub, blub.

"Sure you can," Jon confidently assured him. "You just grab and pull them out. But make sure you get the root."

With exasperation, the boy turned to his dad, wiped away the tears he'd conjured up, and asked, "But what *is* a weed?"

Enough said.

ASSESSING THE LANDSCAPE

Yard work around our home has taken different shapes through the years. At times, we've maintained our yard ourselves. I personally find mowing the grass therapeutic. The monotonous hum of the motor relaxes me in a strange sort of way. Maybe the fact that it drowns out the noise of my often-boisterous crowd has something to do with it. Whatever the reason, I get jazzed from clipping one row up, one row down, one row up, one row down. Spicing up things by adding a little circumference action—going around the edge, then picking up the rows again. The heat doesn't even bother me. Plus it's an easy workout sporting the right price tag: free.

Jon, on the other hand, has never liked the idea of his wife mowing the yard. It might have something to do with an incident some years ago when I was seven months pregnant with our fourth child. A friend saw me mowing the yard while the kids sat watching, sweating it out on the porch until I finished. He called Jon and proceeded with some sarcastic, most likely well-deserved, ribbing…and that was the end of my mowing days.

While he does not care to have me mow the yard, he has less than no interest in doing it himself. Mowing isn't the way he wants to spend his weekends after long arduous days solving the corporate tax problems of the world. So all it took was one of his famous hourly wage computations to solidify his decision to pay someone else. When he compared the cost to the rate he charged at work, it was a no-brainer to outsource mowing to Raymundo and his crew.

So up to this point, none of our kids have dirtied their hands in the yard maintenance arena. Nor will they experience the joys of mowing during this task. Our dad and Big Boss has little—make that zero—interest in adding a lawn mower to the budget, even for the sake of the Experiment. Raymundo's job is safe, for now. But, I'm not going to give up on the lawn mower. We have three boys who need to experience mowing yards in the heat of a Texas summer.

But for this month, anyway, our yard efforts will center on four areas that seem to present the greatest need and opportunity.

Declutter

In the same way we started the Experiment (a loose use of the term "we"), our outside assault begins with clutter control. Remember *Sanford and Son*? Those guys have nothing on us. We might not be dealing the junk, but we've got lots of it. The seven of us somehow have scattered across the

yard shoes, socks, balls, wrappers, clothes, bicycles, scooters, newspapers…
the list goes on and on. And chairs! Are you ready? Twenty-two chairs.
Who needs that many chairs in their yard? We didn't buy the chairs. No,
we're the king and queen of inheriting. Whenever anyone wants to get rid
of something, they call us. For some reason, we've adopted the "we don't
need it now, but we might down the road" mind-set. No wonder Jack has
some hoarding issues.

Twelve of the chairs are logically placed at two patio tables. The rest
Jon has strategically placed…around the driveway, by the playhouse (another item we inherited), by the trampoline, by the…oh, it doesn't matter. Regardless how you slice it, there are too many.

I am *so* tired of looking at a particular set of four—a set we've had for
years, never use, and have even moved three times. So what if the chairs
are vintage (actually just old) Brown Jordan? For some reason, Jon's determined to save them from being sold. There's certainly not any value in
these '70s antiques. They sit with no anchoring table, which was sold
several garage sales ago. Basically, they just take up space. What they need
is a new home.

Weeds
After a wet winter, pesky nut-grass weeds have already infiltrated the beds
and the yard. Our front yard resembles a budding tree farm. It's not
pretty. We, like everyone else in our neighborhood, will have quite a job
getting rid of the prolific green machines.

Odd Job Postings
We have lots of yard-related odd-job opportunities. Sanding and painting
the front porch chairs, washing windows, painting the front door, and
cleaning the porch. These jobs will yield actual cash rewards, anywhere
from five to twenty-five dollars. For a few low-dollar items, I've thrown in
things like sweeping the back porch (something that could be done almost daily), watering the plants, emptying the pool skimmers. (Yes, we

have a pool. Have I mentioned we live in Texas, where it's almost essential to survival and definitely crucial to preserving a mom's sanity?) My newly created job board, strategically placed on the refrigerator so as to be seen, beckons an industrious kid, promising great reward. We'll see if I have any takers.

Flowers

What's better than looking out your window to a view of warm and inviting petal power? If I had planned ahead, or even revealed this task to the kids a little earlier, we could have had some major fun and education by growing flowers from seeds. But due to my tendency to procrastinate, we'll save that for another time. Rather than watching seeds sprout, we will opt for purchasing budding flowers and grown plants. It will be a great chance for the kids to see that, though pleasurable, beautifying a yard can be expensive. I tend to keep things minimalistic, only planting flowers in the spring. Our hot Texas summers make it tough to keep anything alive, but there will be terrific lessons in that too. I can't wait for the kids to enjoy the fruit of their labor, to be greeted by the beauty of color each day as they open the door. It will be a treat for me too. I can just see myself sipping a tall glass of sweet tea, enjoying the spring, and pushing urgent activities off where they belong—in the background.

All four of our target opportunities are intended to give the kids a better sense of the effort that goes into maintaining a presentable yard. *Better Homes and Gardens*, here we come!

Yet even as I start to feel encouraged about the growth opportunities in this month's task, I find myself wondering, how do you inspire kids to take care of things? to be responsible? Although we're making some progress, it continues to take a lot of energy and creativity on my part to serve as cheerleader and coach and team manager.

I'm also discovering many more questions:

- Do they have so much stuff that they can't keep up with it all?

- Do they have any concept that all this stuff they love costs money?
- Do they think they deserve all their stuff?
- Do they realize the privilege of ownership?
- Do they understand that stuff doesn't matter?
- Do *I* understand that stuff doesn't matter?

Maybe as the kids are required to pitch in a bit more—to gain some insight into all the effort that goes into maintaining a home and providing all that they so easily take for granted—they will not only begin to appreciate the stuff and all that goes with it, but also begin to ease up on the obsession with outer appearances that seems to consume tweens and teens—well, all of us really—and realize that character is what really matters. (Possible Pollyanna alert.)

As we begin to deal with concepts that up to this point have been overlooked or only superficially addressed, I'm thankful for the unexpected teachable moments. That's one of the many benefits work has ushered into our home: even more learning opportunities than I planned for—many of them geared to teach me as much as or more than the kids.

We're All in This Together

My kids, ages twelve and fourteen, have graduated past this, but how about all the stuff they bring home from birthday parties and school events? We have become so focused on making each event more special than the last, but we forget it has nothing to do with loot bags full of toys that will be trash tomorrow. I cringe to think how much money I threw away on all that stuff...and how many bags of junk I ended up donating.

—Abbie

DIGGING IN

Since the kids seem a bit tired of, possibly annoyed with, the changes brought about by the Experiment, we decided to kick off our month of yard work with the flowers, a bit more palatable exercise than cleaning out the garage. They have loved helping me plant since they were little. And I've loved their helping. As many times as I've been pregnant, little digging hands came to be a welcome relief to an enormous belly-laden, nesting, wanting-everything-to-look-pretty mother. I've always let them help in a controlled setting, with me close at hand to direct, organize, and determine what will be planted and where. This planting season, however, I intend to remove myself, as much as possible, from the picture and clear the way for them to feel ownership. (Eek! I'm feeling a *The Little Engine That Could* moment coming on. "I think I can... I think I can.")

As we eyed our yard and the rather large job in the landscaping arena, we took a deep breath and considered our resources. I'm sure there are economical ways to add color to a yard. But I'm fairly certain those tend to involve a green thumb, frequent attention, water, and care. This otherwise-occupied family has enough trouble remembering to feed ourselves. I pity the plant that meets our soil, inside or out. I've managed to kill even ivy plants.

So I am thankful for businesses that specialize in fledgling plants and seedlings, where half our job is done before we begin. Here's a big shout out to Lowe's, The Home Depot, and our local nurseries for making it all seem so easy. Rather than needing to research regional soils, temperature indices, indigenous species, and so much more, we can just head over to the ones who have done the work for us (hmm...sounds strangely familiar!) and pick plants that not only have been sprouted and partially grown but are organized according to their requirements for sustaining life.

Do you have a shady spot? Interested in color? Just want a little ground cover? Low maintenance? High maintenance? The choice is yours. Confused? Just ask the guy or gal in the apron, and you'll be all set.

With confidence in the knowledgeable people at the garden center, I loaded up the kids for a trip to the store.

Here's how it usually goes with us. Since we have a little guy and a teen guy, the lengths of our outings are limited. The similarity between toddlers and teens never ceases to amaze me. Toddlers have a short window for errands due to sleep and food requirements. Teenagers have a similarly limited tolerance for outings, unless it has something to do with their own agenda...or the mall. Unlike the tantrum-oriented toddler, the teen expresses disinterest by sullenly walking several steps behind the group to make it clear "I'm not with those people," while heaving a few grunts and sighs for good measure. Teens pepper an outing with frequent queries of "Are we done yet?" and "Can we go now?" to reinforce their disapproval of forced participation.

With these things in mind, our family tends to operate on a grab-and-go basis, also known as the try-it-on-at-home-and-return-rejects-at-a-later-date approach. That's why I've previously run into the grocery store alone. And, dare I say, the reasoning behind one of my primary enabling excuses: "It's so much easier doing it myself." But that would undercut the goal of our equipping exercise. No, these kids need to know, even if they don't care, how to make a yard beautiful.

Ignoring the groans and a few squeals of delight, I drove the whole crew to Lowe's. We arrived and piled out, some more eagerly than others, and made our way to the nursery section. Before letting the kids pick the plants (which I did, fighting my every desire to control color and plant selections), I made them ask for help. We happened upon an employee (we'll call him LG, for Lowe's Guy) who didn't quite appreciate all the crucial learning that was taking place as we tried to equip the newly minted workers. Either that, or he was as clueless as we were.

Snopes (always polite if nothing else): Sir, could you help us figure out what plants would work best in our yard?

LG: Whaddaya lookin' for? This whole area is full of flowering plants. Ground cover is over there.

BARTON: Something really pretty.

BOXSTER (under his breath): Ugh. Just pick something and let's go!

SNOPES: Yeah, those pink ones.

BARTON: No, the purple ones.

FURY: I like the red.

SNOPES: Red doesn't go with purple. Let's get the pink.

MOM: Well, we need to make sure they will grow in our spots. We have to look and see if they like sun or shade.

BARTON (with a bag of seeds in hand): How about these? Please, Mom! Let's *make* a garden.

FURY: I want red. Pink is for girls. They always get what they want.

MOM: Chill. We haven't picked a color.

BOXSTER: Puh-leeze, can we go? I told Brandon I'd meet him at Top Golf.

SNOPES: Oh, how about these yellow ones?

BARTON: Yeah, they'll look perfect in the pots by the fence.

FURY: Yellow is for girls too. I want red.

BOXSTER: Oh. My. Word. I'm walking home.

MOM (ignoring the absurd walking comment): Ask the man to show you how to know where they'll grow best.

Pause.

SNOPES (looking around for help): Where'd he go?

Sure enough, sometime during our "discussion," LG had disappeared. In his place stood Jack, our Future Hoarder of America, pushing a cart full of goodies he had gathered while we were talking among ourselves. Mostly seed packets.

Now for a little lesson in organization and putting things back where they came from.

Nah. We're butting up against our time window.

I sought out another employee to show her our cart predicament, apologized, and asked if we could get some help restocking. Not only did she tell us to leave it, she helped us select our plants. Such a nice salesperson. She showed the kids the tags on each plant that describe optimal planting situations in words and user-friendly pictures. Armed with that knowledge, they chose an interesting combination of plants. We also picked up a bag of fertilized potting soil, then headed to the counter to pay.

The helpful garden-center girl even checked us out.

As the kids pushed the cart to the car, she pulled me aside. "Keep your receipt."

"Oh-kaaay," I responded, appreciative that she cared but not quite clear on her intended point.

"If the plants don't work...or die... Not that I'm saying they're going to die... I'm just, well..." The poor thing couldn't quite get it out. "All I'm saying is, we'll take them back and give you new ones if you have a problem."

How sweet. She didn't have the heart to say outright what seemed so apparent: the poor plants we'd purchased had just received their death sentence. Little did she know—and I didn't either a few months ago—that these kids can produce. With a little direction, they can do a rather fantastic job.

I was looking forward to all of us enjoying many months of beautiful plants. Of course we had to get them into the ground first. But for the moment, the excitement meter had tipped to the positive side on this task. If only they remember to water.

COMBATING WEEDS OF ALL VARIETIES

Planting flowers is one of those tasks that offers instant gratification. Within minutes of finishing (which included taking all the plastic plant holders to the garbage; for some reason the kids assumed someone *else* would be doing that), the workers can bask in the beauty of their accomplishment. The great thing about flowers, especially those already sprouted and partially grown, is that it doesn't much matter whether they artistically match in color, depth, and density. They bring joy just by their presence. Let's face it, even flowering weeds can be easy on the eyes.

Unfortunately, the weeds in our yard are not of the flowering variety. Just the annoying kind. Annoying and prolific. Prolific and incredibly challenging to dislodge. Somewhat reminiscent of our entitlement issues.

Every time we open the front door or drive up to our house, we're greeted by a yard full of nut-grass sproutlings. They're basically little trees produced from a bumper crop of acorns dropped by our trees last fall. If we had taken the time to rake and dispose of the millions of acorns, we might have a smaller job on our hands. But why work when you don't have to? Apparently the yard guys felt the same way. As they walked up and down clipping the grass, they did a terrific job of pushing the nuts further into the ground with their boots and mower wheels.

I can't help but take note of the analogy at hand. (So many seem to accompany each of our tasks!) Those acorns didn't appear to be much of a problem sitting on the ground. No one would notice them unless standing in the yard. In fact, after a few weeks, we couldn't see them anymore. The squirrels helpfully buried the ones that didn't get pushed down by Raymundo and his crew. Then the nuts took on the out-of-sight-out-of-mind status. What you can't see won't hurt you.

But we all know that's not true, especially with our kids. Each day the culture drops seeds into the minds and hearts of our kids—seeds of insecurity and inadequacy, of greed and consumerism, of selfishness and cynicism. As with the acorns, our efforts at combating these invaders will be more effective if we act before they take root. We can have the conversations, present strategies, be honest, and work together to help our kids build up their defenses.

It isn't fair what our children are hit with these days. But I can't pretend the problems aren't real. In fact, I'm determined to be vigilant against the many ways a mediocre culture threatens to encroach on our home. Sometimes the kids think I go a bit overboard. I suspect they think I'm rather a prude.

It's not just culture, but weeds hide in their hearts too. The other day in the car, Boxster, after hearing his sister's menu for dinner, asked, "Why don't you buy everyone's meal tonight?"

"I want to make mashed potatoes, chicken, and corn."

"Can I have a side of cereal?"

"No. You have to eat what I make," she know-it-all sassed at him.

"Shut up, Barton," he muttered under his breath.

Oh yeah. He went there. From the driver's perspective, a less-than-wise choice of words had been uttered.

"Did you just say, 'Shut up'?"

"Yes." (God bless him for his stand-up honesty. I hope he never loses this great character quality. He didn't even bite the temptation to blame either.)

"Well, we don't say those words." In fact, in my midforties I still have a hard time saying the words. I can almost feel *my* mother glaring in disapproval on the rare occasion they pass my lips.

"What are you talking about? I'm *fourteen*!"

What is it with the "but I'm a teenager now" declaration? Is some secret "See and Say Whatever You Want" pass slipped to a kid on his thirteenth birthday? Does the Blue Fairy hide a free-ride card to the word/movie/experience of your choice under a new teen's pillow the morning after twelve bids adieu?

As you might have guessed, the disrespect coupled with sass won Boxster a free trip to the front yard to gather twenty of our uninvited guests. Then it occurred to me that our sapling-riddled yard offered not only a great place for a wayward child to "think" about his or her actions but also a terrific job posting for willing workers. I accidentally uttered a compensation offer of twenty-five cents per weed for anyone else who could use some extra cash. As Boxster grudgingly pulled his weeds, still muttering that he had said nothing wrong, the rest of our gang sped out to the yard. Tom Thumb bags in hand, they raced to gather their plunder as if they were at the White House Easter Egg Roll. Oops. My too-generous offer was instantly rescinded and replaced with a price per bag.

As cars drove by, a few drivers beeped encouraging honks to my chain gang–style work crew (à la Maricopa County's Sheriff Joe, without the striped jumpsuits). The kids each filled one bag, except Fury, who contributed three. He may be stubborn, but the kid can work!

As I watched my kids work, I couldn't help but consider some of those stubborn life weeds that sprout at every age. If only I could pull those weeds as easily as the seedlings in our yard. How I'd love to get my hands on those uninvited guests—you know the ones: eye rolls, insecurity, "it's all about me" attitudes, apathy—and yank *them* out by the root. I want to clean house so that other much more beneficial attributes can grow and not get choked out by uninvited invaders.

And I won't settle for simply yanking out the bad stuff; the good stuff needs fertilizing. I need to hit their areas of strength—such as Boxster's fierce loyalty and admirable character and Fury's strong work ethic—with fortifying measures of meaningful work and responsibility. Doing so will confirm that my admiration and belief in their God-given abilities is more than lip service. As confidence and character take root, they might find the strength to ward off self-doubt that leads to staggeringly destructive behaviors.

Today's weed happened to be in the form of questionable language. In the offender's mind, his words are nothing compared to the trash he hears around friends. To his credit, the kid walks the high road in that area. But does his avoidance of full-out cussing warrant his use of lesser inappropriate language? He thinks I'm treating him like a baby when I jump on those things. I would point out, though, that the adults he respects in his life don't use those words. And I don't think that growing older somehow makes the use of rude words acceptable.

I think my kids, in their hearts, like the thick, Sharpie-black boundaries—whether or not they admit it. I'm convinced even my teenager craves those dark black lines that clearly mark off the danger zones, just as much as he did in the toddler years.

Perhaps, however, in this case I overreacted just a little. I'm far from perfect. Frayed nerves at the end of a long day can catapult me to Enforcer Extraordinaire. But the kids might as well get used to that too, because yet again, life isn't fair. There will be times when a teacher, a boss, a friend, and yes, a mom overreacts or is unreasonable. They need to know how to deal with it.

That said, I'm learning to see the yard from a whole new perspective. Not only does it provide an inherently productive, instantly gratifying, physically demanding environment in which to toil, it provides an excellent location for working out consequences for less-than-desirable behavior.

Meaningful Work

As we were enjoying a meal with our friends Scurry and Barbara, Jon offered a response to the question, "What have y'all been up to?"

"Well, Kay is bent on making the kids productive."

"Oh…we've heard."

I defended myself, "Listen, kids are *way* overserved these days. I'm tired of it. Some might mock, but I can tell you, when I've given them the chance to work—and when I've endured the complaining long enough to actually follow through—the result almost always involves positive self-esteem. Sometimes even a desire to do more."

This couple isn't new to the arena of making kids work. Almost every weekend at the Johnson home, some type of labor, usually hard and hot, takes center stage. Starting when his boys were quite young, Scurry has required them to perform tasks most people would consider beyond their abilities. They were significantly included in construction projects such as fences and sheds by age nine. They were required to mow and keep up the yard by age eleven. At age fourteen—*fourteen!*—the oldest was given the job of sawing out a new doorway in the dining room, then covering the existing doorway with Sheetrock as well as caulking and painting to finish the project. His dad helped, but the kid was the main man on the job. A job he could do because the previous summer he had worked with a painter and learned the necessary skills.

I used to laugh with (sometimes at) Barbara who, more often than not, was as put out as the kids by Dad's incessant demands. It was a bit daunting since none of the kids' friends were doing any of this stuff, some of the jobs involved dangerous equipment, and perhaps hardest for Mom, the chores took precedence over many "fun" activities that the kids were required to decline.

But even in the case of the dining room, the small imperfections, still visible, have been worth all the pride and self-confidence the crazy project provided the kid…and his parents.

Work is not something to protect boys from;
it is something to lead boys toward.

—MICHAEL GURIAN, IN *The Wonder of Boys*

That night at dinner, Barbara shared with us the latest in crazy tasks handed down from father to son. "Scurry decided that we needed a sprinkler system installed in the front yard. Of course, no one in our family knows how to install a sprinkler system. But he decided that the oldest was more than able to figure it out. I mean," she laughed lightly, "after the dining room, why not the front yard? And why pay someone to install a sprinkler system when he has a strapping young seventeen-year-old available in our own home to do the work?"

"Seriously?" I asked, knowing Scurry and the answer.

With a little oh-yes-he-did lift of her eyebrows, she continued. "So the kid went to Lowe's and researched sprinkler installation. He talked to the guys, told them the size of our yard and what we needed. They told him what to buy, which he did. Then he came home with it all and started digging trenches in the one-hundred-plus-degree heat."

"I love it. Did he balk?" I asked.

"Not really. He's been around long enough to know that there wasn't much of a choice. Plus after the dining room thing, I think he kind of likes the challenge—and the accomplishment."

"That's so cool," I gushed. (Is my envy showing?)

"Well, the project took him several weeks. It started to run into school meetings at the end of the summer."

This young man attends an elite all-boy prep school here in Dallas. They have an active scholarship program so not everyone is superwealthy, but most are comfortable. As evidenced by conversations that ensued, whatever their financial situation, very few have any strenuous work stuff going on at home, unless you count schoolwork, which certainly is nothing to laugh at.

She continued, "One day he lost track of time while he was digging his trenches. Looking at his watch and realizing he was late for a student council meeting, he jumped in his beat-up 1991 Chevy Suburban and hauled himself up to school—still wearing digging clothes—filthy and sweaty."

I could totally envision his arrival as Barbara described the scene for us.

"When he got there, the other eight or so student-council kids, all fresh in their pastel polos and khakis, stared at him. They couldn't believe it. Especially when they asked him what he'd been doing. 'Installing a sprinkler system in my yard,' he told them. They didn't believe him. No one did! In fact, just after school started, one of their teachers posed the standard, 'What did you do this summer?' question. When he told his teacher and class about the sprinklers, they, too, didn't believe him. They seriously thought he was lying. The teacher even called in his brother to out the lie, only to find out the kid was telling the truth. I was floored that the teacher was so shocked. He didn't know anyone who could install their own sprinkler system themselves, let alone anyone who would allow a kid to do it."

"What did your son think?"

"That's the best part." Barbara beamed with satisfaction. "He told me that instead of feeling silly or diminished by the other students' response to his appearance and activities, he felt an immense sense of pride in his work and in the fact that his dad trusted him enough to give him a major project like this. I even think that lurking under the clean, scrubbed scorn of the other boys was a small sense of admiration and envy."

"Ohhhh," I cooed. "I love this story." Hoping my kid-chore-averse husband, who thinks it's much more efficient to have it done quickly and right rather than suffer through the learning process, was listening. Not that I suffer from any sort of manipulation disorder, you understand. "It's so rich with truth."

"Yeah, it's pretty convicting," she said. Barbara nodded at Scurry sitting next to her, thoroughly enjoying that his countercultural approach to parenting was receiving the deserved accolades. "Yes, he's loving it. Don't egg him on. But he does have a point. Think about the hundreds of dollars spent on coaches, tutors, conferences, you-name-it to build confidence in our kids. What Scurry gave the kid by letting—okay, making—him do a job outside his comfort zone was worth any penny we might have lost if he had done something disastrous like hitting the water main. Who could pay for the confidence that resulted from this major effort?"

Is that not the question of the hour? Who can pay for that kind of experience? It's not available for purchase. The benefit one gets from meaningful labor is worth every bit of raised eyebrows from other parents, pushback from the kids, moaning and groaning (from both kids and the parents doing the hard work of empowering them). As I listened to Barbara, I could barely stop myself from running home to put my kids on task. But I reminded myself that being able to install a sprinkler system didn't happen overnight. Scurry had spent years with the boy in their yard, raking, building—teaching him how to work. Because his muscles were toned, the kid was able to run the distance when asked.

The rewards of Scurry's investment in equipping his son for manhood are amazing. Fast-forward two years, and this child, who spent more time at home working odd jobs than throwing or kicking a ball, decided to try out as a walk-on for the University of Texas football team. Looking beyond what most would consider insurmountable barriers to entry (thanks in large part to a dad who put crazy tasks in front of him), he pitted himself against athletes who had played football their entire lives, had achieved accolades on competitive Texas high school football teams, and had been groomed from toddlerhood to wear a Longhorn jersey. The unlikely occurred. In the fall of 2011, this young man earned a spot on the UT roster as a wide receiver.

Later that evening, Barbara told me about something Michael Gurian, author of *The Wonder of Boys,* shared with the parents at one of their school's meetings. He said that if they only took one piece of advice away from his comments, it should be the importance of meaningful work for the spiritual and mental well-being of their sons. *Meaningful* work.

She then offered this. "The more I pondered this, the more it became clear to me how powerful his advice was. In our society, children are generally not required to do meaningful work to help their families. Going to school, pursuing their extracurricular activities, and staying out of major trouble is considered their function. In the old days, boys (and girls) had chores and roles that were vitally important to the survival and functioning of their family unit. These roles gave children a sense of self-worth, vitality, and importance. They knew that they were an integral part of the survival of their family and that without their contribution, it would suffer."

Barbara went on to describe the stark contrast she's observed in our current society. "A shocking percentage of children today suffer from depression and other psychological problems. Maybe this is a symptom of our culture of materialism, coddling, and entitlement. Maybe our kids are not given important opportunities to develop a sense of self, a sense of worth, a sense of accomplishment and ability to contribute meaningfully."

Interestingly enough, I'd had this same conversation with the girls' staff leader for one of our area youth ministries. We were hanging out one day when I asked her to describe the biggest areas in which she sees kids struggling.

"Oh, that's easy," she quickly responded. "Sexting, complete lack of interpersonal communication skills, and suicide."

They're all appalling, but that last one leaves the biggest pit in a mom's stomach.

"Why suicide?" I asked.

"You know, it seems to hit all kinds of families these days. Terrific families, genuine, faith-filled homes. I don't get it," she confessed. "But I'll tell you one thing. Most kids, no matter where they're from or who they are, reach a point in life where they feel so sorry for themselves, they think no one would care if they were dead. The problem these days is, kids don't stop with the thought. They follow through."

We both paused to consider that dreadful reality.

She continued. "I've thought about it a lot. And I can tell you that if I had hit that point when I was younger, I would never have followed through. My family depended on me. I helped take care of major things around our house, including my sister. It didn't matter how unloved I might have felt; I was needed—a necessary cog for the machine to work."

Meaningful work.

Her words left me humbled as I considered the ramifications of enabling versus equipping our kids. This Experiment is more than a game or a parenting strategy for empowerment; it is critical to my children's emotional well-being.

Help Wanted—See Management

My job postings have been available for weeks. Finally, I have a taker!

Boxster, in need of some green stuff to pay his monthly iPhone fees, came looking for an odd job or two. I pointed to the chairs on our front porch, which were in conspicuous need of some rejuvenating spa time. The tired old regulars that greet our guests and provide a nice spot for respite and some good neighborly conversation had seen better days. Visitors who took a seat more often than not needed to brush paint flakes off theirs before leaving.

The task required yet another trek to Lowe's. As we entered the store, I noticed that their white rockers were on sale for eighty-three dollars. I felt a small thrill of pleasure knowing that our chairs would sport the same fresh look in a few short hours. But I could almost hear Jon saying, "You know we could just buy new ones for the same amount it will cost to refinish these old ones. Especially taking into account the time spent doing it."

A reasonable perspective, financially speaking—the same plausible logic that has steered us away from many a character-building project. I looked at the new chairs, then thought about the Johnsons and their sprinkler system. I considered how that project continues to produce character and instill self-esteem in their son every time he sees his yard. I reflected again on the boost it gave his confidence. Some things don't translate into a simple profit-and-loss scenario, and some things can't be bought, even with the help of life coaches or trainers.

Our chairs aren't quite the caliber of the yard project, but this endeavor is perfect for us. Kind of like getting farm-team experience before hitting the big leagues.

The Lowe's paint guy fixed us up with a sanding sponge, a quart of white semigloss paint, brushes, and a supercheap plastic drop cloth. Boxster scanned our items through the self-checkout lane, and we were off.

When we arrived home, another able body begged to help. Boxster wasn't pumped about having to split the earnings, but a shared job almost always lightens the load. I helped out at the beginning, showing them how to sand the chairs, clean off the resulting dust, and paint without drips.

The project started out with lots of griping.

"I'm hot!"

"She never said anything about sanding. I wouldn't have picked this job!"

"You're doing it wrong."

"Hey, that was my spot."

"Quit dripping."

"This is taking forever."

I excused myself. Our college-age niece then bravely joined the pair to sand one of the other chairs. She lasted only about five minutes. Compelled by the kids' disagreeable attitude toward one another, I sighed and reentered the danger zone, ready to give the pair an inspiring life lecture on working together without complaining or grumbling. I planned on lobbing a little "only say things that build one another up" homily for good measure.

No go. I was stopped in my tracks.

"Mom, we've stopped griping at each other," Barton informed me.

"Yeah, we're done," Boxster added. "I'm actually glad she's helping. She's really good at sanding. But clearly, I'm a better painter—"

"Hey!" she defended. Then she laughed.

I loved to see them getting along. I looked at them and thought ahead to when they would be adults. They don't know it now, but for the rest of their lives, they will be best friends…if they apply the healing balm of love to the inevitable sibling wounds. I hope they succeed. They're two of the neatest people I know. Well, deep down, anyway. We could do without the surface scum—but I know much of it comes with the age territory.

For today, not only did they earn some cash, they also worked through sibling issues, started and completed a task, and productively used their lazy afternoon. To top it all off, they get to see the results of their labor every day as they bound from the car to our front door.

Those chairs are a daily reminder to me to equip and to empower. To show them how to do something, maybe even walk with them through the first few steps, then to back off and only help when asked. I need to look beyond the paint drips, missed spots, bad attitudes, gripefests, caked on grime, missed opportunities, and so much more—and focus on the incredible outcome of kid-propelled achievement. If I can let go of my own ideas and stop worrying about what people think about me and my parenting, I can better appreciate the genuine growth that's taking place. The self-esteem resulting from this Experiment is exactly what the yard doctor ordered. Those annoying apathy weeds don't stand a chance against the confidence-fortified seedlings of responsibility sprouting up all over the place.

REARVIEW MIRROR MOMENTS

We've seen solid results from the kids' efforts with the flowers, the weeds, and the odd jobs (though a few are still available). But I learned that outside clutter, like inside clutter, requires daily attention.

The great thing about big families is dividing and conquering. The hard thing about big families is the volume of stuff and clutter, both inside and out. One friend, a mother of four, told me that she divvies the work by task, rotating through the kids. One gets dog duty, another yard clutter, another upstairs common areas, and the last covers the downstairs. Each is also responsible for his or her personal space—bed, toothbrush, and so on—and each has to pitch in as needed. The system works well for them.

At our house we're struggling through a phase of finger pointing and blaming because a few of mine are just flaky. They have great intentions about picking up the shoes they flipped off in order to jump on the trampoline, but then they completely forget when racing inside to play. But though some of us are more conscientious than others, we're all in this together and all are held responsible.

I think my knee-jerk tendencies to enable are fading. But why is it *so* much easier just to do things yourself? I'm the absolute worst with the oldest. From catering to his whims, to finding him job opportunities, to organizing his homework, to…well, the list sadly goes on. I've nipped several areas. But it seems the more I stop enabling, the more I realize how many ways I'm doing it.

While at Snopes's volleyball game last night, I had a delightful conversation with a wise and insightful grandmother who had come to cheer her granddaughter to victory. The topic of summer plans came up, and I told her about our Experiment. Since summer employment is just around the corner, I mentioned that our two oldest kids would be working.

She told me work is wonderful for a child's self-esteem and mused about how few kids walk that road even though the benefits are so great. As she thought back to raising her own children, she added, "Building self-esteem and nourishing a child's need to know unconditional love combine to form the most critical role in raising kids."

Unconditional love…a hard thing for a kid to believe: "I love you no matter what you do." So often redirecting, correcting, even admonishing are taken the wrong way. They think we don't believe in them, we don't trust them, we don't love them.

She encouraged perseverance.

I guess the key is to keep on keepin' on, knowing that eventually they will snap out of it and get the message. I'm realizing that putting meat on the bones of the "I love you and trust you" message is important too. It involves lots of letting go, not the easiest thing for this recovering controller. I could do a much better job listening to their opinions about music, movies, and friends and trust them by getting out of the way. I'm not giving up my right to check in (whether we're paying for their phones or not, we reserve the right to view communication on all electronic devices), but I sure can reward with increased responsibilities and independence.

Recently I watched Barton ride her bike out of our driveway and make her way to a neighborhood shopping area, Fury traveling in her wake. Armed with earned cash, they had asked if they could venture out alone to the candy store and possibly a few other places. I forced myself to park my worries about things like teenage drivers who speed and forget to obey stop signs. I trusted my ten-year-old to watch out for her brother and to pay attention to cars. I avoided any lectures on how to spend their money wisely and did my best to simply appreciate their budding independence.

Not long after, I was approached by the parent of one of Fury's friends. "I was at Snider Plaza the other day," she said, "and I saw Fury riding his bike. I looked for you to say hi but couldn't find you. I mean, I looked and looked, but you weren't anywhere to be found."

"Yeah, the kids love riding up there on their own. You know...why not? They're old enough."

"I guess so. I just hadn't ever thought of that... It surprised me."

They *are* old enough. For years I've sought ways to stretch their muscles and spread their wings. I've always tried to be a mom who doesn't hover, but apparently I've done so much more than I realized. Now that my eyes are open, I'll be looking for new opportunities to let my kids exercise their abilities and expand their independence.

WHAT THEY LEARNED THIS MONTH

- You have to pull weeds out by the roots or your work is wasted.
- Working for a positive purpose is more fun than working as a consequence.
- Teamwork—and laughter—makes a load lighter.

- To the worker go the spoils, some of which is fun to spend on sweet treats. (They don't realize yet that the greatest reward doesn't involve cash.)

WHAT I LEARNED THIS MONTH

- My kids thrive on my high expectations.
- The teen years offer terrific opportunities for nurturing self-confidence and responsibility.
- Meaningful work, not work for work's sake, is a gift—for my kids as well as for me.

Working for a Living

The Search for Gainful Employment

> If you want children to keep their feet on
> the ground, put some responsibility on their
> shoulders.
>
> —ABIGAIL VAN BUREN

In this marathon of motherhood, some days I feel like I'm hitting the wall. According to *Runner's World*, it's called "bonking." Here's how they describe the athletic phenomenon:

> Chiang Kai-shek is said to have received news of his army's
> mutiny while still in his pajamas. Chances are you will be equally
> unprepared for the mutiny of your own body—in other words,
> for bonking. We're not talking about the mere cramping of a calf,
> or the everyday slowing caused by lactic acid build-up, or the deep
> muscle pain sometimes caused by downhill running. Marathon-
> ers used to call bonking "hitting the wall," but it's actually a
> bodily form of sedition. In some form or another, it becomes a
> collapse of the entire system: body and form, brains and soul.…
>
>   And then there's the little-purple-men bonk. "After about 20-K,

I started to see little purple men running up and down the sides of these cliffs," says Mark Tarnopolsky, M.D., who wears hats as both a leading sports nutrition researcher and an endurance athlete. "I knew it was an hallucination, but I stopped in the middle of the race to look at them anyway," he says. "It was kind of crazy."[1]

I swear I saw little purple men running across the floor just the other day as I refereed a mind-numbing altercation between Boxster and Fury. We all said ridiculous things, they blamed each other, everyone walked away frustrated and hurt.

Despite my recognizing this as a normal part of parenting life, such scenes sap every ounce of energy, leaving me "hitting the wall" and in need of some major redirection and encouragement. We're entering our fourth month of increasing the kids' responsibilities and work load. It has been stressful, in many ways, for all of us. Mostly because we're working muscles that we didn't know we had.

Each incremental increase in expectation frustrates the kids, who feel that accomplishing the previous assignment should be enough. They can hardly believe when we undertake another task, even if it's something easy and possibly enjoyable. Continuing with the Experiment is hard for me, partly because of the constant demands of being the Enforcer, and partly because I catch myself questioning whether my motives are pure. Am I throwing these tasks at them because I came up with my list and feel compelled to follow through? Am I treating them like guinea pigs, testing my theories as if we're in a laboratory? Am I just doing this to provide entertaining fodder for my blog?

So we all are a bit weary at this point, and our muscles are burning. The thing is, I know that we aren't even running the personal responsibility marathon yet. We're just in training. And I'm learning that it's critically important to keep training and pushing through the pain so that when they really do run the race—on their own—they will be able to press on to the finish line because of the work they put in today.

Still, that knowledge doesn't eliminate the daily pain. Frustrated with my lame officiating (I'm certainly not destined for the job of an NFL referee), I left our house and headed out to a dinner we had scheduled weeks before. Jon stayed back due to work overload, so I was on my own. Thankful for a scheduled distraction, I not only jumped at the chance to leave the house but also chose to work out some pent-up aggression by pedaling my bike rather than driving. It didn't even matter that the temperature outside was pushing one hundred.

A friend of mine was one of the hosts, but other than her, I wasn't sure I'd know a soul at this dinner party. The cerebral group of authors, educators, philosophers, and physicians gathers throughout the year to discuss relevant topics as they relate to our spiritual lives. I'm not sure why I was invited, but I welcomed the break.

Walking in the door, sweaty from my pedaling trek, I searched the sea of strangers and found my friend in the kitchen. She quickly swooped me over to some mutual friends I hadn't seen in years. I started to catch up by asking how their kids were doing.

"We just had our third graduate from college," he reported. "Only two more to go."

"Please tell me I'm going to survive," I begged, still mentally anchored in the discourse I'd left at home.

"You will. I promise. Our oldest presented us with *years* of challenge. You would be amazed at the incredible adult he is today. Just last week we had lunch. Gone are the days of head butting. You'll get there."

"I'm not sure I'll survive in one piece," I said, giving into the pain of "bonking."

"Let me ask you two questions," he offered. "First, how's he doing in school?"

"He's being a dope." I sighed. "He sure hasn't owned it yet. Who knows if he will."

"Okay. How about friends? Are his friends nice kids? Is he making good decisions on the social front?"

Hmm. There might be hope here. "Actually, yes. He has nice friends. He's not a rabble-rouser or a superpopular social butterfly. He's just an all-around good kid." I could have offered a detailed description of his integrity and propensity to make good decisions regardless of what the crowd might choose, but I chose not to.

"You're going to be just fine. You're in for *years* of frustration," he acknowledged. "But keep your head down and keep going. Don't let the stubborn pushback discourage you too much. I promise there is a light at the end of the tunnel."

Just those words were food to my soul. The "years of frustration" might seem like a downer. But I'm not asking for rose-colored glasses. Give me reality and I can work with it. In parenting my teens, I just want to know what's normal. If we've entered a danger zone, please tell me so we can seek and get appropriate help. I greatly appreciated my friend's clarity. Does your child have good friends? You're okay. Not without mind-numbing annoyances, but okay. Questionable friends? That's a yellow, maybe even red, flag. Heed the warning signs and take action before bad decisions usher in potentially lifelong consequences. I know these aren't the only concerns we deal with in parenting, but for tonight the reassurance that our issues are normal put some fuel in my tank.

As I took my seat, the strangers next to me exchanged pleasantries and proceeded down the same conversational path after learning the number and ages of our kids. Having five kids of their own (the youngest age twenty-two), they instinctively offered soothing words of encouragement without my saying a word: "You will make it. Don't let this phase define your relationship with your kids."

I loved that comment: "Don't let this phase define your relationship with your kids." Wow, I need to let that advice take root in my mind and remember it. Often. I hope I remember the next time I'm in the heat of the moment.

I guess on the mom marathon, this is what we need to keep pressing on: encouraging, realistic words from parents who have walked the road.

They might not be carbs or a protein drink, but wise words of encouragement sure got me over a hill that night. I think the bike ride helped too.

Time to tackle the next incline: the hill of the legitimate employment.

WORKERS, START YOUR ENGINES

"Which job do you want to do this summer: the youth center or selling papers?" I asked Boxster.

"I'm not getting a job, Mom!" followed by a can-you-believe-my-mom eye roll to the friend sitting next to him in the backseat. Yes, we're in the car. And I just might have embarrassed him in front of his friend. Why can't I learn to hold off on conversations when a friend is around? Even the best friends can be a bit stinging in their comments after I've left.

Nonetheless, his response was rather strong, especially given that we'd already covered this ground.

"You *will* be getting a job," I said. "You know, work isn't always fun. But it's still something we all have to do."

Silence.

"Are *you* going to get a job this summer?" I asked his friend, suggesting it would be a lot of fun if they did something together. Yes, I'm still a geek.

"Oh, I do lots of chores around our house. I don't work in the summer." He thought for a moment. "Not unless it has something to do with playing golf."

Score another point for Boxster's argument that none of his friends have to work.

Even so, we're not budging on this one. He has forgotten, or maybe never even realized, the wonderful benefits of working last summer at Youth Believing in Change (YBC), a local youth center focused on helping lower-income and refugee children. The overall result of his time at

the youth center? A big, fat healthy dose of self-esteem. I could have finagled for months and never achieved such success.

The kid worked two days a week, arriving at 7:30 a.m. and leaving
around 2:30 p.m. The center runs a program for the kids while their
parents work that includes all sorts of activities, ranging from music and
reading to games and field trips. Boxster hung with the kindergartners. A
group of supercute kids, along with Raymond, his summer nemesis. To
say Raymond has lots of energy is an understatement. He basically has
one speed: full throttle. Boxster's most memorable day featured a lovely
incident involving Raymond and urine. Boxster had to handle the whole
thing himself, including changing PeeBoy's clothes, disinfecting the floor
and surrounding area, and trying to keep hurling jokes at bay.

Despite the horror, great stuff stuck. First of all, a rather entertaining,
bordering on heroic, story entered Boxster's repertoire. Second, self-esteem
seeds began to take root in the heart of a kid who now knows he can face
a fairly unsavory situation, conquer it, and live to tell. Let's face it, would
any of us have wanted to do that task? I don't like cleaning up those kinds
of messes from my own child, let alone a virtual stranger. Boxster did
something hard, exponentially hard for his age, and enjoyed a deep sense
of accomplishment that came from completing a challenging task.

He didn't want to work last summer, but he did. And he'll be doing
so again this year.

To be clear, our definition of *working* doesn't mean eight hours, five
days a week. It means answering to some authority other than a parent,
a predefined schedule (not subject to the kid's whim), and some sort
of compensation. Since our kids are younger than sixteen, we take care
of the money component, considering their employment more of an
apprenticeship.

Sometimes I wonder why we go to so much trouble instead of just
creating work opportunities within our home. But as much value as we
find in nurturing capable kids through household responsibilities, nothing quite equals the experience of reporting to an adult who isn't related

to you by blood. Not only will a boss feel free to demand a kid's best effort, but kids tend to perform better for people who aren't family. How many times have we watched our kids behave and perform so beautifully for someone who is not related to them? A part of me wishes they would consistently put in the same effort at home. But another part is thankful they feel safe and comfortable enough to show their warts around me.

The evidence suggests that kids who are insulated within the safety of a loving home until adulthood are in for a rude awakening. Ann Burnworth, executive director of Youth Resources of Southwestern Indiana, noted in an article, "Most of us thought our primary job was to make sure our children felt good about themselves. After childhoods filled with praise and ego-boosting, many of today's young people are experiencing 'Adulthood Shock.'"

Ann continued, "As parents, we owe it to our children to help them learn how to deal with criticism now in preparation for the inevitable day when it is not delivered as gently as we—or they—would like. The first step in doing so is backward—away from our natural tendency to step in and make them feel better."[2]

We don't have to stand by helplessly and watch this generation become Gen Me. These kids have so much more to offer than we could ever dream of doing. If parents can paint themselves out of the picture, I think our kids can become Gen XL: XL-erated by ingenuity, work ethic, and crazy-good technology skills. Working for someone outside their immediate family will stretch them and offer challenges beyond our sphere of thinking.

So, while the younger kids gain experience at home, Boxster and Snopes will be finding gainful employment for a good portion of their summer vacation. Okay, so it's highly likely that I'll be finding it for them and giving them a choice of one or two options. But we've got to start somewhere. I wonder if helping in this area is a form of enabling, but I'm thinking that at their ages some direction is definitely in order.

I'm Too Young to Work!

While passing by Office Depot, I noticed a sign on the door that I hoped Boxster, who was walking with me, missed. Of course, Eagle Eyes spotted it about the same time I did.

Now Hiring
Apply Within

Applicants must be 18 years or older
and
have open availability for evenings & weekends

I was happy to see that jobs were available but cringed as I readied myself for the inevitable "I told you so" remark. For weeks, not only had he been running through his list of friends who had not been forced into finding employment, but he'd also been claiming that no reputable establishment would hire him. When I scolded him for not even trying to find a job, he always retorted, "I'm too young to work!" And here was the proof he needed to support his claim.

"Look, Mom!" Then, "I told you I was too young to work!"

"That's just one sign." I lamely attempted to regain my footing.

"Well, Henry and I called lots of places. Office Depot isn't the only one."

"I bet you could get a job at Wal-Mart."

"Nope. Sixteen."

"What about Tom Thumb?"

"Eighteen."

"Central Market?"

"Mom. They're *all* over fourteen. We checked."

Apparently they had done their homework, but I couldn't resist conducting my own research to see just what the law has to say about age-appropriate working. According to the US Department of Labor, one can legally have a job at age fourteen, with certain hourly limitations.

> However, at any age, youth may deliver newspapers; perform in radio, television, movie, or theatrical productions; work in businesses owned by their parents (except in mining, manufacturing or hazardous jobs); and perform babysitting or perform minor chores around a private home.[3]

Youths fourteen and older can work in an office, grocery store, retail store, restaurant, movie theater, baseball park, amusement park, or gasoline service station (as if those still exist!). The hard part is finding an employer willing to give a kid one of these jobs. Child labor laws coupled with insurance requirements and, let's face it, apathetic teens have left businesses less than eager to hire younger employees.

People in small towns seem a bit more open to the idea. Snopes came home from a weekend in Lubbock not long ago reporting that kids get to bag groceries at the local store. "You never see kids doing that where we live!" she moaned. It looks fun to her. It seems appropriate to me. Either way, that door appears to be closed in our community.

All of which helped to prove Boxster's point.

Legitimate, paycheck-earning work might not be an option this summer, but we do have alternatives. The first question to address: What does my child enjoy? Work isn't always fun, but it can be tailored to suit kids' interests or aspirations. Considering aptitudes and passion might save a lot of heartache (and money!) by helping us steer our kids in a valid career direction. It would be nice to know, sometime before they complete an expensive degree program, that accounting drives them crazy but photography floats their boat.

The other day, chatting it up with a friend, I shared that, although my kids are working—and learning great things—I'm not sure both have found work that builds on their strengths. She was quick to tell me that her college major and her giftedness not only didn't match but couldn't have been more opposite.

"My dad pushed me into the business school, but I drooled over the work my friends in the art department were doing. Not just the art department, but anything that included 'fashion' in the description. Knowing the fairly limited career mobility and need for financial stability, my father convinced me that practical is better than passion. He said, 'You can do the passion stuff as a hobby that will be paid for by the career.'"

My artistic friend followed the advice of her dad and got a business degree. Her job after college? The institutional equity desk at Merrill Lynch. Lots of young grads would have killed for that job, but she tolerated the work. Barely. "Every day I would wake up and get on my game face," she told me. "I'd put on my blue suit. Get in character and do my job, sneaking to the bathroom throughout the day for a quick fix from the *New York Times* fashion page." She was miserable.

Eventually she found the courage to risk her financially secure job and go after something in line with her interests. Now she's a photographer, loving every supercreative minute. Well, almost every minute. It's still a job. To her dad's credit, she is using that business degree. But still, she looks back and wishes she had followed her heart sooner. The miserable grind and years doing a job she despised just might have been avoided.

Finding employment that complements my offspring's aptitudes might take a few tries. And the kids haven't been much help in the search. All I hear around my house is the "none of my friends have to work!" moan. And you know what? For the most part, they're right. But I don't want them to miss out on a valuable discovery: meaningful work actually makes you feel good about yourself. Experiencing this benefit outside our home, from someone other than me, will help solidify this truth.

What to Do?

With it firmly established that our work crew falls below the employable age in Dallas, Texas, the kids and I will be getting creative. Not a problem on this front. We love a good challenge, and I love work. The kids might not have realized it, but they've been working for years. Not so much around the house, obviously, but I've jumped on any opportunity to get them thinking about others and to help them capitalize on skills I'd like them to hone.

Also, we have a dad who asks us to keep a tight rein on our schedule. He prefers activities that are close to home and, if sports related, with limited practices and games. More often than not, only two of the kids are participating in an outside activity during a season. Anything school-sponsored is fine, since they will be practicing there. If I can double up—on music lessons, for example—that's great too. Jon wants us to use our time efficiently and do our best to avoid extended times in the car. Well, at least as much as possible.

This means plenty of downtime at home. Lots of close-quarter, sibling-infused free time—especially in the summer. Since crabbiness can quickly infiltrate free time, for years I've encouraged creative activities ranging from raising money for our school by selling crafts to mini home-based businesses and making movies. You name it, we've probably done it. Here are some of the options we and other families we know have explored for employing underage able-bodied workers.

For the Self-Starters
For the entrepreneurs, there are countless possibilities to use their skills and passion and maybe bring home a little green.

- *Car wash service.* Boxster and a friend did this a couple of summers ago. They basically detailed cars, doing a much better job than the local car wash. They may not have optimized their hourly rate, but car owners still approach me and ask if Boxster and his friend are washing cars.

Other home-related services include:

- *Window washing.*
- *One-off yard jobs like sweeping and/or raking.* Lots of
  avenues here. Unfortunately, most of the homes in our area
  have yard services, so mowing hasn't produced many takers
  for friends' kids who have tried. But one-off jobs can prove
  successful. One group of boys we know pooled their
  resources and started a power-washing service.
- *Dog walking or pet sitting.* Great help for neighbors heading
  out of town. There might even be neighbors whose dog
  could use some attention while they are at work. It's fun
  and financially rewarding.
- *Day camps.* Kids can make a flier and invite neighborhood
  children to a "Day Camp" at your home. The idea is to
  provide crafts and other activities, read stories, play games,
  and offer a fun respite for a mom so she can have a couple
  of hours to run errands or visit the nail salon for that long
  overdue mani-pedi. In our area, a few junior high girls
  get together and offer an entire week with varying themes
  each day.
- *Lemonade stand, homemade cookie booth, or snow cone
  vendor.* A few years ago, our next-door neighbor held an
  estate sale. When Boxster saw the line of people waiting to
  get in, he quickly asked to put up a lemonade stand. For
  two days he sold drinks and cookies to a captive audience
  and cleared over ninety dollars—a lot of money for a little
  kid. Banking on that success, he contacted a family friend
  who runs a local estate sale company and asked to put up
  a stand outside her sale. He sold at only a couple of events.
  It was very profitable but a little labor intensive for me since
  the kids were too young to be there alone. It works best for
  a sale closer to home.

Key to all of these business ideas is that crucial accounting component: cost of goods sold. My kids seemed to think the lemonade and cookies appear from the sky. We now work on net profit rather than gross. Have I mentioned I'm a mean mom?

For the Budding Salesperson

Our neighborhood paper often has jobs available for kids eager to sell subscriptions door to door. We encouraged Boxster to do this with a friend one year. He did okay, but maybe the biggest benefit was learning that he is not destined for a career in sales. He had done well selling lemonade, but door-to-door sales were excruciating for the poor guy. By contrast, one of the girls who sold subscriptions cleaned up. She was motivated and loved meeting people. She's so sweet, people couldn't say no.

For the Service-Oriented

So many great options here! I'd start with a local church and their surefire summer programs. They are almost always looking for able bodies to help herd kids to and from activities. In Dallas, several youth centers and day camps need help, even with something as simple as reading to kids. Do your kids like organizing? Head to a food bank, Goodwill, or any charitable thriftshop and offer to help them restock or display their inventory. Do your kids love sports? Try one of the Boys & Girls Clubs of America and see if they need help getting the kids to burn off their energy. Ideas are endless in this area, and organizations love the help.

CONVENIENCE TAKES A BACKSEAT TO COMMITMENT

Boxster decided to take up our friend Vincent on his open invitation to come work at YBC any summer he'd like, quite a testimony to the kid's work ethic and proficiency the previous summer. Vince can't put him on the payroll yet due to age but has told him that, when he reaches that point, the job is his if he wants it. Boxster is too young to appreciate a standing offer of employment, but I'm delighted.

This summer he's working two full days a week, arriving at seven thirty and leaving at two thirty. We consider it an apprenticeship and will pay him accordingly. The rest of the week, I'm hoping Boxster will take on some of our odd jobs to get some extra cash, hopefully to put toward a car.

The kid has been placed in a room of first graders and given the role of teacher's assistant. He's basically there to do anything she needs. At lunchtime, he works with the older boys to serve and clean up after lunch. Without a doubt, he's gaining experience in many work facets. One day he came home and proudly mentioned that he knew how to sweep and mop when the other boys didn't. I found this simultaneously encouraging and appalling. Are his coworkers not helping around the house either?

A few weeks in, however, my kid was ready to take a break. "Please don't make me go. Please. Please. Please. Please."

"Sorry. It's part of work. In order to do it, you have to show up."

"Just this one day," he begged. "Please let me stay home."

"No can do."

"*Pleeease.*"

"Sorry."

"Fine." The reluctant worker seemed resigned to his fate.

But when we drove up to the youth center, the kid pretended to not notice we'd arrived. He just sat there, apparently hoping that I wouldn't see him or maybe that I would forget or maybe that I'd give in and let him go home with me. Memories of toddlerdom flooded my mind, specifically those times I had to peel him off my body to leave him at Mother's Day Out. I had no problem ignoring the wails then because I knew it was good for him to spend some time apart from me. His protests bounced off my impenetrable mom shield.

More than ten years later, I had to employ that same resolve as I sat in the driver's seat and listened to my teenager's protests. I finally had to kick him out of the car.

Clearly, the kid had hit the wall. No longer was he eager to hit the ground running. Well, he was never actually eager, but at this point he was downright averse to going. His body ached to just sleep in. I'm no slave driver. The job required only two full days each week. But with odd jobs peppered in, he was actually getting a small taste of what most people do every day: they go to work whether they feel like it or not.

I'm convinced that despite his protests, the experience is worthwhile. It's good for him to answer to someone else. It's good for him to get up early. It's good for him to work—not at his convenience but at the employer's need and requirement. It's good for him to hit the wall and keep going. It's good for him to get an idea of what his strengths are and what he might enjoy.

And maybe a little misery will encourage him to be more proactive in finding his own employment. I was incredibly encouraged when Boxster told me the places where he'd like to work next summer. This is a huge step in the right direction. I think he's actually realizing that the world isn't here to serve him.

Now if they would only hire him!

ADVENTURES IN BABY-SITTING

Snopes elected to baby-sit for her summer job. We encouraged her to do something to advertise her availability and expertise. She decided to create a flier that she could both snail mail and e-mail to people with young children, preferably families within biking or walking distance. She went online and found a cute summery clip-art picture to brighten up her ad.

I forced my designing self to keep my mouth shut and my hands off. This was her effort. I needed to support her efforts instead of forcing my ideas on her. My actions should mirror my words, the ones that keep telling her how talented and great she is. Maybe if I sit on my hands, they'll stay out of her stuff.

She planned to e-mail her flier to a few family friends who know her, then follow up with a phone call and specifically ask. She decided to leave the amount she charges off the flier. I found that so interesting. Probably revealing of her nonconfrontational personality. I think she was afraid to ask for the money lest she offend someone or ask more than what some-one might think she's worth.

So many good teaching opportunities arose as she tackled this task— opportunities I otherwise might have missed. We talked about compen-sation and that families expect to pay their baby-sitters, so she shouldn't be worried about offending anyone. We also walked through the secrets of doing a job well, not just the minimum but exceeding the client's ex-pectations. I've told my daughters that when they baby-sit, they should be sure to clean up everything—even to the point of loading the dishwasher if there happen to be dishes in the sink. Small things like that cement you favorably in someone's memory.

As Snopes embarked on her summer work, I realized we also needed to talk about putting a client's needs ahead of her convenience, similar to the "you can't work if you don't show up on time" conversation with Boxster. Her initial reaction to the employment edict was to accept a gig only if it fell favorably on her terms. We made sure she understood that sometimes friends and fun activities have to take a backseat to someone else. Another tough yet valuable lesson about being the kind of person others rely on to be dependable and responsible: we generally have to plan fun around our work commitments, not schedule work around our social calendar.

With her sweet, nurturing personality, Snopes had plenty of requests for her services. Especially after passing out her homemade business cards. It was agonizing to watch her struggle to get out of her comfort zone, to enter homes of people she only knew from a distance, to care for kids whose house rules differed from our family's. But she loved the compensation and was careful to set aside a portion to give away, to keep on hand, and to save. I watched her begin to swell with confidence and pride.

Then came the job that was more than she could handle. I have three dear friends with special-needs children, all of whom are truly amazing in their own way and whose personalities couldn't be more different. One of the moms, a huge supporter of my whacky projects, was quick to call and ask Snopes to baby-sit. She knew that at Snopes's skill level, it wouldn't be a good idea to leave the almost-teenager home alone with her son, but a mother's helper situation seemed the perfect solution for everyone.

It sounded good to Snopes, who adores my friend and her child. What could go wrong? Well, for a quiet, young lady who wanted to do a great job and give this mom a break…lots. Though Snopes has known the child her entire life, he's recently grown quite a bit not only in stature but in strength as well. He's not as tall as Jon but easily as strong. And he's full of energy and life, eager to make the most of any situation as he bounces from one thing to another within a blink of an eye—sometimes with his clothes on and sometimes not.

Snopes knew she was in trouble when he overpowered her and locked himself in a neighbor's car. The sweet girl, having heard on the news stories of babies dying in cars during extreme heat, was instantly overcome with fear. Determined not to bother the boy's mom and reluctant to leave him outside alone, she went into stress mode, jumping from driver's- to passenger's-side window while constantly pleading with the smiling kid to open a door. He thought it was all a great game. The more frantic she got, the greater his resolve to stay in the car. I'm not sure how long this scene played, but when I came to pick her up, she was a shell of the girl I had dropped off. She was mortified at her inability to control the situation, and she had literally been in fear for the kid's life.

I'm not sure why she didn't just ask my friend for help. Such circumstances are not new to this absolutely amazing mother who goes with the flow of her young firecracker. Granted he knows little about boundaries or cause and effect, but that's a part of his beauty. He lives in the moment and passionately embraces the joys of life. But the situation proved too much for a tender young soul, who is apparently too insecure and timid to ask for help. We both learned that she was too young for this job.

But I'm not sorry she gave it a try. We salvaged some great lessons

We're All in This Together

My husband knew that our daughter could never save enough money to buy herself a car he deemed safe for her to drive around town, and ultimately off to college. He master-minded a plan that was one of the best parenting decisions he/we ever made. He told her that he would buy her a car—most likely a used one—but it would sit in our garage until she could put gas in it. Yes, she had to buy her own gas. How would she do it? She would have to work in the summers to save enough money to fuel the car for an entire year.

So the summer before she turned sixteen, she began to work. Her first job was as a tennis instructor for her varsity tennis coach. She worked nine to noon every day, teaching little ones how to serve and volley. It was hot. She complained a little. But it was a job, and she got a paycheck. At fifteen, we had set her up with a checking account, savings account, and debit card, so she was ready for business.

Requiring your teens to purchase their own gas is brilliant for several reasons: (1) it limits their driving, (2) they are forced to budget their money through the year, and (3) they learn to work and save. Unfortunately, many students are graduating high school and college without ever having had a job. No employer, no résumé. They don't know how to work.[4]

—Lisa Clark

from the experience, the most pressing of which was that she needs to ask for help, especially if she feels someone is in danger. Another positive was that she lived through an experience that was off her chart on a challenge scale. Yes, it burned her from baby-sitting for a few weeks. But the best way to put a challenging encounter behind you is to get right back out there and try again, which her mean mom made sure she did. Another great lesson in perseverance.

THE APPLICATION SITUATION

We're not the only ones hitting the streets in search of employment. I just got off the phone with my BFF. We met on our first day of kindergarten and have been friends ever since. About eighteen years ago, she cemented our lifelong friendship by marrying my older brother. Now we talk on the phone pretty much every day, which was a bit of a sore spot for my brother until long-distance plans moved to unlimited minutes. Our efforts to sneak in a "short conversation" (not more than forty-five minutes!) were always thwarted by Eagle Eye when he opened the phone bill.

As a mother of seven, ages six to eighteen, she has loads of hilarious, pertinent stuff happening around her house. In fact, she can take credit for a big part of our in-home revolution against entitlement. She was the one with whom I first discussed our overserved kiddos. We were both spurred to action by the entitled mentality in our families.

So summer started with *her* fifteen-year-old hunting for a job. The kid is looking for a little something more than odd jobs around the house. His mother wants him to have an employer other than her. First stop, the neighborhood Publix grocery store. My best friend dropped the teenager off at the front door so he could go in and fill out an application. We, of course, happened to be on the phone—our second call of the day.

Within minutes of his heading into the store, her phone started beeping.

"Uh-oh! He's already calling me. I've got to go. I'll call you right back."

A few minutes later my phone rang. My sister-in-law was laughing hard enough to bust a gut. "Okay, so he went in to ask for a job. They pointed him to a kiosk where he could fill out and submit an application electronically. He started but couldn't get past the question, 'What is your phone number?'"

"What?"

"Oh yes. He kept entering our area code in the 'Pager' box."

Poor kid. At least he's trying, forging into uncharted territory to reach the great land of Grocery Bagger or Cart Boy. As his mother walked away from helping him, he yelled after her, "I'll call you if I have any more questions!"

Reading the directions might be a good place to start.

Here's a shout out to Cousin Cart Boy. Keep on keepin' on! You're an inspiration to us all. Hey, I've never filled out an electronic application, at least not successfully. Last year the camp where we send our kids made me mail in their birth certificates when I registered. A requirement that might have had something to do with the fact that the year before I inadvertently typed in our eleven-year-old's birth date on the nine-year-old's online application. Nothing like sticking a third-grade girl in a cabin with fifth-grade girls. It wasn't pretty!

If I couldn't accurately answer a simple question like my child's birth date, how in the world could this young man be expected to answer, by himself, these questions that Publix asked?

- An employee keeps showing up for work twenty minutes late. Everyone has been covering for him. What should you do?
- If you were to leave your job, would you wait until a replacement is found?
- If you were to observe ways in which our store could be safer, would you report them? If so, how?
- How would you handle a dissatisfied customer?

These weren't the real stumpers for my nephew. For him it was, "What's your mother's maiden name?" He called his mom again, seeking guidance.

In disbelief his mother replied, "How can you not know my maiden name? I've fed you, loved you, wiped your bottom…"

"Is it Robinson?"

"Close enough."

It's Robertson.

JOB POSTINGS

In my home when I was growing up, certain words and phrases simply were not tolerated. As we've seen, shut up was one. (Maybe my mom won't see that if it's written supersmall.) Of course any cursing and references to bodily functions were off limits. Plus, certain body parts were spelled instead of spoken, like "b-u-t-t." We still tease Mom about that one!

But the one phrase she truly despised was "I'm bored." Watch out if you uttered those off-limit words! Now that I'm a mother, I totally appreciate her disdain for the expression—every little entitled, serve-me, slothful syllable of it. Come on! Do I have to think of everything to fill the humdrum of adolescent life?

So we started what I call Job Postings/Bored Chores. The rules of engagement are as follows.

If, for instance, a child comes to the mother and politely says, "Do you have anything I could do?" the mother will quickly reply, as little birds sing gaily above her head and mice happily scurry around her feet, "Why, yes. Here's a list of little jobs ready and waiting for eager hands. And since you came to me, I'd like to generously compensate your hard work and willing attitude." This being our employment month, I'm looking for as many opportunities as possible to fill the gaps left open by days off from YBC or between baby-sitting gigs and also to help younger siblings fulfill their mom's whacky directive to find gainful employment. A zippy song just might spontaneously erupt as the children joyfully embark upon their delightful adventure.

If, on the other hand, said child comes to the mother and utters the phrase "I'm bored," the mother will swiftly present the Job Postings list that has morphed into Bored Chores opportunities, lifting that pesky burden of free time and replacing it with good, clean, character-building work—unpaid, as a consequence for the "I'm bored" complaint.

Here are a few of the Job Postings/Bored Chores (depending upon the attitude) that appeared on our list:

- *Weeds.* Yes, despite all the yard work, they continue to poke their annoying little sprouts out of the ground. I loved watching Snopes clean up on this posting. She nabbed Jack's trike and sat on it rather than break her back bending over.
- *Windows.* This is a fine two-person job. One inside, one outside, working together to ensure clean panes and learning a little teamwork to boot. My takers here were Snopes and Barton.
- *Drawer Organization.* This one beckoned Fury. The kid loves to sort...and to make money.
- *Car Wash.* This one can even be a treat on a hot, muggy day if you're a glass half-full kind of person. Boxster is our resident pro on this chore.
- *Brushing the Pool.* Since I'm sleeping with our cute pool guy (okay, so we're married and he's too cheap to hire a professional), I don't think he'd mind the help despite a slight aversion to relinquishing duties. Plus, a kid can jump in afterward.
- *Data Entry.* Maybe I'd actually send our Christmas cards this year if I just had to print a sheet of labels instead of hand addressing. Perhaps typing camp (yes, there is such a thing) will pay off!

- *DVD Organization.* It's so frustrating to open a box to find it empty or housing the wrong movie. Fury was all over this task too. He brought in Jack for backup. In spite of his young age, our Future Hoarder of America has an amazing ability to find and match discs to jackets.
- *Furniture Refinishing.* Boxster and Barton did such a terrific job on the chairs, and we have a couple of benches in need of some attention and care.
- *Fun with Math.* I'm happy to reward nonrequired summer study.
- *Decluttering Common Areas.* The need here is never ceasing.

I have no problem keeping the kids busy if they can't find productivity themselves. And while I'm not opposed to a bit of summertime relaxation, I don't want the kids to enter adulthood expecting every day to be

Expert Advice: Raising Future Leaders

Setting up our kids to believe they're the best, or need to be the best, causes some major problems when they hit the real world, as noted by Rick Burton and Norm O'Reilly in an article for *Sports Business Journal:*

> We believe strongly that a disconnect exists between parents' excessive coddling and their children's ability to learn valuable leadership traits. It may be a parents' right to assist their child, but keeping a young person from starting at the bottom may alter his or her capacity to master group dynamics and truly seek out servant-leadership moments on thankless tasks.... Entitlement without hard work is a recipe for disaster.[5]

fun, another message I suspect we've mistakenly planted in this generation by our parental tendency to entertain rather than challenge our children.

"I'm hot. I've been working *really* hard! I think I've done enough," Snopes said, though her Tom Thumb shopping bag was only one-quarter filled with nut-grass weeds. She wanted some cash so she could ride bikes with a friend to Chick-fil-A and grab a snack.

"Pretend like you're working for someone other than your mom," I said, knowing she would not give up or complain for anyone else.

Indignantly, she informed me, "Mom, I'm working for God!"

There you have it.

I tend to chalk up any lack of initiative or a poor work ethic to laziness. That might be part of the issue. But maybe lofty expectations also play a role in their aversion to work. Better to avoid it all together rather than perform at substandard levels. I watched Snopes almost paralyzed by unexpected failure (at least in her mind) after the challenging babysitting experience. Maybe they feel pressure to be perfect the first time. Have we finagled, raced in to save, focused on awards so often that our kids have warped expectations?

Society labels these kids the trophy generation, the kids who expect gold stars, showers of accolades, and positive reinforcement at every turn. Adults roll their eyes and respond with all kinds of "Let me tell you what it was like when I was a kid" lectures about youth hardship, which can't hold a candle to what our Depression-era grandparents knew.

When we're tempted to write them off, repulsed by their entitled attitudes, should we pause for a moment to consider the folks who led them to believe their every action deserves praise? Yes. It was us. All in the name of love. All in an effort to encourage, to fortify, and to build up our kids so they could withstand the meanies of the world. That's what parents do, right? We tell our kids how great they are, then we remove any hurdles that might stand in their way, doing the hard things for them so they're protected from pain and disappointment and failure. When the time comes to leave our nest, they will fly, strong and beautiful, on their way to the land of plenty that's already been prepared for them.

Of course, that's not reality. So maybe their reluctance to take initiative isn't due solely to our failure to serve up responsibility and meaningful work; maybe it's also because we feed them unrealistic expectations that life should be easy.

I can't think of many individuals who have come out of the gate a winner. A lot of people…well, most…okay, nearly *all* the people I know tripped and fell a few times on their maiden voyage. In fact, looking back, I suspect it's often the falls that lead to success. Not an infusion of positive words but tripping, stumbling, reeling, and persevering until you finally gain momentum.

Attempts followed by failure pepper the background of most successful people. Those challenges gave them perspective, tenacity, and a huge dose of reality. Here are just three examples:

"Failure is just a resting place. It is an opportunity to begin again more intelligently."—Henry Ford, who failed twice in business before he finally went on to build the Ford Motor Company

"If I find 10,000 ways something won't work, I haven't failed. I am not discouraged, because every wrong attempt discarded is often a step forward" and "Many of life's failures are experienced by people who did not realize how close they were to success when they gave up."—Thomas Edison, who failed 10,000 times trying to invent the light bulb

"I made a resolve then that I was going to amount to something if I could. And no hours, nor amount of labor, nor amount of money would deter me from giving the best that there was in me."—Colonel Harland Sanders, who started out as an entrepreneur at the age of 66, developed a "chicken recipe" business idea

that was turned down over a thousand times before Kentucky
Fried Chicken was built

So what do these success stories have to do with housework and Job
Postings/Bored Chores? My kids may or may not be a wild success in the
eyes of the world. That's not a priority for me. But I do want them to
persevere at whatever they put their minds to. It's critically important that
they try and complete tasks they think are impossible or irrelevant. They
need to learn that no task is beneath them and that getting to the prover-
bial top begins at the bottom. It's also important that they fail. Only
through failure can they learn to get back up. From what I hear, kids
these days don't get back up; they quit.

Here's to hoping our quirky, sometimes lame, often bemoaned
home-remedy Experiment teaches them that quitting just isn't an option.
No matter how menial the task.

WHAT THEY LEARNED THIS MONTH

- Work isn't a function of convenience but of an employer's
  need and/or requirement.
- Filling free time with odd jobs can actually be as lucrative
  as youth employment.
- When hit with tough situations, quitting just isn't an option.

WHAT I LEARNED THIS MONTH

- Fourteen-year-olds really do have limited employment
  options, and my son isn't always trying to get out of a job.
- I need to be careful not to push the kids into situations over
  their heads and to make sure I trust a potential employer.
- Being creative and staying focused bring tangible benefits
  for all of us.

Domestic Dirty Jobs

*Introducing Lysol, Tilex, Soft Scrub,
and the Dreaded Toilet Bowl Brush*

> The Rose Bowl is the only bowl I've ever seen
> that I didn't have to clean.
>
> —Erma Bombeck

I overheard a recent conversation between the girls. "Did you put those there?" accused a sister who didn't appreciate that her roommate had thrown shoes in the wrong spot.

"At least they're off the floor!"

"They're supposed to be on the rack."

"What difference does it make? They're in the closet."

"I work so hard organizing it all!"

"Well, so do I. Just look at our desk," she indignantly responded. "Plus, I made your bed this morning!"

"I wish we could go back to normal. Don't you?"

"Sometimes… Not always… I don't know."

Disillusionment has definitely set in. What started out as a semi-entertaining novelty has taken on a somewhat detestable quality for the kids. I'm not sure if it's because they're tired of the whole thing, which I think we all are, or if the nature of this month's task is especially distasteful. But they might as well realize now rather than later that bathrooms are the same as every other room in the house. They just involve wipeable, waterproof, desperately-in-need-of-disinfection surfaces. I was hoping a few might find this month's task fun. Maybe an adventure. A trip to a place where you can slosh water around on purpose. Spray Tilex, scrub, and use potty language at will. Plus, unlike most other rooms, after cleaning a bathroom, you walk away feeling especially confident and purpose filled because you can see and smell the results of your labor.

No such luck.

Cleaning the bathroom seems to be not only incredibly daunting but also ridiculously giggle producing. What's up with a kid's need to snicker or fake gag about any matter associated with a toilet? Seriously.

But I'm determined to push through all the verbal protests, resistant attitudes, and expressions of disgust. Because I know from personal experience that this truly matters.

COMBATING THE CYCLE OF CLUELESSNESS

By the time I got married, I had traveled to every state except Alaska, received a master's degree from the number one international business program in the United States, worked with or for heads of state, finance ministers, ambassadors, famous business leaders, and national and international news correspondents. I had achieved great successes and endured colossal embarrassments (including a ripped skirt incident while working a Hispanic Chamber of Commerce event for Vice President Quayle). I had received public accolades and suffered public humiliations. I had learned that perseverance, honesty, and a strong work ethic pay off.

Despite all that, I was worse than inept when it came to running a household. I stumbled repeatedly and felt ridiculously ill-equipped to do what mattered more to me than all my accomplishments.

My kitchen skills, as pathetic as they were, actually exceeded my knowledge in the cleaning arena when I first entered adulthood. By the time of my nuptials, I wasn't a slob anymore, but I had never really *cleaned* a bathroom. Maid service fell into the "essential" category of my nonexistent budget before marriage. Not so with my new husband. We had a few school loans that took precedence over Merry Maids.

Crippled by my lack of experience, I did what I would do in any situation in which I might find my skills lacking: seek expert advice. I hopped in my car. Drove to Wichita Falls where I grew up. I picked up Bea, a spunky little fireball of a woman who used to come every day to clean our house and whip us into shape when I was a child. Many a day she would get after us with a yellow fly swatter (the pink one was reserved for bugs) and keep us in line, all while watching her "stories," the CBS lineup of soaps.

I loved Bea. She may have thought I was crazy driving back and forth from Wichita Falls to get her help. She might have been a bit disappointed that I was pushing thirty and still in need of housekeeping assistance. If so, she never let on. We both were delighted to have a reason to be with each other, even if it involved cleaning products. We had such a sweet time together as she walked me through the steps of cleaning our little Dallas rental house. I'll never forget the two of us on our hands and knees, scraping the grime from that old bathroom floor. She, in disbelief that I genuinely had no idea what I was doing. Me, grateful for this nonjudgmental teacher who showed me the ropes.

I was a tad embarrassed that I didn't know how to do simple life tasks when I entered the on-ramp to adulthood. My early days in marriage and parenting could have gone much more smoothly if I'd been better prepared. I especially felt that way when we made the decision that I would stay home after Boxster was born. Though my education had prepared me for international banking transactions, I wasn't sure what to do when the director of domestic affairs became my new vocation.

Clearly, my parents ran a tight ship and pushed us as children. We were never allowed to quit. We were never allowed to see obstacles as deal breakers. We were always expected to do our best. But I guess I was a bit spoiled—not rotten, but definitely spoiled. My mom, in the name of love, had made many aspects of life easy so we kids could excel in school and sports. Looking back, there was plenty of time to do both. And looking ahead, I'm hoping the Experiment will not only equip the kids but help them merge safely the day they hit life's highway on their own.

That's why I want my children to face reality—and cleaning bathrooms is a reality in nearly every person's life at some point. It's dirty. It can be gross. But it's part of life.

I have no idea what the future holds for my children careerwise, but my hope is that by helping them master the basic essentials of functioning on their own, we are freeing them to tackle the tougher challenges of

We're All in This Together

I am a mom of two girls, ages fifteen and eleven. For years I did all the laundry, shopping, cooking, and so on. Then my husband was laid off, and we decided to open our own business. This meant lots of hours and absolutely no money coming into the household.

Reality quickly set in for my children. No more mom at home all day to take care of the everyday things. My girls now do all their own laundry (including sheets and towels). They clean their own bathrooms, run the vacuum, pick up dog poop, unload and load the dishwasher. Before my eyes they have matured and become more responsible. Their friends think I'm the "mean mom" for making them help. They don't care because they know what they are doing is helping our family survive.

—Texas mom

life with more energy and confidence. It takes so much brainpower and emotional vitality and physical energy to do the so-called big things in life (work assignments, refereeing sibling fights, making your spouse feel valued)—but if all their verve is drained because they're overwhelmed by the simple tasks of cooking and cleaning and shopping, how can we expect our offspring to be world changers?

Since the kids are a bit worn out by the Experiment right now, we're approaching this task lightly. A few will genuinely enjoy cleaning our bathrooms. A few might consider outright mutiny. I don't want to make them hate working around the house. I just want them to know how. So rather than require a thorough cleaning of every room in the house, we're limiting this task to their bathrooms, where they can pretty much do it all in one small space: clean, mop, disinfect, and so on.

Last week when I introduced Barton to a toilet brush, I was met with an indignant, "*Eww.* That's *gross!* Why would anyone have to *clean* a toilet!"

I am amazed once again that my kids have lived this long without giving thought to the workings of the world around them. Not in the grand sense, but in practical daily living. Has it never dawned on them that the toilet is cleaned? Have they never considered that a toilet gets dirty? That their sheets are washed and why that's necessary? I can only attribute their cluelessness to the fact that I have been opting for the easy way out, doing it myself. Yet again, this leaves me baffled. Why have I been so adamant about encouraging independence for the kids in so many areas, but not in and around the house?

I guess up to this point, I've bought into controlled independence. I've decided when, where, and how things are done in and outside of our home. This exercise is opening my eyes to where I can equip and teach—and then let go.

So often along this road, I've been overwhelmed with the parallels between our Experiment and my own relationship with God. I'm grateful that God doesn't approach me the same way I've dealt with my kids.

I can't think of many times throughout Scripture that he stepped in and did. He almost always instructed, taught, provided materials, encouraged, commanded, then said, "Go." He never sends us alone: "I am with you always" (Matthew 28:20). But he sends us, nonetheless. I think, too, about how most of those sent felt completely inadequate. But God didn't let them off the hook. In fact, by going forth even when they felt ill-prepared, they were compelled to rely completely on the One sending. (See Adam, Noah, Abraham, Moses, Joshua, Gideon, Samuel, David, Elisha, Elijah, Isaiah, Jeremiah...okay, so pretty much everyone.)

I think I'll take some cues from the Master Instructor. Whether or not they feel ready, my kids are about to go forth and conquer grime.

Gearing Up for the Battle of the Bathroom

Up to this point, I have kept our cleaning products in a plastic caddy and transported them from room to room, a frugal solution. But in the name of hard work, we're changing that approach and supplying each bathroom with necessary cleaning products. I, for one, could live without sibling battles over who has the caddy or who lost it (because it's bound to be misplaced, mostly in some lame effort to avoid work), or who used up all the _____ (fill in the blank). To avoid World War III, I headed to Target to gather supplies for each of our three bathrooms.

I feel like I'm living in a Laura Numeroff world:

If you give a mom some Pine-Sol, she'll want a new cleaning caddy to put it in.

She'll take the caddy to the bathroom and notice all the junk under the sink.

When she sees the junk, she'll want to organize and cull.

She'll gather the under-sink nonessentials and race for the back door, planning to add them to the pile destined for a garage sale.

As she runs down the stairs, she will trip on the shoe left in the middle of her path.

The shoe reminds her that children should be the ones cleaning and culling.

So she goes back up the stairs to "inspire" her kids to toss trash and gather future sale or Goodwill items.

When she enters a room in search of kids to inspire, she sees a made bed. And smiles.

She drops the culprit's shoe, picks up the pj's forgotten on the floor, turns to leave…and sees the Pine-Sol sitting by the bathroom door.

She decides she needs a break and chooses to forget the Pine-Sol, remembering instead her Keurig coffee maker.

She blows off the bathroom, ignores the chore for one more day, and settles in for some Coffee People french roast and the lazy enjoyment of some well-earned procrastination.

Clearly I'm in need of adult interaction.

Eventually, realizing I couldn't avoid it any longer, I decided to hit the chores head-on. We're definitely moving into deeper territory. Our family meeting yielded the toughest pushback thus far.

"Well, how would you all like to handle the bathrooms?" I asked.

"We wouldn't."

"What?" (I couldn't believe Boxster actually said that!) "That's a pretty sorry response. Way to be a leader."

"It's true."

"Listen work isn't always—"

"We know. 'Work isn't always fun. It's something we *all* have to do,'" quoted Barton and Snopes in unison.

Hmm. Apparently I need some variety in my repertoire. "Yes, okay. I know I've said that a few times."

"Mom! This is crazy. We've done everything you've asked. *Why* do

we have to clean bathrooms? None of our friends do *anything* like this!"
Boxster defended his comment.

The moaning chorus chimed in, "Yeah! *None* of our friends!"

When entering a conversation of this sort, the first thing I should
have done was to park my prickly, prepared-for-combat baggage at the
door. Rather than being on the defensive, I should have come to the table
with a bit more empathy. Empathy and creativity. Because they're right.
On the whole, their friends aren't cleaning toilets. All the kids needed to
do was ask if I had to clean toilets when I was their age, and I'd have been
toast. I myself am the poster child for housework ineptitude.

I wish I had entered this arena with spunk, excitement, and loads of
praise for jobs well done. I wish I had celebrated their efforts thus far by
maybe taking them out for dinner. Why didn't I surprise them with a
little Benihana hibachi-grill action rather than hit them with my standard "work isn't always fun" lecture?

None of this entered my thoughts, however, in the heat of the moment. I came ready to spar.

"If you all have no opinion, I'll decide it for you."

Moaning. In stereo.

"Stop complaining," I barked. "Rather than just cleaning your own
bathroom, you will each get a day where you clean both kid bathrooms."

"What?"

"That's not fair!"

Oooh. Clearly I'd hit a nerve.

"Fair schmair," I retorted with motherly maturity. "You all need to
know what it's like to clean someone else's area."

"That's *disgusting*!"

"Maybe. But you'll certainly get a chance to appreciate what I do.
Plus it will be easier to keep track. Trust me. You need to know how to do
this in life."

"Noooo. Puh-leeze. No-ho-ho-ho-ho." Sob, sob, sob.

My sentiments exactly.

Doing Their Best (to Do the Least Work Possible)

Our bathroom adventure has revealed much about our kids and their characters. I can't decide if it's an age thing or if it's an indication of wiring. Two of the kids have stepped up. No complaining. Okay, minimal complaining. They needed direction to get started, but both did their best from there forward. The other two went through the motions, but I can't say they truly cleaned. They got the job done—sort of; but I'm not sure they cared about the quality of their work at all. I was intrigued by their lack of concern or effort. My diligent ones went over and beyond what was asked. The get-me-out-of-here kids did just enough to be able to say they did something.

I'm hoping the disregard for excellence has something to do with the job and is not indicative of deep-seated character flaws.

Just the other day, a small-group leader who works with the girls at our church came for a visit. I started delving into her life, asking about dating and such things. Then I asked about her job, what she liked and didn't like. When talking about the challenges of her work, she summed it up in one word: apathy. The people she works with just don't care. They're competent, well-educated, and completely disinclined to take initiative. Not only do they exert the bare minimum effort to get a job done, they also shift responsibility to a coworker's plate any chance they get. Being a diligent worker, she's baffled and bewildered. She would never consider opting for mediocrity.

Curious, especially considering the fact she's in her late twenties (part of Gen Me), I asked where she thinks her own work ethic originated.

"Listen, my home life was a mess," she said. "I had smothering parents who wouldn't even let me ride my bike to school unless one of them was following me in their car. Throw in some major dysfunction—a different story for another day—and I was screaming for a way out. So I found a job as soon as I could. It started when I was fourteen with a paper route. Then I made my way to steady employment after school and on the weekends. It was the only environment that I got to put in some time, away from home, and succeed. Nothing glamorous, but I loved it."

"So you had a job when you were a teenager?" I prompted.

"Yeah. It was a lifesaver for me. Besides giving me a way out, I learned how to work. To work hard and with excellence—even when my job was nothing more than making copies and binding books. I was so grateful to have it," she continued, "I would never have done anything but my best."

"That's so interesting." It really *was* interesting to me—that a kid would escape home by getting a job. Then actually care enough to do her best.

"I just don't understand the attitudes of people we hire," she said. "Granted, most of them are in their early twenties, and I get the Facebook and texting thing. I'm right there with them. But they actually opt for that over a job well done."

She went on. "I'm constantly amazed at the lack of critical thinking. Only on the rarest of occasions will someone take the time to think about what they are doing and go beyond the task itself to find possible solutions or new, more efficient ways to handle an issue. It's like it's chronic. No one is going the extra mile. They're limping to get through a half mile. Then they decide they've done enough, and someone else can finish for them."

Yikes. She was describing my bathroom workers to a T. My not-so-inspired pair have been completely content with mediocrity. They've even convinced themselves that the halfway mark of finishing this bathroom task is the finish line.

Refusing to give in to my old habit of taking the easy route by doing it myself, I forced myself to grab the pair and open their eyes to unfinished business. I don't want them doing less than their best when they enter the workforce. If they're going to learn, they might as well get schooled here. Where someone loves them.

The response was strong. One of them even squeezed out some dramatic tears. "I can't believe you're saying I didn't finish. I was so proud of my good job."

"Please… You can't look me in the eyes and tell me you think your work is done in here." I pointed at a bathtub still full of toys from the night before. Clearly, no cleaning action had touched the porcelain. "There are still toys in the tub. You cannot be telling me you cleaned it!"

Silence.

"Well?"

"Okay, so maybe I didn't clean *all* of it."

"Really? Did you even clean some?"

"Mom! *Yes!*" Mumble, mumble, then to herself, "She never thinks I do anything. *Fine.* I'll just start over." *Stomp, stomp, stomp.* (Those are figurative stomps. She didn't really do a drama dance for me. But she made clear her frustration.)

I decided to ignore the immature reaction and offer words of encouragement. Of course, she wanted nothing of the sort, so I left. Her compadre in crime worked with her to finish the job—really finish the job. I'm glad they did it together. The muffled grumbling soon ceased, and they surrendered to the job at hand. Toilet humor and outright belly laughs replaced the moans of self-pity.

Maybe that's part of the equipping thing too. Not giving in to the inevitable bucking. I guess a child is kind of like a wild stallion, desperately trying to ditch the uncomfortable saddle of responsibility. Yearning for freedom to roam the range. But carefree wandering is not reality for most adults. And if at some point in their lives, my kids decide to walk the vagabond way, at least they will know how to clean a service-station bathroom.

A key principle continually brought home to me by the Experiment is that parents need to start the equipping process when the kids are young. Preteen pushback lacks the intensity, strength, and relentless attitude so frequently dished out by older siblings.

I've also learned that taking the cheapest road isn't always best.

Rather than equipping each bathroom with the incredibly handy disposable toilet cleaning wand system, I initially forced the kids to use our existing brush and Clorox Toilet Bowl Cleaner. When kids are struggling through a chore, it's probably not a good idea to make it more difficult than necessary. Squeezing the bottle and getting the gel to hit just the right spot in the bowl caused much grief and frustration—for all of us. I wised up about halfway through the month and purchased some wands. Though cost-inefficient, somehow they made a seemingly terrible job exponentially easier. I even heard one child utter the word "fun."

My kids aren't the best bathroom cleaners. In fact, clean is a bit of a stretch. I find it hard to believe a basin was washed when I can still see toothpaste remnants from the night before. On the positive side, at least the kid brushed his teeth. Still, I don't get it. How hard can it be? But they're trying. Maybe succumbing to the force of my insistence is a better description. But I'm not giving up. They think I will, but I won't. Taking responsibility and completing their tasks needs to be second nature. Plus, I refuse to let a simple task like this get the best of me—or of them. In fact, I'm going to stick with it until I get the best *from* them.

That said, something happened in the kitchen today that is worth sharing.

While standing next to a sinkful of dirty cups and plates, I opened the dishwasher and found it full of clean dishes. I just couldn't force myself to empty and fill it again. With all that we've been requiring of the kids, we've had to shift around a few responsibilities so they could still have time for homework and other things. Being a bit unorganized, I couldn't remember who was doing what when. So I grabbed the closest able body, knowing that after their Month of Meals, they all have complete ability to rinse, load, and empty this dishwasher.

Fury got the call.

"Hey, come empty the dishwasher."

"What? It's not my turn," he protested. "I did it yesterday." Actually he did it a couple of days ago, but when chores are involved, it seems like only minutes, not days, have passed between assignments.

"Well, do it again." Better to not debate the details.

He did do it again. And he did it well. Drying off each cup and every plate. Methodically stacking and sorting before putting it all away. I was genuinely impressed.

Later that afternoon, I stopped his play and asked him to look me in the eyes. He thought he was in trouble, poor kid. But all I wanted to do was thank him for his terrific work. We shook hands, and I once more told him how proud I was of his effort and a job well done.

When dinnertime hit, the dishwasher had run its cycle and the sink was full. I needed another "volunteer." As I began to delegate the job to

Expert Advice: Differing Standards of "Clean"

Cynthia Townley Ewer, the creator of OrganizedHome.com and author of *Houseworks,* suggests that, when it comes to the quality of our kids' efforts, we may do best to focus on the big picture of preparing our kids to manage a home, rather than getting caught up in the perfection trap:

> Cleaning methods are a frequent bone of contention between parents and children. A parent's insistence on "the right way" can add another element of conflict to the housework issue. The answer? Avoid this by focusing on the "good-enough" job. A 10-year-old's skill with the vacuum cleaner will increase with practice...if he's not derailed by arguments over too-high standards or demoralized when a parent redoes the work.[1]

the girl cooking dinner, a voice from the other room piped in, "I'll do it! *Please* let me do it."

Round two! He even went to bed asking what he could do tomorrow.

Research studies have explored the power of positive (and negative) words. A positive word can actually change an average Joe into a person who strives for excellence. The opposite holds true for the negative word: it takes excellence and spirals it down to mediocrity.

The positive word must be truth based. No lip service allowed. Interestingly, it takes around ten positive comments to reverse the effects of one negative remark. For a few residents of our house, one simple negative comment could outweigh one hundred positives. In fact, the negative word could be 100 percent fluff and still zing home an esteem buster. Negative words strive to prove that our deepest insecurities about ourselves are true.

I've witnessed more than once the transformative power of positive reinforcement. It's not as easy as dishing out a quick, seemingly effective (in that I might get the desired behavior by force) negative swipe, but it inspires like nothing else.

Sticking to the positive in a house full of strong personalities, whining, stubbornness, moods (oh, how I could go on) can be a challenge. But today I witnessed, in case I had forgotten, just how wonderfully inspiring a positive word can be.

Oh, that I would spend a lot more time on that side of the fence.

Best Foot Forward

This weekend I ran into a friend whose very talented, accomplished, capable son is applying to colleges.

"Where's he looking?" I asked.

"Oh, A&M, UT, and a couple others out of state."

"How's the application process going?"

"Really great. I'm submitting two for him tomorrow. And we just finished the essays."

I didn't say anything, but I almost gagged on two words in those sentences: "I" and "we." At times I wish I had never started considering the problem of youth entitlement. In some ways life was simpler before I realized that my attempts to rescue/fix/help/save weren't really sending the message I intended—and before I grew concerned about how our society is being shaped by other parents who race in to save.

No need to point out that this family is terrific. The parents are wonderful people who, in the name of love, are helping their child complete what they consider one of the more important processes in life. But as with all this "help," that annoying little message keeps presenting its nasty face. The one that loudly implies, "I'll help because I can do it better than you." Or, "I'll help because you can't do it."

It's so hard to let my kids handle their business, especially when 1) I'm fairly certain I can do it better, 2) I know other parents are stepping in for their kids, 3) I equate helping them with loving them, and 4) I'm just not sure my kid will actually get it done. To the latter, I need to genuinely let my brood swim floaty-free much earlier than senior year applications so I know they can do it and so *they* know they can do it.

Ugh. Why is it so hard to embrace solo-flight opportunities? I may not have college staring me in the face, but I feel like this hits me every day.

Everyone is padding life for these kids. The schools, the parents, even many coaches who, in fear for their lives from a berating parent, give equal playing time or awards to all the kids lest someone's self-esteem be negatively affected.

I love my friend Ron Harris's approach when college-level students walk into his class expecting extra-credit opportunities. Why wouldn't they? Safety nets are the norm every time they turn around.

One of the common things I have heard from students in almost every class and each semester is this: "What can I do for extra credit?"

Sometimes it comes in a panic near the end of the semester when the handwriting is on the old blackboard, as it were. Sometimes, to my surprise, it comes at the start of the semester. On both occasions I have a ready answer. In fact, at the start of each course as I walk students through what to expect, I let them know there won't be any work for extra credit. And then I share my philosophy, forged from both academic experience and life in the working world.

Take the effort you would use on extra credit and use it on the regular work.

Try that on your kids, and you'll probably get the same response I usually get. A blank stare, a rolling of the eyes, a shrug. However, the advice is sound, both for the classroom and for life. Whatever we anticipate it would take to do the "extra" to pull a grade up is probably more than it would take to do the work the right way the first time.

There are actually terms for that. Effort. Time management. You get the idea. They are principles that serve us well throughout our lives. And if we can teach that to our kids early, they will benefit, and so will our corporations, our ministries, our families, and our communities.

Here's how the alternative plays out in the work force. "Hey, boss. I know I didn't do too good of a job on that big contract, and we lost the account. However, if I could straighten everything in the supply closet, would that make up for it?" In the sports world it would sound like this: "Coach, I realize now that I haven't been giving my best effort out in the field, and our team is in last place. What if I ran laps after the game tonight? Would that 'extra credit' make up for that?"

No, in life, like in school, the best time to do our best work is the first time. It is what is asked of us, it is how we are gauged, it is the expectation for the job at hand, and if we can't perform at that level, we may be asked to step down. Or worse, we will be an inhibitor to a company or a ministry.

The Lord is clear in Scripture on the topic of work. In Proverbs 21:5 we are taught, "Good planning and hard work lead to prosperity, but hasty shortcuts lead to poverty."...

There may be a time for extra work for extra credit. There may be circumstances that warrant the extra effort to put something over the top. But we cannot let our kids think that later effort will always make up for a lack of effort at the start.[2]

I think about the extra credit often. It helps me persevere on what seems a bit ridiculous. Maybe when I don't give in to my daughter's stubborn defense of her minimal, at best, efforts at tub cleaning, she'll realize that by doing it right the first time (which she knows and has been shown how to do), she could get it done faster and more efficiently. So it goes for all our tasks.

At the same time, and even though I've again been dubbed "Mean Mom," I'm not expecting perfection. Friday morning I returned to school to drop off Boxster's project that inadvertently fell into the backseat as he raced out of the car to beat the bell. That's not enabling, is it? Nah, that's giving a hand up to my kid who worked hard on his presentation. He knows I'm there for him. His school doesn't offer much extra credit.

What Happens in the Bathroom...

Despite the complaining, these kids reached previously unknown summits in this little Lysol climbing challenge. Unlike a Kilimanjaro ascent, this task probably won't be something my kids brag about to their friends. I'll do my best to not embarrass them by bragging in their presence.

I recently walked in on the girls during their pre-bedtime routine.

"The toilet's clogged, Mom."

"Yeah…won't flush," chimed in Snopes from her shower.

"I'll fix it," I replied and reached for the plunger conveniently located behind the toilet and next to our nifty bowl brushes. This particular commode is a bit high maintenance. As I lifted the plunger, I couldn't help but notice that it was wet.

Then from the shower I heard, "I already tried to unclog it!"

Visions of toilet yuckiness sloshing from the bowl onto the floor invaded my thoughts. We didn't cover unclogging a toilet in our task education. Mostly because her father, Mr. Clean, prefers to handle this particular job. That way he's assured of complete cleanliness and disinfection. It helps him sleep at night.

As I stood there holding the wet plunger, the kid read my mind. "I washed it off after I tried. It was too hard for me. The stuff looked like it was going to flow over onto the floor, so I decided to wait for you."

"Yeah. It's soooo gross!" chimed in Barton.

"You did a great job," I told Snopes after I flushed the toilet and discussed plunging strategies. Such fun girl talk. Mascara and curling irons have nothing on the plunger.

I was fairly certain that, when he heard about the evening activity, their father would put the kibosh on plunging (probably to everyone's relief). But I was delighted to see evidence of personal initiative, which I'm convinced never would have happened in our pre-Experiment days.

WHAT THEY LEARNED THIS MONTH

- Toilets don't magically clean themselves, and neither do mirrors or sinks or tubs.
- Any time gained by slopping through a job is lost when you have to go back and do it right.

- If you're going to claim you've done a job, it's probably a good idea to remove any evidence to the contrary.

WHAT I LEARNED THIS MONTH

- Teaching responsibility when the kids are young is much easier than trying to introduce it during the turbulent teen years.
- Even teenagers can kick the entitlement habit, with a little boost from Mom and Dad.
- A single phrase of positive reinforcement packs a wallop of influence.

Roll Tide

Diving into Our Family's Dirty Laundry

> The only place where success comes before work is in the dictionary.
>
> —V. SASSOON

"Not the laundry too!"

"Is this part of that Experiment thing?"

"This must be Mrs. Silva's fault!"

They know I appreciate her approach to chores. Mrs. Silva and I have been friends for years. She's the queen of putting her four kids to work. I so admire the quality of their lawn service—provided by her teenage son! Plus, we get to commiserate about the whines. It really is nice knowing you're not going it alone.

Even though I shared the kids' dread of taking the plunge (no pun intended despite last month's challenge), their reaction confirmed our need to learn to swim in Lake Laundry. Goggles on. Nose clip and ear-plugs in place (for obvious reasons), we're diving in.

Step 1: Declutter

Have you noticed a trend here? As with a few of our other chores, before we can really start, we first have to clear some work space. I've decided that Jack's hoarding tendencies are constantly reinforced by our family's propensity to pile stuff—lots of stuff—anywhere and everywhere. Some of that is the inevitable result of seven bodies living in sufficient but far from expansive space.

Our laundry room is more of a laundry closet. Though a monumental step up from our last house where the full-size stackable washer/dryer unit shared space with a water heater and furnace, the space is fairly small. Since we have no closets downstairs, I use every available spot to pile extras. Our laundry room/closet is located right outside our kitchen, so I tend to conceal behind its door whatever overflow can't find a spot in a kitchen cabinet. Then the "out of sight, out of mind" adage takes over. Several old art projects from school, the penguin ice shaver, a box of one thousand water balloons hidden for reasons apparent to any mom—all this and more had been tucked away for months, maybe years.

Decluttering has been one of the keys to success in our equipping activities. I've noticed that with the kids the less clutter they have to deal with, the better their ability to maintain a clean space. Okay, so maybe that's true for me too. I guess I can chalk clutter-control issues up as a side-effect of my procrastination tendencies.

Expert Advice: Decluttering

Peter Walsh, organizing expert for *The Nate Berkus Show*, suggests a Trash-Bag Tango to get started decluttering your home. Give everyone two trash bags and ten minutes in which to fill one bag with trash and the other with stuff to give away. Do this once or twice a week and watch the clutter disappear. Walsh confirms the truth we all know deep down, "Happiness does not come with more stuff. But life has got to be about experiences, not about accumulating things."[1]

As to the task at hand, with all the extra stuff in that small space, only one body can fit in our laundry room. So decluttering is critical if I'm to bring the kids in for a laundry how-to workshop.

Step 2: Strategize

Thanks to great advice from friends, I gave the kids two options, both of which start with each child taking one day a week to wash, dry, and put away clothes and towels. No sheets or bedding; we'll save those for another day. Let's face it: I still fight with folding a fitted sheet. Asking my kids to wrestle with that thing would be like inviting them to go on strike.

With the nonnegotiables established, I explained how they get to take ownership by choosing one of two laundry plans.

Option A: On their assigned day, each child handles whatever family laundry needs washing. This would hone the skill of serving one another and foster teamwork. But it also could set the stage for the blame game. I can hear it now, "Where are my black shorts?" directed to a sibling. "It was *your* day to wash… Mommm!"

Not only will blame be tossed around like socks in the dryer but pity parties will be thrown: "He only had to do towels. I had to wash four loads of shirts, shorts, and *underwear*!"

Option B: On their assigned day, kids will wash only their personal items. The buck stops with them.

They chose B. Maybe one day we can mature into option A.

Step 3: Implement

We'll start on Tuesday. Why not cave to a little procrastination? I'm trying so hard everywhere else.

Step 4: Incentivize

I'm catching some flak about limiting their earnings to a dollar a day while I keep adding jobs. I'm thinking I might add a buck each day they launder their loads. This would increase their potential earnings to a whopping thirty-five dollars per month—if, by some chance, they fulfill all their other daily obligations: bed, bathroom clutter, bathroom cleaning, and room clutter.

Tonight when I retrieved Barton from a friend's house, I was surprised and delighted to learn that their family had been discussing our idea of incentive for chores. Barton had shared an earful about our crazy antics—from the money jar to the dinners to our new and exciting adventure in Laundry Land. The mom, a sweet friend of mine, encouraged my kid to tell it all. The dad happened to be on hand, taking it in.

As I stood in their foyer, waiting for Barton to come down, he commented on the brilliance behind the thirty-one-dollar-bills jar idea. He thought we had strategized the dollar-docking system. Isn't it nice he would assume something so cerebral and premeditated? Doesn't he know we're totally flying by the seat of our pants? As with most of the Experiment's strategies, the idea was not mine but a friend's.

Anyway, he was impressed by the use of a stock-market psychology known in the business world as behavioral economics. One of the central tenets of behavioral economics is that people are "loss adverse." On an emotional level, a loss appears about three times larger than a gain of equal size.

So what does this have to do with the money jar? It's all about the emotion associated with losing a dollar versus the incentive of gaining a dollar. Boy, have I seen this played out with my kids!

When our Experiment started, I offered cash incentives (thirty one-dollar bills and coins in a jar). Our core plan, based on the great suggestion of my friend Lauren, was that for every day they completed their tasks, the kids could keep one of the thirty dollars. It seemed streamlined and easy. It spoke to my memory disorder, the one that causes me to forget to dole out allowance. (So maybe the jar is enabling my own problem, but that's a separate issue.) Plus, they see the money. Some of them count the money—daily. If they miss a chore, I simply take a bill out of the jar. Bam! It's done. No negotiation needed.

However, not wanting to be considered mean for taking something away for a job done poorly or not at all, I initially gave the kids an option: they could either see the bills in their jars and deal with docking, or they could start each month with an empty jar that could be filled as chores were accomplished. Either way, they're not allowed to spend the cash until the month has concluded. My motive was to avoid the focus on negative consequences and instead operate from a positive reward system, if that appealed to them.

All the kids chose the dollar-docking approach, except for one. You guessed it: our oldest preferred that the dollar be put in rather than taken out of the jar. A killer for me since I never seem to have any one-dollar bills on me, and I really do struggle with remembering. It never mattered, though, because only one party has paid minimal attention to our bed-making/chore efforts. (Well, maybe two if you count me.)

How interesting to discover from this successful businessman that a stock-market principle was hidden in those jars. The motivation associated with potentially losing a dollar is much greater than the incentive to gain a dollar. Who knew? I think I must have been absent, or possibly asleep, when this theory was discussed in business school.

Ironing Board Tip

Regarding money management, we opened checking accounts for our kids at age thirteen. We put money in, and they managed it however they liked. This not only stopped their constant requests for money but also stopped us looking over their shoulders all the time at what they spent it on. We decided an amount—and from that they were to buy clothes, lunch, and so on.

—Lucina Thompson

My equitable efforts have failed miserably. I thought letting them choose their method of payment was a good idea. Apparently, not so much. It's just like the meal thing where I let them pay for dinner if they didn't want to make it. Boxster was the only one who opted to buy—another less-than-positive experience. Good intentions led to my offering options I hoped would build decision-making skills and self-esteem. Instead, just the opposite resulted.

If you hear a beeping sound, that's my truck backing up to start again. Boxster's jar now starts out full, just like his siblings'.

Detour from the Path of Least Resistance

As you may have guessed from the blame targeted at dear Mrs. Silva, news of the month's laundry task was not met with universal enthusiasm. When I asked the kids to pick their days, Boxster was the first to speak. "I'll take Wednesday!"

"I want Tuesday," chimed in Barton.

"Give me Thursday," said Snopes.

Since Fury was at camp, I gave him Monday.

I heard a hushed but victorious "Yes!" coming from Boxster, possibly accompanied by a fist pump, though I couldn't be sure since he was way in the backseat. Yes, we're in the car again. We get some of our best conversations handled while en route to our various activities. I think I save the potentially dicey ones for when they are imprisoned by seat belts.

I admit I can be a little slow on the uptake, but when a teen is pumped about laundry, something fishy is going on. It didn't take me long to realize that he had instantly assessed the advantage of selecting a day that coincides with one of Clara's regular visits to help me out. One thing about that kid: he's no dummy. Oh, how I hope he uses his tenacity and quick wit to do good for the world instead of using it to take the path of least resistance and effort.

"Just so you know," I quickly piped in, "if you pick Clara's day, you'll still be doing *your* laundry. Just after she leaves."

"What? You can't be serious!"

"Oh yes. I'm serious."

"Why do we need to do our own laundry? I'm only fourteen," he moans.

Hmm. The "I'm fourteen" phrase can take on such different meanings. There's the "I'm *fourteen*" sarcastically thrown my way when a PG-13 movie comes up for discussion. Then there's the "I'm fourteen," as in *only* fourteen and obviously not equipped to do an adult job.

Oh, I have such a long way to go. I wish I had started this stuff when they were much younger. Oh yeah, I did. But somewhere along the way, I began taking the easy way out, doing it for them.

As I embarked upon another steep climb, wondering if I'll ever even glimpse the summit of youth responsibility or if I'll be doomed to wander forever in the valley of entitlement, I remembered something my friend Andy Kerckhoff guest-posted on my blog. Andy is an educator, coach, and dad who has a great deal of wisdom to share when it comes to adolescents. He's seen it all.

Give them real work.

Yes, give them real responsibilities, as much as possible, so they get the sense that they are important and that their good work is greatly valued by real people (and that shoddy or incomplete work is a problem for real people). Give them some things every day to do around the house that are legitimately helpful to others, and then reward them for sticking with their task and doing a good job.

To underscore his point, Andy quoted teen-behavior expert Mark Gregston: "Kids need to be given responsibilities in the family that they can claim and make happen without parental badgering. It builds a sense of value and belonging."[2] Andy concluded,

> It's pretty easy to protect and provide for kids. You keep them physically safe, give them an abundance of fun things to do, and they grow on up easily. That's the American way. The better way is to prepare kids for independence, but that is a much harder task. As they develop, we should slowly reduce the protection and provision, while increasing the preparation.[3]

Good to have some mental reinforcement. Yes, they legitimately need to wear clean clothes. Not all of them believe that, but at some point they will realize an oft-worn shirt tends to repulse rather than attract. Plus, I like the idea of building "a sense of value and belonging." Sounds wonderful.

Now…how long does that take? And at what point will "parental badgering" actually cease to be a part of the work release program? I can't say we've reached that glorious milestone. I will say the length and volume of my badgering has started to diminish a bit. At least we're walking in the right direction.

We're All in This Together

I told my girls I am on strike from doing their laundry. It has been a week and still the only action the washing machine has gotten is from my pile. The clothes might be hairy by the time they get to them!

—Lauren

Washers and Dryers And Lint. Oh My.

At the start of week one, I collectively introduced the kids to the washing machine and dryer, knowing I would need to do it all over again when their individual days arrived. I showed them the knobs, the detergent, the dryer sheets, the lint filter.

Aah…the lint filter. If you're thinking that our generation was hip and ready for action when we left home, think again. I'll never forget visiting my brother and his wife shortly after their first child arrived. We were chatting with a group of mutual friends when my sister-in-law rejoined us after a visit to their laundry room.

"Honey, you've got to call the repairman," she said. "Something is terribly wrong with our dryer."

Frugal man that he is, he said, "I'll fix it. What's wrong?"

"I leave the clothes in there for at least an hour on high heat, but they still come out wet. It's just not working."

"How long has it been doing that?"

"At least a month. Sometimes it takes like five hours to dry a load."

"I'll look at it," one of our friends volunteered.

Shortly afterward, he walked back to our little gathering with a brick of lint in his hand. The thing had to have been at least ten inches thick. How he got it out of the filter still baffles me.

"What in the world is that!" my sister-in-law gasped.

"Uh, it's your lint. Have you ever cleaned the filter?"

"What filter?"

Enough said.

At the conclusion of our Laundry 101 class, I heard a chorus of "Oh, that's easy."

"Yes," I said, "it is easy. In fact, the washing and drying can almost be fun. However, the job isn't over until all items are folded and neatly put in their proper location."

An in-stereo response of "Awwww!" filled the air with their collective disillusionment. Quite frankly, I'm with them. I could wash and dry all day, but folding and putting away have never been my friends.

Then there's our biggest problem: Clara, who helps me on Wednesdays and Fridays, is entirely too efficient! She gets in there and whips the house into shape before I can stop her. I've tried to explain what we're doing. She's even enjoyed the benefit of the kids' labor. But I think she doesn't like them working her out of a job. Even though her primary role is to help me with our little hoarder, she has such a strong work ethic, she just can't stop herself from doing more.

Ironing Board Tip

If you haven't yet watched Cesar Millan, the "Dog Whisperer," on the National Geographic Channel, then you are missing out on a wonderful parenting tool. I don't say this because your teen is an animal—although he or she may seem to be at times! But after my son convinced me to watch the show, I saw what many have seen: his principles apply perfectly to parenting.

For example, you must be the pack leader. Lead by example. Take control of the room, the situation, and the energy exchanged in your interactions with your teen.

One thing Cesar does well aligns with what I have told parents in every seminar I've ever given on discipline: *be detached.* I'm not suggesting that you be detached from your teen, but that you be detached from all the *junk* they send your way.

Here is a key point to remember: your brain works differently than the brain of your teen. As the adult, you

"Go upstairs and get your laundry. Today is your day," I informed Boxster.

"I don't have any laundry."

"Yes. Yes, you do."

"No, I don't."

"Yes. You. Do."

"I *don't* have any!"

"You *do* have some!"

"I'm telling you the truth. I don't have any."

"Get upstairs and get your laundry right now. If you don't get it right

---

usually use the rational, logical, planning part of the brain. By contrast, your teen often reacts first from the emotional part of the brain. If you then react with your own emotion, you ignite their emotional fuel. *Kaboom!* And who wants that in our homes?

So the secret is, remain calm. Stay detached. Respond rather than react. Speak softly but be firm. Use your eyes and body language. And, especially you dear moms, you have to remember to lower your voice as you speak, rather than increasing in pitch and ending with a shrill, "Do I make myself *clear*?"

And remember this: the owners having the dog problems always want Cesar to come in and fix the dog. They are surprised to find out that, more often than not, *they* are the root of the problem. So don't go into a parenting issue thinking, *That lousy teen...*, as hard as that is to resist! Be the parent. Not their BFF or their parole officer.[4]

—Jody Capehart

this minute, you…well…" I searched for a suitably effective threat. "You won't get any TV for the *rest* of the week!" (So there!)

"I don't *have* any laundry," he muttered as he schlumped off.

I mortify myself sometimes with my ridiculous comments. Why can't I avoid the verbal back and forth? We enter these "Ping-Pong" matches almost daily. I think sometimes he actually enjoys it. Forehand. Backhand. Forehand. Backhand. Volley. Lob. Forehand. It's a ridiculous game. Basically he enjoys arguing. I hate it but can't seem to stop myself.

But today he was right. Clara beat us all to the punch. He didn't have any laundry. Not only had she washed it all, but she had put it away. Truth is, we both were a little bit relieved to have avoided the day's laundry lesson. Maybe someday soon I'll master the first rule of engagement when parenting teens: *don't* engage.

FIELD TRIP

After an excruciatingly long day of debacles ranging from a swarm of bees in our yard (estimated to be around five hundred by the guy in charge of removing the hive) to a crown on my tooth coming off in a bite of chicken salad, I got a call from Clara. "Kay, the dryer has stopped working. It's no longer getting hot."

All I could do was shake my head and wonder what else could go wrong.

So I came home, gathered up the three wet loads and a crew of kids, and headed to the Laundromat. Despite the inconvenience and the dreaded cost of fixing or buying a new dryer, I was actually excited about our pending adventure. We arrived at the Spin Cycle late in the afternoon—not the most exciting time of day. Televisions were tuned to Judge Whoever, and most of the machines sat idle.

My wide-eyed kids had never seen anything like it before: an entire store solely devoted to laundering. Of course, Jack was thrilled to find a bank of shiny washers and dryers in which to hide his accompanying treasure of goods. He snagged a rolling laundry basket, then proceeded to entertain himself by opening and closing doors, moving his stuff from place to place like a paranoid pirate protecting his treasure from imagined looters.

I quickly explained the purpose of a Laundromat to my crew, handed each kid a dollar bill, and sent them for change. They loaded the dryers with our stuff, put in the coins, and watched the laundry spin—finally aware that drying clothes costs money. I explained that it costs at our house too, via the electric bill. (*Hmm.* Bills. Sounds like a great task for next year.)

As they took in their surroundings, they realized that having appliances is a privilege, not a right. Okay, so maybe they didn't realize it so much as they heard me lecture on the subject. Even though the clothes dried fairly quickly, I heard several "This is boring" mutterings. In fact, it sounded something like this, "This is boring. Not a little, not a teeny, not a smidgen...but *a lot* boring!" Boring isn't always bad. They got to drink a dose of reality today.

Maybe more than I bargained for. While we were folding our clothes, a snarly old lady stood with her back to the kids and released a few expletives at her dryer. Some beauties featured prominently in her string of verbal frustration. My daughter looked up at me alarmed.

"Mom! Did you hear what she said?" the kid loudly whispered.

"I did, honey. I think she's frustrated because she put her coins in the wrong machine."

After putting in quarters to dry her load, she had walked away, not realizing the coin receptacle was on the left side of the dryers, not to the right. So for who knows how long, the machine she'd fed the quarters into had been drying nothing while her things sat just as she had left them in the neighboring machine.

"Mom, can I share my quarters with her?" the kid asked.

I smiled inside and nodded.

The lady was stunned. She couldn't believe that a little kid would notice her and offer to help. She also couldn't believe that she had let loose that string of profanities in front of my children. She turned to us and profusely apologized. Her tough demeanor melted.

"Oh, I'm so sorry I said those things," she groaned. "I would never have said something like that in front of my kids. I'm so sorry." She gave us a sincere toothless smile while adjusting her flimsy T-shirt so as to appear a bit more presentable. The smell of alcohol drenched her words. "I just was a little mad to see my clothes still all wet."

"No worries," I assured her. "We were just as confused on where the quarters go when we loaded our clothes." Hand on her shoulder, I urged, "Please let us start it for you. We have plenty of quarters left, and the kids would just love putting them in the slots and firing that thing up."

She tried to protest, but it was too late. My brood was fighting one another for the chance to start another dryer. The sweet lady shared memories of laundering clothes with her kids. It was fun to watch her disappear to what was clearly a happier time. We were on common ground. She existed and we had noticed—something I'm not sure she had experienced in a long time.

She thanked us, apologized again, and went back to her business. Our dryers buzzed, and the kids began to fold the rest of the clothes. Yes, they made the expected "Eww! Underwear" comments, but they folded and organized it all the same.

This little laundry detour was peppered with such great lessons. The most important: even characters who seem utterly hardened are still people (maybe even somebody's mom), soft and tender inside if you can get through their tough crust.

So by the end of the day, I'd had my tooth repaired, hundreds of bees were removed from our yard, and we'd survived open-concept Laundry 101. And miracle of miracles, all our socks matched up.

Go-To Girl

Barton exceeded expectations big time on the laundry front this week. Thanks to my younger brother's wife and her generous parents, we had the chance to escape our Texas heat for a brief reprieve and spend a week in their lovely home nestled in the Colorado Rockies. Our family might have been on vacation, but the chores weren't. The kids had the opportunity to cook in different pots, shop in a new store, and flip a different kind of disposal switch. It was actually good for them to learn that not all machines are created alike.

When Barton saw the laundry piling up in the rooms, she jumped right in to handle the task—without my asking. She needed some help with the machine, though. Instead of opening the lid to add soap like our machine at home, she had to pull out a drawer. And instead of our powder detergent, our friends use liquid. Also, the controls were a little different. No buttons to push. Barton had to turn the dial and pull it out in order for the cycle to start. Small things, but still surprisingly practical lessons. The kid did everyone's laundry (not just her own), never uttering one word of complaint.

This little vacation exercise prompted me to rethink our current strategy of making the kids launder only their own clothes. As Barton gathered the goods, I noticed that someone in my brood had contributed only two items to be washed. No need to identify which kid apparently decided to go dirty rather than wash clothes. The same child later informed me that he/she hasn't used soap in the shower since we've been here "because there isn't any."

What in the world? "First of all, come tell me if you don't have soap! Second, there *is* soap. It just looks different because it's body wash."

Said the surprisingly nonstinky child, "No wonder my hair has been weird. I thought it was shampoo!"

Oh my word. Yet another testimony to my enabling issues. I've always bought their shampoo and soap for them, and I've made sure to refill their supplies as needed. To think kids will go without washing, either because they don't feel like getting more soap or they're determined to wait for someone (me!) to bring it to them. I grabbed a bar of soap and directed the offender straight to the shower.

Back to the laundry: not only did Barton wash everything, but I was greeted tonight by folded clothes on my bed. I couldn't believe she had gone the extra mile.

So here's a kid who has embraced her newfound work skills and started to make them her own. The interesting side-effect: her attitude toward hard work has made her my go-to girl. I know the others will do their jobs, but often only after I chide them into it or endure the moans of "Why?" "It's not fair," and "No one else has to do this." This doesn't happen every time, but I never know when I'm going to get pushback. I'm not giving up on them or making them second string; it just takes a little extra effort. The result? I'm slower to give them as much responsibility.

On the other hand, I find myself relying on Barton because I've come to trust her work and the spirit in which she does it.

Barton trusts me, listens to me, obeys me. In turn, I'm eager to pull her in and get her integrally involved. It doesn't change my love for the other kids or my desire for them to learn. But the fact of the matter is, she's learning more, gaining more independence (because I don't have to stand over her every minute explaining how to do things), feeling a wonderful sense of accomplishment, and growing into a closer, more mature relationship with me.

That leaves me with a bit of an "aha" moment as it drives me (yet again) to consider my relationship with God. Should I leave it there or walk down the obvious road? As if the countless Bible stories, the parables, the admonitions hadn't given me enough of a clue, this kid has offered a compelling confirmation of what I know to be true. The stronger my faith (resting in what is known rather than seen), the more I listen, the faster I respond, the less I complain and push back...the deeper my intimacy with God, the more often I'm called to serve, the greater my peace and contentment.

The lesson for me, and the one I'd love for all my kids to grasp? Be the go-to, uncomplaining, submitting, teachable worker. In a counter-intuitive sort of way, peace and freedom accompany that path of surrendered obedience.

WHAT THEY LEARNED THIS MONTH

- Showing kindness to others brings joy to us as well.
- Having appliances located right in our home is a privilege, not a right.
- Stepping in and helping without being asked gives the greatest sense of accomplishment and gratification.

WHAT I LEARNED THIS MONTH

- Serving without complaint is a beautiful thing—for them and for me.
- Badgering my kids into compliance is less effective than letting them face the consequences (dollar docking) of not doing their chores.
- A dollar lost is more compelling than a dollar earned. Who knew?

The Handyman Can...
Or Can He?

Do-It-Yourself Home Repair and Maintenance

> One only needs two tools in life: WD-40 to
> make things go, and duct tape to make them
> stop.
>
> —G. M. WEILACHER

A t this point in the Experiment, we've gotten to where a few chores
are becoming second nature—the nonnegotiables, like making
their beds and keeping their desks, floors, closets, and bathrooms fairly
clutter-free. I have a few highly creative free spirits who struggle with
completely clean, so we accept "presentable" as defined by the parent. Yes,
we have to go so far as to define it with some specificity. I have one child
who's destined for the courtroom. He can argue opposing sides at the
same time and win both. Defining "clean" is a bear with this kid.

Although Laundry month has officially ended, we will most certainly keep that chore going. And regarding meals, I have moved from
the kids cooking Monday through Thursday to them preparing our meal
once or twice a week. With four able-bodied chefs (and cleaning crew),

they will each end up cooking twice a month. I hope this will keep their kitchen skills honed, help them realize that these jobs don't stop, and promote creative thinking as they try to come up with new and appetizing menus. That said, the girls have so enjoyed their venture into the kitchen, they help me with most meals. Nearly all their favorite television shows are now found on the Food Network, and they're determined to own a cupcake store in the future. The boys tolerate the requirement, only pitching in on their assigned days. Whether they're cooking or not, they still have to load and unload the dishwasher when asked.

My kids have balked at all the extra work. Okay, so they balk at *any* extra work. I don't really care, though. We need to have a family meeting to talk about the method by which we'll incorporate all our newfound abilities into daily life. Assigning certain chores by the month might work best, or maybe trading off chores each week might be preferable. If I was more organized, I would have a chart already, but I'm in that annoying creative category where lists tend to take a backseat to just about everything. All they do for me is cause great pain because I only remember after the fact that I forgot to do whatever is on it.

Organization seems to come more naturally to some of my friends. One mom lists daily responsibilities on her kids' doors. (I think they should be called Door Chores.) All four of her kids expect to pitch in as a matter of course. Each day she tacks the day's assignments on their bedroom doors so they know exactly what needs to be accomplished before they can pursue their own agendas.

Here's a sample of what might be found on her sophomore's door.

READY FOR CAMP CAROLINE
CHORES, June 23, 2010
clean room
1 load of laundry
finish packing for camp
do work sheet on discernment

read 45 minutes

exercise

Yes, the kid completely packed herself for camp. Forgot the sunscreen? Use your own money to buy it from the camp store. Not enough underwear? Learn how to discreetly wash it in the sink before the next day. We all forget stuff. How nice for her to learn early how to handle a curve ball on her own...without crying to Mom for help. Plus, she'll remember next year to pay more attention.

This mom even puts a chore list on the door for her younger kids, ages five and eight. This week their list includes:

clean room

get dressed

read on your beds for 20 minutes

be nice to each other

listen to Taylor and Caroline

complete 1 page in math book

How lovely to point out that being nice to one another really can be a chore! I have a couple of kids who would like to see that chore posted on my door.

At this point in the Experiment, I'm convinced that responsibility is a gift that keeps on giving. It gives our family an increased sense of teamwork and collaboration, and it gives each individual worker much more than we could ever imagine. Not only have they gained self-assurance in doing the chores themselves, but they have greater confidence to meet new challenges with a can-do attitude rather than dreading anything outside their comfort zones.

So on the days when I worry I'm pushing too hard or being too tough, on the days when I watch them caving under the weight of adolescent pressures, on the days I can't quite see the color of their warning flags and catch myself praying it's not red, I cling to the message I've heard from wise parenting survivors: the key to it all is love.

A fellow mom shared with me the following quote from child psychiatrist Dan Myers's book *Biblical Parenting*, which I thought sums up our job well:

> In a nutshell, the answer to childrearing is to love one's children, use good common sense, and be guided by the Bible, not worldly standards. For parenting, "Do as I say and not as I do," is not sufficient. You must be the person you would like your children to become. Jesus, *Matthew 22:37–39*, said you can do this by (1) loving God with all your heart, soul, and mind and (2) by loving your neighbors as yourself.... Remember that the goal of parenting is not to provide a successful childhood but to grow your child into an adult who is a good person.[1]

It's not about the tasks; it's about loving my kids. The tasks in and of themselves are nothing more than a means to an end. The end I crave is a young adult prepared for life and confident in the person he or she is created to be.

Loving them by making them work puts energy behind my claim to believe in the kids. The assurance that "you can do anything you put your mind to" has greater meaning now that I've gotten out of the way. I've seen this prove true for an eight-year-old proudly setting a homemade meal in front of his family and for a fourteen-year-old getting up and going to work. Though his actions are clearly induced by an "unreasonable" mother, he is genuinely aware that his presence and assistance make a difference in other people's lives. He can look at the kids hanging on him, begging him to read just one more story, and quickly grasp that he's needed and loved by someone other than his mother.

No longer are my kids sitting on the couch waiting for someone to smooth the way for them. They have started to understand that they are capable of far more than they realized…even things they don't want to do.

What better preparation could there be for adulthood? Day in and day out, we are hit with things we don't want to do. Just ask me about the toilet I wrangled to address a nasty clog. Or the countless diapers I've changed. Or the mind-numbing "discussions" lobbed at me by argumentative tween/teens. Or serving as the Enforcer for our Experiment. I don't *want* to do those things, but I do them anyway. Rewind several years and ask me about my first office. It literally was the copy room. I lived the "Making Copies" *Saturday Night Live* skit before it was even a comedy writer's thought. Working while people wander in and out of your "office" to make copies isn't the culmination of a career dream for any determined young professional. Did I collect my pencil caddy and walk away? No. That's not what adults do. That's not how my dad taught me.

At least, that's not what adults used to do. These days, employers see a disturbing trend of exactly that: employees who walk away from the job when the work proves more demanding or less interesting than they expect.

Ironing Board Tip

The thing I would change about my mothering would be doing too much for my kids! Both of my girls (now thirty-three and thirty) have told me they wished I had *made* them do chores. I tried but got tired of nagging so just did them myself. I wish I had been stronger and stayed the course!
—Peggy Zadina

New research has found that a similar attitude to work is burgeoning among the group of people known as Generation Y—usually defined as those between the ages of 11 and 25. A study of more than 2,500 people born after the early Eighties found that they were rebelling against their parents' values and were determined not to lead lives that revolved so heavily around the world of work.

Instead, they were ready to resign if their jobs were not fulfilling and fun, with decent holidays and the opportunity to take long stretches off for charity work or travel. Salary and status were not high on the priority list, according to the study by Talentsmoothie, a firm that consults companies in banking, professional services and the law on the changing workforce.[2]

Ironing Board Tip

In seasons of smart mouths, heightened hormones, and stinky attitudes, if we can take a step back and view such times as God's heavenly sandpaper sloughing off the rough spots on both mother and child, we might keep our sanity.

Here are some tools to help us maintain a healthy perspective as we parent through difficult times:

- *Respect.* Look at your children with respect for who they are as individuals. They may have different dreams, different gifts, and different ways of expressing themselves. Give them some space (within reasonable limitations) to be who they are. Look at them as future contributors to the world.
- *Mutual interests.* Find activities that you and your child can enjoy together. This will give you great

One of the great things about this generation is that it's less obsessed with the pursuit of financial gain than was the previous generation. But rather than overcoming "the world revolves around me" syndrome, it seems they've simply exchanged the goal of personal wealth for another egocentric objective: the determination to do whatever feels good in the moment.

In our house, we've seen the tasks produce exactly the opposite of me-centeredness. After we deal with the initial pushback, our work activity ends up taking the kids' eyes off themselves. So not only do they experience the satisfaction of accomplishment, but they also get to enjoy the pleasure that comes from serving others.

I hope the kids grow accustomed to forgoing momentary comfort in the interest of long-term gain, in the same way an athlete enjoys the

pleasure and create special times to share well into the future.

- *Kind gestures.* Find something specific you can do for your child that would be especially meaningful to him or her, something out of the ordinary. Ask, "How can I pray for you this week?" or "Is there anything I can do for you today?" A little extra thoughtfulness goes a long way in improving relationships.

Consider this: "Children are like Jell-O salads; we want to pour as much good stuff inside them as we can before the mold sets" (author unknown). In the teen years, the mold is beginning to set up, but it is still jiggly in the middle. We still have time to pour, stir, and make a difference in the flavor of their lives.

—Jane Jarrell

workout burn. I'd love to see hard work and determination become second nature to them, translating to a lifelong mind-set that hurdles are
something to be cleared, not something to sidestep.

This month, the hurdle is handyman projects.

Boxster tried to help Jon fix our broken laminating machine today,
but he lost interest between removing the third and fourth screws. It
didn't help that Jon wanted to fix it himself and was all but pushing the
kid away. Since an electrical cord was involved, Jon was wearing his Safety
Sam hat rather than capitalizing on a learning opportunity. Both he and
Boxster were relieved when Jon took over the project entirely.

Clearly, we face some challenges in this area. The handyman task
promises to be our biggest hurdle. Not because the potential handyman
projects are so difficult, but because handyman opportunities around our
house involve tools…and our reluctant dad.

A Truly Hairy Situation

After a frustrating day involving a misplaced wallet, a less than helpful
conversation with an AT&T call center in India, switched lunch sacks,
misplaced keys, back-to-school sign-ups, another less than helpful India
call-center conversation to fix the problem resulting from the first helper,
and two trips to Costco (not realizing I had left my wallet at home on the
first trip), I met my son coming down the stairs around 9 p.m.

"Um, I might have some water in my bathroom."

"Huh?"

"Well…my shower. It got water on the floor."

Being that it was Handyman month, I'd been eagle-eyed for things
that might need fixing. With the laundry, dinner, beds, and yard, I knew
we'd always have plenty of chores to go around. But for the kids to achieve
fix-it-man status, things had to break. I must admit, I geeked just a bit
each time a prospective task surfaced.

So when the kid described this repair opportunity, I was thrilled. We finally had a true-blue handyman chore at our fingertips. In fact, excited would be an understatement. I ran to get Jon, who wasn't so thrilled.

When he and I arrived to check out the situation, we saw that at least three inches of water had backed up in the shower.

"When did this happen?" I asked the dumbfounded kid, referring to the drain backup.

"I don't know. It just started going on the floor tonight."

We all knew the drain must have been clogging up for weeks. Hopefully not months. Why he didn't tell us earlier is a mystery. Maybe he thought that it was normal. Maybe he was afraid of getting in trouble. Whatever the case, I was determined to take advantage of the moment. I raced to tell Jon.

"*Please* let Boxster snake his drain." I nipped at Jon's heels like a yippy puppy.

"I am not letting one of the kids snake the drain," he said. "It's a mess in there. They're all bathed, ready for bed, and have school tomorrow."

"But, honey, it—"

"Don't push me on this. I know you're all excited about some work thing, but I don't have time for this tonight," he replied. "Really, just let it go. I'll show him how another time."

My heart felt heavy and sad, but I agreed.

Such a terrific opportunity staring our family right in the face. And having learned so much about the connection between work and self-esteem, I suspected Dad was unknowingly sending several unspoken yet loud and clear messages to his son:

- "You screwed up, and now I have to come clean up your mess."
- "I have to fix it because you're not capable."
- "You can't do anything but mess things up."

None of which Jon would ever think or believe about his very capable boy. But add an age-induced negative self-view to the mix, and the boy's ears were ready to confirm what he already believed to be true.

All the kids had gathered around to see the excitement. This, of course, was my fault. I had been so pumped about a real-live handyman opportunity, I might have audibly squealed with delight while Jon went to the garage to retrieve his plumbing tool, before my heel nipping had been zipped.

Grumbling a bit as he worked, Jon struggled with the snake. Getting it situated in the awkward shower space, turning the handle, fighting the gunk. The kids, at least the younger ones, pushed one another to get the best vantage point to view their dad in action.

I stood at the back of the crowd, behind Boxster who watched the whole thing transpire with a rather downcast expression. He's so at the age where he wants less than no attention. The oohs and aahs were more than he desired.

I tried to encourage him. "Honey, it's not your fault. It's an old house. That gunk has been building up for years." Then, ever the manipulator, I spoke the wrong words, words that added fuel to my husband's ire. "Get in there and ask your dad if you can help." Oh, how I cringe thinking about it now. Why did I not stop myself?

The kid inched forward, as if he actually might ask. He was met immediately with a furrowed brow and a glare meant for me, which implied, "We agreed, not now!"

It really didn't help that the other kids had taken up the chorus, "Yeah, let Boxster do it."

At this point, I could see the open wounds beginning to fester on my son's spirit. He looked at me, then at his siblings, and actually said the words for me and them to hear, "Oh, I can't do it. Dad has to. I'm only fourteen. Maybe I could do that when I'm sixteen or eighteen. Maybe when I'm a man."

It was one of those slow-motion moments, where everything around me came to a grinding halt. The words took on a life of their own, flashing in my head—"Maybe when I'm a man," "Dad has to do it," "I'm only fourteen," "Maybe when I'm a man," "I can't do it," "Maybe when I'm a man."

I ached at hearing such self-doubt come from my son. The kid is taller than I am. He's smart. He's capable. That's the truth. Nothing in that response was true. All that he believes about himself was revealed in that moment as we stood in a flooded bathroom, Dad working furiously, kids standing around watching. A young man uttered the words he believed about himself—words that seemed to be proven true the minute his father stepped in to do rather than let his son try.

I could feel the anger rise up my back and through my neck as I witnessed the destructive power of the unspoken message my children hear each time I deny them an opportunity to prove that they are capable. My son's shoulders sank in an effort to disappear inside himself, away from the eager eyes of his siblings and mother, in front of whom he was so ashamed, and the father he thought he had failed. I could have strangled Jon right then and there. He wanted to do the same to me since I had not trusted him and treaded into territory we had agreed to avoid.

A hairball the size of a rat came out of that drain. Everyone chorused "Eww" and squealed at the grossness. Everyone except Boxster, who was relieved to get people out of his bathroom, and me.

We all left.

One dad still muttering about how we don't take care of things and barking at everyone to get to bed, its being a school night and all.

Four siblings excitedly talking among themselves about the evening's plumbing adventure.

One mother filled with warring emotions of anger and deep sadness.

One young man who didn't believe his mother when she responded to his self-proclaimed loser status by saying, "But you are a man, honey. A fine man."

His response? "No, Mom. I'm not."

The Battle for Control

Within moments of leaving that bathroom, I wanted to pack my bags, put all the kids in the car, and leave. I wanted nothing to do with the hurt that transpired in that cramped shower stall. But that isn't what I agreed to when I pledged "for better or worse." And I knew that even by walking away, I couldn't escape one of the key troublemakers in that whole scene: me.

Jon and I acknowledged the ickiness we each felt the night of our plumbing incident, but we still needed a few days between us and the situation before we could even begin to discuss it objectively and productively. I needed him to acknowledge the depth of hurt his son felt. Jon needed me to trust him and to acknowledge his desire to be treated with respect—particularly in front of the kids. I do trust him. He's a terrific dad. And of course, even as the words left my mouth that evening, deep down I knew I was making things worse by trying to manipu-finagle the scene into what *I* wanted it to be.

The fact is, in that ugly bathroom scene, both Jon and I were dealing with the same issue: control. He wanted to be free to handle the situation as he deemed best—and that did not include trusting a young teenage boy with a plumbing tool that could cause further damage when there wasn't time for instruction. I wanted him to handle the situation my way. And our mutual insistence on control not only damaged our relationship with each other but also damaged our son's view of himself.

And isn't that same desire for control what lies behind the parental tendency to do everything ourselves and our way? Do we even slow down long enough to realize that by taking the helm and dictating the way things should or shouldn't go, we're charting a course into the same troubled waters Eve chose so many years ago? A course that puts us in the place of God.

When I step in and assume that my way is best, I've decided right then and there to play God in my kids' lives. Don't get me wrong; at certain times responsible parents must intervene to ensure a child's safety and well-being. It just seems we've expanded that to include everything. We've decided that almost every situation qualifies for "safety" status. Grades, teams, schools, friends—all require our hands-on interference in the name of protecting our children and securing their future.

In this case, my safety-conscious husband stepped in to keep his kid from potential harm that might occur with plumbing equipment. Okay. But he also stepped in because he could do it faster. He could do it right. And he could get it right on the first try. In the pursuit of efficiency and expediency, he controlled the situation. And in the pursuit of affirmation of my "mother knows best" perspective, I tried to wrestle that control away from him.

When I started the Experiment, I focused on all the great things my kids could and needed to learn. I wasn't really thinking about the lessons that might shake up my own approach to life. Here's a big one: I am not in control. When God created the world, he didn't establish it as a dictatorship. Instead he ushered in a relationship that has boggled the minds of theologians for centuries—the relationship between an all-knowing, all-powerful God and a mortal being with the ability to choose. Not only do my choices matter, but so do my husband's—and so do my kids'. Why would I try to rob them of that?

Lesson number two for me: I'm so thankful that God, who could *always* do every task right, efficiently, and in the ultimate timely manner, doesn't step in and do everything for me every time. Not only do I glean experience from hands-on learning, but I also gain confidence—in him and in my unique role as his child. With increased confidence comes widened boundaries.

The other day, my kids grabbed their bikes and headed for our neighborhood shopping area. Our niece happened to be over playing. She called her dad and asked if he would bring her bike so she could ride along with them. We had bikes, but not one in her size. He agreed and brought this sweet eight-year-old girl the bike on which she had learned to ride. Granted the training wheels were off, but it was tiny. Her wheels were less than half the size of her same-aged cousin's bike. She got on that thing and pedaled her heart out. For every ten rotations of her wheels, her cousin did five. A ride that normally takes them ten minutes took twenty as the older ones stopped and waited.

This was a new experience for our niece—and for her parents. My brother couldn't help but get in the car and do a little drive-by checking on the sly to make sure they were okay. The kids busted him.

"You know Uncle Charles was checking on us the whole time," Barton told me when they got home.

"What do you mean?" I asked.

"We saw him looking for us when we were at JD's Chippery. Then again when we went to Learning Express. Yeah, he didn't think we could make it."

She was wrong about his not thinking they could make it. He checked on them because that bike was so small for our niece. Plus, she had never ridden such a distance without an adult along, so he was just making sure everything was okay. Isn't it interesting, though, that the kids defaulted to someone thinking they couldn't succeed?

After the ride, my brother realized that his daughter was ready to graduate bike sizes. Though it was scary, the kid hoisted herself into the saddle of a new bike where her feet could no longer reach the ground. She couldn't instantly stabilize herself they way she could on her old bike. She had to learn how to balance in a new way. But by allowing her to stretch into the more dangerous endeavor of a bigger bike without a crutch like training wheels (the bike is harder to control, the falls are farther, and gears enter the picture), her parents effectively grew their daughter's world. She gained new confidence, could ride farther, felt more grown up, and so much more as she seized the opportunity to conquer an exciting but uncomfortable situation.

Am I doing the same thing, widening my kids' boundaries? Allowing my kids to work through difficult situations, to test their skills—even ones they aren't aware of having? Or am I stuck in training-wheel mode, ensuring their safety but holding them back?

In much the same way, I'm learning to lean harder into God and continually let go of my desire to determine the outcome, especially as it relates to the nearly nonexistent handyman tasks for this month. Not because our house is in such perfect repair, mind you. In fact the number of home-improvement projects that have emerged this month is almost comical. But each time, our resident handyman has come to the rescue, rarely including any eager young sidekicks.

Our icemaker broke. He fixed it himself.

A shower needed caulking. He caulked it himself.

Our yard needed new edging between the rocks and grass. He did it himself.

The dead bushes needed to be removed. He removed them himself.

The sprinkler heads needed repairing. He repaired them himself.

Light bulbs needed changing. He changed them himself.

A cabinet door is falling off its hinges. I've been instructed to leave it alone.

The wisteria needed trimming. He trimmed it himself.

The car needed new wipers. He changed them himself.

Why? you might ask. He just can't stop himself. He can do it faster alone. The job will be done right and to his specifications. It keeps the kids out of danger's way. It's easier. The list goes on.

And guess what? I know that list of reasons by heart because it's the same list I've been working from and struggling with since the beginning of our Experiment.

More often than not, I think, parents miss opportunities to nurture responsibility because we buy into the line that doing it ourselves will be safer, more convenient, less time consuming. Or we procrastinate, telling ourselves, "I'll show them next time." Each time we opt for practicality, our kids receive a message about their own ineptitude. Is it any wonder this generation struggles with critical thinking and problem solving? It seems a hefty price to pay for our convenience and control.

Even so, instead of getting angry or argumentative, which we know just leads to hurt for everyone, I've decided to make my case, then leave the final decision in Jon's hands.

I still beg. "Please let them change out the faucet on my sink. Pleeease." He endures, sometimes laughs at, my relentless search for handyman jobs. He also lets me know when I've crossed the line from opportunity hunter to manipulator.

And our kid isn't completely emasculated. I provide many opportunities for him to be handy on his own. Just the other day in the car, I found another one. "Hey, look at that." I pointed to the digital reading that details how many miles until we run out of gas (key for the Wymas), how many miles we get per gallon, temperature, and a few other points of interest. For some reason, the temperature reading had changed from Fahrenheit to Celsius and from miles to kilometers. Since I'm too old to have learned metric conversions in school, I was at a loss, wanting my readings back to normal.

"Did you do that?" I asked Boxster (though it may have sounded slightly like an accusation).

"Do what?"

"Did you change it to Celsius?"

"Huh?"

"That!" I emphatically pointed. "The numbers. Did you do that?"

"No."

Ugh. I tried a new approach. "Can you fix it?"

"Uh. No."

At this point, I decided to capitalize on the equipping opportunity and introduce him to an owner's manual. "Well, open the glove box and get out the big book. It explains pretty much everything about the car."

"Huh?" (Is the magic age of fourteen also when boys devolve into cave men?)

"Just get the book. You can figure out how to get the numbers back to normal."

"That's okay." By which he means "no thank you."

"Seriously. Open the glove box and get the owner's manual!"

He wasn't moving. So I decided to employ a strategy that has worked well in the past: reverse psychology. "Well, I guess that means you *can't* do it."

"Huh?"

"Apparently you *can't* do it." I was laughing to myself, anticipating the moment when he would jump on it and "show me."

Pause.

"Okay. I guess I can't."

"What!"

"Well, you said it. I *can't* do it. Guess someone else will have to do it."

We're All in This Together

We live on one and a half acres, and when we moved here, we had our kids start mowing and such. Wow. We had no idea how inept they were until that time. Our oldest drove the lawn mower into the side of one of our cars by accident within the first week we lived in our current house. Funny thing is, that's now the car he drives (with the dent still in it, I might add). He loves to mow, though, because he can listen to his iPod and not be disturbed. Our second son is the chief weed eater of the family. He moves quickly, but that's mainly because he is only allowed to hang out with his friends when the chores are done. Our youngest child is happy to do any job as long as someone is with her.

—Lisa

He smirked and snuggled into the passenger seat, content to do absolutely nothing.

Note to self: The old reverse-psychology strategy doesn't work too well with teenagers. Thank goodness it still flies with an eight-year-old.

After a few minutes of silence, Boxster looked at me, sighed, rolled his eyes, and with a subtle smile, reached up to punch the E/M button right above the digital readings. Lo and behold, the numbers changed back to Fahrenheit. Apparently he knew all along how to fix the darn thing.

I'm easy pickin' for the kid. Biting every time.

Aah. He makes me laugh.

ALL IS NOT LOST

Although little of what I hoped to accomplish this month has actually transpired, I certainly learned a lot through this task. The bulk of my education centered on taming the desire to step in and handle things because doing so is supposedly easier, faster, safer. I'll continue in my recovery program, hoisting controller right up there to the top of the list of issues to address, along with enabler and procrastinator...and a few other things as well.

Thankfully, all we're looking for is steps in the right direction. Slow and steady wins the race, right? We're definitely at the *slow* end as it relates to kid fix-it projects. I'm keeping my eyes open for great projects on which to cut our teeth.

I've yet again bumped up against the fact that one of the biggest obstacles facing my kids—all our kids, really—is parent-induced overindulgence. In this task, overindulgence resulted not from coddling but from avoiding. While we avoided teaching opportunities, the kids received a big fat load of free time, reinforced expectations of being served, and confirmation that they belong on the sidelines of life. We made it easy for them to assume that many doable tasks fall outside their realm of competency or responsibility.

But what is the antidote to overindulgence? Give them work…
meaningful work.

My friend who posts the daily expectations on each child's door has
seen her kids reap the rewards of meaningful work. That wasn't her goal,
however. Ann only posts the jobs, as she says, out of necessity. The kids
help out in a very real way because they have to. Not long ago, when the
family needed to cut back on nonessential expenses to make ends meet,
they trimmed to the nub. Part of the trimming included saying good-bye
to their two-days-a-week cleaning help. With four kids, my friend can't
keep up with the household by herself, so the kids were required to contribute their efforts. They help out of necessity.

The truth? All of us should have our kids doing the same thing out
of necessity. Not to earn some "work" badge of honor, but because the
family genuinely needs their help and relies on each member to do his or
her part. We should view daily household chores as a necessity because
the kids themselves need to work. Our kids need to know how to persevere. They need to know that no job is beneath them. They need to know
what it takes to operate a home. They need to know that sometimes you
have to get dirty to get things clean. They need to know how to serve.
They need to know that a family operates as a unit, everyone pitching in.
They need to know that they belong, that they are a part of the group,
that they are needed.

Out of necessity, we all need to redistribute the work load, decreasing
parental or paid assistance and increasing the burden of able-bodied family members. Because we love them. Because they can. Because even
seemingly mundane tasks equip them to do much greater things.

We just might need to beef up availability of home-repair opportunities, out of necessity. We can keep an eye out for electrical repairs around
the house so the kids can learn about the fuse box, for bathroom issues
that might call for turning off a water main or unclogging a drain before
the shower overflows, for a leaky toilet that needs attention, for caulking
opportunities—and even for conversations about when is actually the

right time to call in a professional. We can also keep an eye out for fix-it opportunities outside our homes through volunteering at church, Habitat for Humanity, and so many other places.

If we fully equip the kids in this technologically advanced generation, what could stand in their way? Not much. In them lie the cures to countless diseases, the engineering solutions for travel to different galaxies, the development of environmentally friendly fuels... Who knows what they could accomplish if we stop indulging and start empowering?

I considered this as I watched my girls fold and put away the day's laundry and as I chuckled at a three-year-old "helping"—methodically doing what he could by folding dish rags. Later I noticed an eight-year-old eagerly emptying the dishwasher and a teen finding an alternative solution for reading the book he'd lost. True to his tech-savvy generation, he downloaded an audio version so he could finish his studying. And just for the record, instead of talking with Charter Communications about our cable outage myself the other day, I handed the phone to Boxster and let him handle the problem. It felt good to tell the Charter guy, "Here. Talk to my son. He knows more than I do."

Items of Interest

What did the kids get to hands-on fix during our month-long effort? Not much. They changed a couple of light bulbs and batteries (to my mind, it's a huge stretch to consider those tasks handymanish), hammered a few nails, pulled some hair out of a sink drain.

Nearly all our handyman opportunities were hoarded by our resident fixer-upper. He wasn't too keen on the kids fixing things that could be broken even more.

Of all our tasks, this one has had the greatest impact on me. This is the only one in which we have failed. And let's face it, we have. The kids didn't fail the tasks. The parents failed the kids.

And the realization that one of them put it into words is a bit hard to stomach. He uttered what I suspected he believed but hoped he didn't: "I can't do it." A genuine "can't," not an excuse.

We'll be working on this. Together.

Though Jon has not yet fully embraced my harebrained Experiment, I love him and am so thankful for him. He grounds me and all my crazy ideas. He sees the edge when I don't see the cliff. And he loves and is completely committed to our kids. He's definitely trying to loosen his grip on his handyman toolbox. Last night he asked Boxster to help him install blinds in one of the bedrooms. It was a two-man job, emphasis on *man.* Just as it takes an exponential number of positive comments to outweigh a single negative remark, I think it will take lots of two-man jobs to reboot from the snake-drain jolt. But all a parent can do is admit mistakes and try again.

After consulting me about color and slat-width preferences, dad and son headed off to The Home Depot together. Upon returning, drill and screwdrivers in hand, they unboxed, measured, fumbled, laughed, helped each other, and hung a terrific set of blinds. They both shrugged it off as no big deal, but with countless oohs and aahs escaping from the sibling crowd, you know one young man felt good. It didn't hurt that, upon viewing the completed project, a little brother started begging for his chance to help dad, whining an "it's not fair" that Boxster got to help. It warmed my heart and, I think, inspired another.

WHAT THEY LEARNED THIS MONTH

- A man and his tools are not soon parted.
- The concept of entropy: the only way to stop the process of degeneration throughout the house is for someone to exert some energy.
- Plungers are our friends.

WHAT I LEARNED THIS MONTH

- I still have a long way to go in conquering my controloholic tendencies.
- Respect for my husband is more important than having things go my way.
- The fact that God trusts us to help him with the tasks of the kingdom is proof positive that he loves us deeply. And I want to show that kind of love to my kids.

The Entertainers

Party Planning and Hospitality

> Hospitality is the virtue which allows us to
> break through the narrowness of our own
> fears and to open our houses to the stranger,
> with the intuition that salvation comes to us
> in the form of a tired traveler.
>
> —HENRI J. M. NOUWEN

People sometimes tell me, "You have the gift of hospitality." I guess since I've been surrounded by it most of my life, I've just assumed that to be true. But after a little contemplation, I've decided it's not so much a gift as it is the result of purposeful training.

My grandmother grew up in a little central Texas town near Waco, called Ocee. It was the size of town that warranted a *Hee-Haw* "Saa-lute." Her mother and father worked hard but were far from the elite social invitation list. She and my grandfather were sweethearts in their youth and married after college. They didn't own a home at the beginning of the marriage but lived in one of the hospitals where he worked as a physician.

As he became more successful in his medical career and in his on-the-side wheeling and dealing (the man just loved a good trade), they moved to Dallas to live in a house off Farquhar Lane. That was where their open-door policy began. Folks started to flood in as my grandmother welcomed and fed the masses.

She wasn't a great cook but sure could whip up some mean chocolate chip and sugar cookies as well as a show-stopper chocolate cake. By sharing goodies, drinks, and a generous spirit, Margaret and Corkie created an environment that made people feel welcome, especially people who had unhappy homes. Many hurt kids and adults came through those nonjudgmental doors to find respite. They knew they were welcome anytime and could stay as long as they'd like. My grandparents' home wasn't big or grand. The food was far from gourmet. But people came and kept coming back.

My grandmother modeled for my mother the secret of hospitality: "Don't worry about what you're serving, just serve." My mother followed suit, creating a home that invited people to feel at ease. My folks built their house with guests in mind, focused on ways to welcome people, especially their kids' friends. By the time we were in junior high, they had converted our garage into an extra room large enough to house a jukebox, along with air hockey, Ping-Pong, and pool tables. We also had the coolest phone booth salvaged from the City National Bank building during a remodeling project, the perfect spot for junior high phoning and giggling.

People came.

We had plenty of rules at our house, including no alcohol, no inappropriate behavior, no foul language. Plus respect for the hosts and other guests in attendance was nonnegotiable. My folks' generosity and hospitality did not include an invitation to a free-for-all.

More people came.

My brother had a friend whose father died and, shortly thereafter, his mother went off the deep end and left. So he came to live with us through high school and college. After he moved out, a series of others moved in: a newlywed couple, a young FCA rep (a husky Baylor football player), and more—all at different times sleeping on a bright yellow corduroy pull-out couch in a tiny room off our converted garage. No one cared about the less-than-grand digs; they felt at home. When my folks left Wichita Falls and moved to Dallas, the hospitality tradition continued. They hosted Sunday lunch for anyone who wanted to come. Mom never knew who or how many, but she always had an extra casserole in the freezer just in case. Countless times I would call my parents' house from college, and even when I traveled for work, to discover my friends at their house eating lunch. "Welcome" was the operative word in our home.

The precedent of hospitality set by my parents and grandparents is one that Jon and I try to emulate. But rather than being a gift that runs naturally through my family genes, as I'd sort of assumed, I've recently realized that my family's tradition of hospitality was built brick by brick through acts of purposeful selflessness. Training and intentionality provided the foundation, and each generation has built on to the structure in ways that reflect their personal style and flair.

Now it's time for our kids to take up the trowel and add some layers of their own.

Task for the month: I'd like each of them to experience firsthand the pleasure of hosting a party. They can choose the size, type, and venue. A budget of fifty dollars will be allotted to cover expenses and invitation costs, if they choose to send something via our postman, Walter. Anything more will be funded at their own expense.

I want them to learn two major lessons:

1. Hospitality gets your eyes off yourself and onto others—a good thing, no matter your age.
2. Hospitality is always appreciated. Some people use all kinds of excuses to avoid hosting. "My house is too small." "I can't cook." "We don't have anything fun to do." Yada-yada-yada. I'm convinced that people love to be included and enjoy fellowship. If someone's petty enough to dis your efforts, they must really need some loving. So get over the excuses and get on with the party.

Ironing Board Tip

I'm a big fan of having opportunities for guys and girls to "occupy the same space" but not necessarily in matched pairs. They need to be where they can move among people freely, practice conversation skills, have a chance to observe what works and what doesn't. In common parlance, "to practice their moves"! Think…

- less screens/more face-to-face interaction
- less sitting/more goofing around
- less formality/more comfortable
- less money required/more affordable for everyone
- less pairing/more mixing it up

With those thoughts in mind, here are a few party ideas:

- *Talent Night.* Think of all those piano lessons, violin lessons, the new move from gymnastics class, that goofy skit from camp. One mom and son invited kids to a talent night party where each guest was to perform something to entertain the group. One guest did a joke; another performed magic tricks. The *big* hit of the evening was the pair of girls who performed a silly skit from camp. The clear takeaway was the delight kids had in sharing their various talents and the confidence they gained at being recognized for their contributions.
- *Do-It-Yourselves Dinner.* Another group gathered to make a lovely meal together. The host family came up with a simple menu of spaghetti, green salad, garlic bread, and candy-bar brownies. The host wrote each

step of food preparation on separate slips of paper. As guests arrived, they drew one from a basket. For example, one girl was to wash and cut the tomatoes for the salad; a boy was to help mix the candy-bar brownies. Work stations awaited with recipes and materials assembled. People were partnered randomly. The evening harvested some bragging rights on who was the best cook. But best of all, kids grew in competency at social skills as well as kitchen skills, something which should serve them well for years to come!

• *Food Sculpting Fun.* At one university, a campus group initiated a fun new party: food sculpting. The food-service chef agreed to make a massive quantity of mashed potatoes. Party hosts bought "tools" and purchased prizes to be awarded to winners in various categories, like tallest forms, most lifelike forms, comedy-theme forms, and so on. After they loaded lunch-line trays with mashed potatoes, the fun began. Without going into great detail, suffice it to say that it was a good thing the event was held outdoors, it was a warm spring night, and the hose was connected.

The point of any gathering is for kids to entertain themselves, to have fun together, to experience socializing together.

—Kathleen Fischer

That's why my plan includes each kid serving up some fun. It may seem like a crazy topic, but I really want them to personally walk through (not just watching, but doing) the ins and outs of hosting. I expect the task will be enjoyable for some, a hurdle for others. My challenge is to keep their eyes focused outward, seeking what will bring joy to others, instead of inward, worrying about how they might fall short or look weird in front of their friends—an especially pertinent concern when dealing with teens.

Between you and me, I've had my doubts as to whether they can *all* do this task. I've even thought the focus on hospitality might seem a bit inconsequential. But as I considered the things I want them to learn before leaving our house, this is definitely in my top twelve. Quite possibly in my top two.

WHAT REALLY INCREASES A GUY'S COOL QUOTIENT

As already mentioned, part of my goal with the hospitality task was to help my kids focus on others rather than self. This seems to be an ongoing challenge for all of us, particularly in our consumer-oriented culture.

On a recent afternoon Boxster and I were in the car yet again. It seems half our family life takes place on wheels.

"So do you think I'd look good in a Porsche?" he asked nonchalantly.

Struck by a strong sense of déjà vu, I took my eyes off the road to stare at him briefly. Is this not the conversation that started it all, opening my eyes to how self- and stuff-focused my kids had become? We were even traveling Preston Road just like before.

Stifling my exasperation, I said, "Work hard in school, and you can get what you want. Of course, I hope by that point you won't care what kind of car you drive."

"Yeah. I'll want a Porsche, for sure. And a Rolex."

"I think you're a little off on what's important," I said, while thinking, *Have you learned* nothing *in the past six months?*

"Look! There's the car I want right there. And there."

Sure enough, we were sharing the road with two lovely Porsches: one on our right, one on our left. A Porsche sandwich. Yippee.

So he's a boy. That's certainly part of the explanation for his automotive obsession. Furthermore, his social world is one in which a blingy car can shoot him up quite a few notches on the cool scale. He'll grow out of this. Right?

Though I would have preferred his attentions were elsewhere, this particular conversation didn't bother me as much as others because of the event it followed. We were driving home from a ditched trip to Costco. Who knew they vacationed on Labor Day with the rest of the country? We, like so many others, had driven to the parking lot only to discover a huge Closed sign. A bit sad, we were headed back home when we noticed someone having car trouble.

I stopped, rolled down the window, and asked the stranded travelers if we could help. They explained that they'd run out of gas, so we offered to take the driver to the closest station, then bring him back. After accepting, he and his wife, who we later found out was three months pregnant, started pushing their car out of the way.

Who jumped out of our car to help so the wife could be steering instead of pushing? You guessed it. Boxster. Without so much as a word or a moan or a directive from me, he went to work and helped to push their car out of the way. Then he shook hands and walked the man to our car.

Aah. I'm still savoring the moment.

So as I endured the Porsche-coveting conversation for the gazillionth time, I chose to smother my impulse to lecture; instead I focused on his earlier selfless act.

I changed the topic from bling to our task at hand.

"So you may not know, but this month I want you all to learn about hospitality."

"Mom. No... Is this for the Experiment?"

Brief intermission here: I've noticed that many of my little equipping tasks are meeting a new level of resistance. The kids seem to think of the Experiment as a game I've invented, and they're just waiting for life to go back to "normal"—with everything being done for them once more. Granted the month-by-month tasks lend a game sort of feel, but they will soon realize that this *is* their new normal.

Back to my conversation with Boxster.

"It might be part of our Experiment, but I think it's important for you to learn hospitality."

"What do you mean by 'hospitality'?" His fingers formed air quotes while his face formed an expression of suspicion.

"Well, I need to sit you all down and talk about this, but basically I want you to throw a party." I winced, waiting for the onslaught of protest.

"What kind of party?"

"Anything you want. You'll get a budget of fifty dollars to use for invitations, refreshments, and party favors."

"Can I just invite Brandon and Henry?"

Oh my word. He's not freaking out! "Sure," I replied. "You can invite whoever you want. But you must send an invitation."

Then, as if on cue: "Why can't I text them?"

I sighed and did my own eye roll. Mmm. Those do feel good. I know why the kids throw them my way so often.

"Look, that's why you have a budget. There are several ways to do it, but for our purpose you will either send an invitation through the mail or hand deliver it."

"Okay."

He surrendered! I think he realized I was on the warpath and resistance would be futile.

"I'm going to have a video-game party," he said. "Then maybe we can swim. They will love that." I actually heard his enthusiasm starting to build. "Yeah! The new Halo comes out this week. That will be fun. I can use all the money plus some I've saved and get it."

All right, no need to go into the positives (if there are any) and negatives of Xbox gaming at this moment. At least he was excited about having his friends over—or maybe he wanted a free fifty dollars to help buy a game. No, I'm going to be optimistic here.

I explained that the budget needed to cover everything, including food and favors—a little something to celebrate his guests and thank them for coming.

"You mean like at the Dollar Tree?" he asked. I considered dishing out another eye roll, but then he quickly changed course. "No. I'm going

Expert Advice: Technology Versus the Real World

The jury is still out as to whether technology and the pervasiveness of social networking helps kids connect with one another or hinders their emotional development. In the meantime, it's probably a good idea to encourage our kids to engage in activities that involve real-world interaction with their peers. A study by the Pew Research Center, referenced in a *New York Times* article, found that 54 percent of American teenagers text their friends once a day, "but only 33 percent said they talk to their friends face-to-face on a daily basis."[1] The same article quotes Professor Jeffrey G. Parker, who has been studying children's friendships since the 1980s: "These good, close relationships—we can't allow them to wilt away. They are essential to allowing kids to develop poise and allowing kids to play with their emotions, express emotions, all the functions of support that go with adult relationships."

to the candy store at the mall and getting a bag of mini jawbreakers. They love those."

At this point, I released a happy sigh of contentment. He's getting it. He actually stopped thinking about himself for a moment and started thinking about how to serve his friends.

I took note of his knee-jerk reaction to text his invitations. Texting is a great tool, but I hope to teach the kids through this exercise some of the benefits of other forms of communication. It's a temptation for kids to sit falsely insulated in the networked world, assuming it provides some sort of safety because they don't have to risk face-to-face interaction. They can say or share just about anything they want without considering all the ramifications; what they don't seem to realize is that countless people can see and hear it all—and once their words (or photos) are out there, they can't reel them back in.

PAR-TAY

I found that preparing to host a party provides some terrific opportunities to talk with our kids about related subjects, such as being careful not to talk about the party beforehand, lest someone not on the list be offended. It's also a great time to discuss what to do and how to act when you're not the host but the guest. Things like asking the host if you can help with anything, assisting with the end-of-party cleanup, taking a little gift as a thank-you, or writing a note within a day of the party.

Above all, I wanted to emphasize for my kids this truth: when we resist the urge to make practicing hospitality about ourselves, we can all revel in the true joy of serving. Max Beerbohm said years ago, "When hospitality becomes an art it loses its very soul."[2] Beerbohm reveals the truth that we often fail to see: When hospitality becomes something other than pure other-centeredness, it loses its meaning. When people say hospitality is an art or gift, the act becomes more about the one hosting rather than the ones being served. I've found that the most successful events aren't an expression of oneself but an opportunity to celebrate others.

That said, every child's unique personality came through in his or her party planning and preparations—or lack thereof. Here's how one invitation took shape:

Hey peoples!!
This month I am hosting a "White Elephant Party!!!"
It is going to be off the hook!
If you can it would be awesome if you could come!

Friday, 4:00 at my house

Bring a wrapped gift $10 or less that will be exchanged.
It can be cool or crazy.

If you come you will be trampled by elephants!!! JK :)
See ya!!! If you dare!
(we only could invite a few so could you please
keep it away from others?)
Thanks!!!!! ME :)

I loved that this particular host came to me only for permission on date and time; she planned all the rest on her own. Then she hopped onto Evite, searched through her school directory, added her classmates' addresses, offered her own bit of humor, and came up with a creative and welcoming invitation.

I had never shown her the particulars on how to use Evite, but clearly the girl got it. A white elephant party—what a fun idea! I also loved how trendy, clever, and sensitive she was. She did a much better job than I would have, though I did laugh to myself at the lack of address ("Everyone knows where I live," she said) and her prolific use of exclamation points. And she actually hit Send. I can't tell you how many times I've composed something and never sent them. Hmm. Apparently I'm a recovering slacker too! So many things on which to work.

The invitation part of hosting a function worked great. But the date of her affair rolled around much faster than Snopes expected. Either that or she is so accustomed to things magically appearing or happening on their own she never quite realized the effort that goes into hosting a function in your home.

Party Tips

The kids went straight to the Internet to find tips and ideas on hosting a party. The tips almost overwhelmed them. One site divided planning into different stages from weeks to days out. We found it all a bit stressful. "We" because they came to me for help, and we all know my issues with calendars and planning ahead. Plus, they needed some direction. I tried to soothe their worries with a few pointers:

- *Guest List.* If it's your first time to host, go small. The larger the guest list, the better it is to have more than one host.
- *Menu.* Some menus are easier than others. I told the kids that my mom, the queen of hosting, made it simple by serving the same few menus. She had chicken enchiladas for the Sunday after-church crowd and beef tenderloin for fancy sit-down dinners. Her theory: different guests come almost every time, so they will never know it's the same food. Plus, any repeat guest must have enjoyed the food enough to have returned. This alleviates much of the menu stress.

She basically ignored my suggestions to prepare ahead of time. So when the day arrived, instead of enjoying a leisurely ride home from school to get there before her party began, we had a few stops to make. Nothing like scheduling a party at four when you don't get home from school until three thirty. She asked me to stop by Tom Thumb on the way home. Armed with her budgeted cash, she ran into the neighborhood market to grab a few savory items. Nasty icing-laden cookies and Dr Pepper. My stomach hurts at the memory. Beyond those delectables,

For the kids, snacky things are great. The key is to remember that people don't come for the food but for the fellowship.

- *Entertainment.* Anything fun will do. Remember to keep an eye out for the guest who looks lonely or out of place. Then park yourself next to them, somehow working them into a group's conversation. This is a terrific life skill to learn. Plus it gets thoughts off themselves and off any "are people having fun?" insecurities.
- *Timing.* Try to keep a party under two hours. An hour to an hour and a half tends to be great.
- *Logistics.* As much as possible, have the food and fun prepared well in advance of the guests arriving. It's a nice idea to have the preparation tools, pots, and pans in the dishwasher before the party starts. You'll be thankful to have that much less cleanup afterward.
- *Relax and Have Fun.* If the host is comfortable, it's highly likely the guests will be too.

she had accepted a neighbor's offer to share leftovers from her own party earlier that day, and one of her friend's mothers volunteered to pick up cupcakes. Sprinkles Cupcakes, no less. The cupcakes ate nearly her entire budget, but the splurge certainly made her guests feel extra special.

Rather than go it alone, she also accepted a friend's offer to help with shopping and setting out food. I guess she hasn't reached that age where we women feign self-sufficiency by never accepting help when offered. Decorations were minimal. All right, nonexistent. Did anyone notice or miss them? No. No one ever does. I loved that. I also loved that she didn't let the lack of a centerpiece stop the fun. I can't tell you how many friends I know who have wrestled with self-imposed stress over the perfect floral arrangement.

She had one small problem: time. She entered the store at 3:37 p.m. to find and purchase her preservative-infused snacks. When we pulled out of the parking lot to head home, she was already late to her four o'clock affair. Three guests had arrived by the time we pulled into our drive. The truth is, not one of them cared; all her guests are good friends and familiar with our home. But she still should get a clue that greeting guests comes with the territory.

Welcomes were exchanged. Snacks were served. Then the white elephant exchange began. The girls had a blast! Laughter and squeals of delight echoed through the house. The gifts were a hoot. Middle school hilarity.

The party was a huge success. As departing girls headed my way to offer thanks for such a wonderful party, I directed them straight to Snopes, who not only came up with a great idea but provided a fun environment to bless her friends.

The Heart of Hospitality

Our other kids followed suit with their own affairs. For the boys, the most challenging part was the invitation. For all of them, time management was a bit of an issue. Barton hosted her friends for a cake-ball-making party. Her two-hour window didn't allow enough time for the dough to freeze, thus making it a bit difficult to form and coat those crumbly little balls so they could look cover ready for *Martha Stewart Living.*

To varying degrees, each of the kids struggled with being at ease as host or hostess in charge. But the kids' guests were incredibly gracious. They just loved being together and eating yummy food, although their definition of yummy differs quite a bit from mine.

It's been great for the kids to learn that things don't just appear when they want them to, that a social event requires the coordination of many different pieces. It's been good for me to realize again my propensity to step in and plan for them and do so many other things. I had to exert every ounce of strength in my untrained muscles of self-restraint to not step in and do it all for them! There's nothing I like more than throwing a party. An intimate dinner party, a neighborhood coffee, a huge fundraiser—it makes no difference. People gatherings jazz me.

In fact, in a former life before marriage and kids, one of my jobs revolved around huge events for the White House's office of the vice president. I quickly learned to walk into a planned gathering, assess angles, see the whole picture, and be able to adjust accordingly to keep everything seamless and beautiful for countless camera lenses. I absolutely loved every bit of the game—the stress, the pace, the people. So on this hospitality task, I had to work extra hard to keep my hands off the kids' business and let them do it themselves. I bit my lips and held back the abundance of suggestions that threatened to spill forth. It was hard to watch them flail. It was even harder to stop myself from saving, fixing, finagling, manipulating—you know, overparenting and enabling.

Among the more painful of my cringe-inducing moments was seeing one of my kid hosts bail for a better offer while two girls stood waiting for their moms to pick them up. Totally out of character for her. Is it wrong to chalk all these whacky decisions up to hormones? Anyway, though I didn't intervene at the time, I later made sure she picked up on the lesson: don't exit your party until the last guest has left.

As I allowed them to bumble along, we all confirmed something I've believed for years: One of the secrets to hospitality is that people are just excited for an excuse to get together. They don't care about the timing, the food, the theme, the décor, the [fill in the blank]. They just love to be included, welcomed, and cared for.

We watched this truth play out in the life of a dear friend who went home to be with the Lord recently. The queen of hospitality, Dottie Wicker, was recently diagnosed with liver cancer. A gracious woman in her mideighties, she met the diagnosis like she did everything in her life: glass half full.

I'm not sure I ever heard Dottie complain about herself. She approached aging issues with matter-of-fact acceptance. When her sight began to fade, she increased the size of her telephone and television. (The lady loved her Fox News.) When the hearing left, she punted any pretenses and got a hearing aid. She even put a handwritten sign on her door with her phone number for visitors to call so she could come to the door since she couldn't hear a knock or bell. She didn't want to miss a guest. When she started shedding a few more tears than normal, she openly took her prescribed "mood elevators."

Her glass door welcomed any visitor with time for a chat. Toys lined the floor for the broods that accompanied young moms willing to stop by and receive a dash of sunshine in her living room. Dottie had a lovely set of silver containers on the front table in her modest dining room. What would an eighty-year-old woman hide in those treasured keepsakes? Hershey's Kisses—a promised treat for any little visitor (and sometimes their mothers). She expected visiting children to follow just two rules at her house: stay out of the formal living room and collect their Kisses on the way *out*. She wanted them close to her on their visits, not rummaging through the candy jar.

I hope to grow old as gracefully as my lovely neighbor did.

We met the first week my family moved onto that block. Dottie was sitting on her front porch on a white painted wrought-iron chair. Well, "porch" is a stretch. She had a stoop. Eight and a half months pregnant, I lumbered up her walk with my three little kids and began a friendship I will treasure the rest of my life.

With her other-centeredness, Dottie exemplified the heart of hospitality. She welcomed me, a stranger, into her home, and we sat on her couch, getting to know each other, watching my kids politely scamper through her toys. Dottie's grandchildren lived in Baltimore. Those toys were for guests. Her house was warm but not fancy. There wasn't food, but conversation flowed. She never burdened; she always loved.

I'm so thankful I dutifully walked the street that day, going out of my comfort zone to meet new neighbors. We could have stayed in our house, opted for a rear garage, kept to ourselves, and busied our schedules. Our lives would be fine. But I, for one, will be eternally grateful that we weren't crazy busy, that we made the effort to know our neighbors, and that the friendship we forged blessed not only me but my children as well.

Even today as I stopped by her house, the open door invited visitors to step in. Kathy, another neighbor who lived life with Dottie for years and who sat with our friend as she struggled through these last days, was already planning for the meal after Monday's memorial service. She

We're All in This Together

You can have the mind-set of social entertaining, which is stressing, or you can think of it as Christian hospitality, which is a blessing. Always set your table the day before and choose dishes that can be prepared beforehand.

—Lyn

wanted Dottie's children and family to be able to grieve without a worry in the world. In the midst of her own loss, Kathy acted swiftly and like a seasoned orchestra conductor, directing those of us whose lives bear Dottie's fingerprints on what to bring, where to clean, how to serve. If all goes as planned, my equipped children will be with me, serving and gleaning lessons in generosity.

Even through her death, our sweet Dottie is teaching my girls about her favorite subject: hospitality. It isn't just a word, a gift, or an act. It's a lifestyle. And it just might be what life's all about.

Something along the lines of loving "your neighbor as yourself."

A Good Time Was Had by All

This month's exercise was quite the unexpected esteem booster. Hosting a party solo proved a remarkable confidence builder, particularly for a ten-year-old and a twelve-year-old whose friends had never done such a thing.

They all agonized over the thought of putting themselves on the line by hosting something from beginning to end on their own. But once the ball got rolling, they realized their inhibitions were false. By pushing through the anticipation of failing in front of their friends, having people complain about their food, or whispering judgment behind their backs, the kids reaped rich rewards from serving people they know. I think their success was highlighted by how many of our party guests told us they were eager to host something themselves.

The result was that each host truly felt a sense of achievement. Who cares if I was picking up broom-resistant cupcake crumbs two hours after one of their functions. Okay, so maybe not two. It felt like it, though. And yes, the host had already, along with her friends, swept and cleaned up, but despite their best efforts, an extra hand was needed.

Our crew was showered with praise. Our guests were showered with love. A win-win on all fronts.

WHAT THEY LEARNED THIS MONTH

- Consider a little time management on the front end.
- Guests don't need supersnazzy; they just love being together.
- Try to show up at your own party at least thirty minutes before it starts. Guests just might arrive early.

WHAT I LEARNED THIS MONTH

- Though easier for some personalities, hospitality is a learned practice, not a natural gift.
- Given a little freedom, my children are incredibly creative thinkers.
- Watching my kids fly solo is far more gratifying than stepping in to do it for them.

Team Players

The Benefits of Working Together

> No one can whistle a symphony. It takes a
> whole orchestra to play it.
>
> —H. E. LUCCOCK

Any successful achievement rarely rests on the shoulders of a single individual. Even athletic victories in individual sports such as golf, tennis, and swimming are not solo accomplishments but result from the joint efforts of coaches, trainers, and teammates working and playing with the star. Everyone can benefit from sharpening teamwork skills. And let's face it: if you can work with your own siblings, you can work with anyone.

Really, who wants to go it alone? Ecclesiastes 4:9–12 tells us,

> Two are better than one, because they have a good return for their
> work: If one falls down, his friend can help him up. But pity the
> man who falls and has no one to help him up! Also, if two lie
> down together, they will keep warm. But how can one keep warm
> alone? Though one may be overpowered, two can defend them-
> selves. A cord of three strands is not quickly broken.

Our family is a cord of seven strands! Just think of the possibilities—
if we can arrive at a consensus.

In 1964, the *New Yorker* started its "Talk of the Town" on teamwork
with a simple statement written by a nine-year-old kid in a letter from
camp. "Dear Mom and Dad: I am feeling fine. You don't have to worry
about me in the water this year. We are using the buddy system. This
means I can't drown alone. Love Martin."[1]

I guess that's what I hope to teach the kids. Two is almost always
better than one. With a whole team, you get these benefits:

- Efficiency. In teams, work gets done faster. Maybe because
  large tasks can be broken down into pieces. Maybe because
  there is a collective effort. Maybe because other nagging
  voices help keep a wandering mind on task. Maybe because
  it's less daunting to complete smaller individual tasks than
  to take on the whole enchilada.

- Combined Skills. Even the most talented individual can't
  supply on his own the diverse set of skills that are available
  in a group.

- Strong Relationships. Working toward a shared goal creates
  unity and a sense of belonging. Individuals get a chance to
  shine in areas of strength and to appreciate those whose
  strengths are different. Even when bickering or disagree-
  ment brews, a team offers opportunities to learn about
  conflict resolution. Relationships are always stronger on
  the other side of resolved conflict. On top of that, better
  solutions often flow from ideas that might have caused
  conflict. Oh, there's hope for us!

- Creativity. When we go it alone, we tend to focus on
  the few ideas of which we're aware. But with a few additional thinkers, we can get lots of potential solutions and
  ideas.

- Self-Esteem. Being a part of a team, being needed, belonging to a group sends quite the positive message—especially to our kids, who more often than not think the world is against them.

A family unit provides an ideal opportunity to experience the rewards of working together rather than going it alone. I tell the kids all the time that those siblings who nonstop drive them crazy today will be their best friends one day—and for the rest of their lives. Siblings will be the ones who drop everything to come and help. They will be the ones offering unconditional love. They will be the ones who pick you up when you fall. It's tough to believe, but it's true. The key: don't ruin those potential best friendships by letting youthful stubbornness, competitiveness, and pride guide your decisions.

However, I suspect that before they'll believe me, the kids need to learn how teamwork functions in life. They need to appreciate one another's strengths and maybe even recognize weaknesses they can help their siblings overcome, rather than let those weaknesses drive them crazy.

Not to go all business school, but I love management guru Steve Denning's take in one of his blog posts at Forbes.com, in which he contrasted the formal manager-led teams promoted by most of corporate America against the higher performance associated with self-organizing teams. He notes that self-organizing teams tend to focus less on the individual performance and more on the group:

> This means that sometimes an individual may need to do less than what that individual thinks is the very best in order for the team to achieve more. So if the individual knows an esoteric technique that is objectively the best, but the rest of the team doesn't understand it, that individual may need to set aside that technique so that the team as a whole can produce more.

Individuals have a tendency to optimize their own performance. Team vision and discipline goes beyond that to discover how are we going to make the most progress together.[2]

What I love about this is the reminder—once again—that I need to give up some control. Rather than appointing one child to lead on any particular project or, worse, trying to lead it myself, I can let them self-organize and just be sure they understand the emphasis is on what's accomplished together. Plus, self-organizing supports the concept that people tend to participate more eagerly when they help set the agenda rather than simply executing ideas that have been pushed upon them. This longtime management theory may seem a bit contrived and manipulative, but it actually promotes individuals working together.

The truth is, kids will be facing a team environment in their education and in almost any career they choose. It's critical they learn skills in this area so they can rise to their calling.

I also love what Pat Lencioni recently posted in his "A Penalty for Discounting Teamwork" article for *Businessweek:* "Virtually no one will tell you teamwork isn't important when it comes to an organization achieving its goals. Even cynics understand that groups of people willing to put their individual interests aside for the good of the team will outperform those who do not."[3]

Okay, so I did get a little business schooly and maybe even soapboxy, but I'm realizing that a team-building project is more important than I thought when I haphazardly threw together my list. It holds the potential to help us meet much larger goals; in our case the "organization achieving its goals" just happens to be a family.

Our overall family goal is to grow in wisdom, stature, and favor with God and man. Okay, so I might have stolen that from someplace. (See Luke 2:52.) But since it's attached to someone worth emulating, I think we'll keep pursuing it.

Now the goal for this organization as it relates to our task at hand:

The kids must come up with a project that requires all of them to work together. They will define the problem and the resources needed to solve or fix the problem, divvy out the jobs (hopefully complementing each of their skill sets), and complete the task.

Enough *about* teamwork. Let's see how it fits when they try it on for size.

THE PROJECTS

With a little help from Mom, the kids identified their projects. I wish I could emphasize "little"; let's just say I'm trying! Anyway, an impromptu family meeting (the kind that occurs in the car when running from one place to another) to pick our project yielded not just one undertaking but two. The kids wanted to be able to play Ping-Pong and volleyball. We have the table. We have the net. But both areas supporting such games are encumbered by various objects. Our table by a garage full of stuff taking up all the room. Our net by a yard with an enormous stone path.

Project Ping-Pong: We have no game room, so the garage offers our only table tennis location. Like in Where's Waldo? our table has hidden itself somewhere in the mass of murk that fills our garage. Lest one think our garage is large enough to lose a Ping-Pong table, it could barely house one car. Hmm...more clutter. Yes, apparently there is a pattern.

Project Volleyball: In order to enter our front door, visitors can either walk the driveway or take their lives into their hands by navigating a precarious rock path through our yard. It looks beautiful, but "dangerous" aptly describes the stone placement and deep crevices surrounding the path. Not only that, but those wretched stones impede our ability to erect the volleyball net. Since Jon has given the green light, the stones will soon be living in someone else's yard, courtesy of our homegrown rock-removal crew. Jon prefers that Raymundo and his crew get and lay the sod, so the kids will only be responsible for the stones. Fury, always up for hard labor, was instantly ready to jump on the opportunity to get dirty.

No go, though. Dad has directed that work be on the weekend so he can supervise. I'm glad about that. The kids enjoy working with their dad, and more often than not, he makes it fun while teaching them to keep at it until the entire job is complete. The kids tend to think they're done before they actually are. Brooms, rakes, and such are sometimes left behind as monuments to a day's effort. Not so if Dad is around.

With our problems defined, the kids began to brainstorm strategies. I loved that they chose two projects. I would have been happy with one. But once they got started, they wanted to work on more than one thing. Granted not every child was equally delighted. With a group our size, you will never please all the people all the time.

I also was thrilled that on the other side of this task, games will be played. Games that take place outside (since our Ping-Pong table is in a detached garage) and involve at least two, if not more, players. Another thing, both of the projects involved stuff needing to be hauled away. I was curious to see how they would handle that.

I had confidence that they would succeed. Little did I know how quickly and how well.

Ironman

Sometimes when you're in the middle of a marathon, it's hard to see if any progress has been made. Long training sessions feel burdensome, heavy, stagnant, all uphill. Our family may not be logging in miles for an actual race, but the Experiment sure leaves us feeling like we signed on for an Ironman. We've finished the swim, suffered through biking over one hundred miles, and started to settle in on our twenty-six-mile run. We can't see the finish line, but we know it's close. Our noodle legs aren't sure about the terrain and continue to flash warning signs of overuse. Then a water station emerges at the horizon and offers fuel to our tired bodies, reminding us how far we've already traveled.

Recently I encountered that much-needed station.

I had left the kids at home while I attended a meeting. I've tried to pare down on meetings since motherhood entered my life. I withdrew from boards on which I'd previously served and reduced my commitments as much as possible. I figured if I was leaving my job to have free time for my kids, I should probably keep that time as free as possible…or at least fill it with kid-related stuff. For my sanity I added a few girl things, such as the garden club, but I made sure whatever stayed in my personal planner offered great flexibility. We try to keep our family calendar clear too. The kids each participate in one activity at most each semester. I sign on for a minimum of school and church commitments, and I steer clear of many wonderful-sounding "me" activities. That said, I still have a few meeting-centered commitments, which always seem to fall on nights that Jon has to work late. So the older kids get called on deck.

A few years ago my friend Nancy shared her brilliant "baby-sitting" strategy. She has three boys, the oldest of which is fourteen. One might think fourteen is prime baby-sitting age, but as mothers of the male species know, put a boy that age in charge of two younger brothers and that area has disaster written all over it. Still, what a drag to pay someone to watch your more-than-capable kids. Nancy came up with the brightest idea: she pays all her kids to watch themselves. After an evening out, she divides among her crew, weighted by age, the amount she would pay a sitter. She takes a survey upon returning home to ensure that everyone behaved. Each kid gets to rate the others. No good, no green. This terrific checks-and-balance system has given the boys independence and confidence.

I love her approach and have employed it often, as on this particular evening.

When I walked in the door from my meeting, I was greeted by an eight-year-old screaming, "Mom's home!"—an announcement that was followed by squeals from elsewhere in the house.

Not quite sure what to expect, I started toward the kitchen.

"Don't come upstairs!" Pause. "Mom! *Don't come upstairs!*"

Great, I thought, but I said with fake cheer, "Okay, I won't."

I walked into the kitchen and stopped short, stunned. When I left the house, the room had resembled a culinary war zone: pots everywhere, food on the stove, dishes on the table, baking remnants on the floor. Now it was magazine-worthy pristine. I couldn't believe they were capable of such a cleaning. The dishwasher was even running!

Then I glanced to my left. The living room—normally a pillows-everywhere scene of chaos and clutter when I arrive home from an evening out—was picked up, the television was turned off, and every Wii controller and toy was put away. What's more, the backpacks that usually get abandoned there had already been repacked and placed by the front door for school the next day!

I went back outside to check the address.

Yes. I was at the right house.

After I closed the door on my reentry, I could hear feet scampering upstairs and squeals of "She's coming!"

"Can I come up?" I asked.

Before I had covered the last few steps, two boys jumped from behind my door at the top of the stairs.

"Tah-dah!" the eight-year-old proudly yelled while holding his arms out to parade his pajama-clad younger brother. "We did it ourselves."

"You gave him a bath?"

"Yeah," the kid proudly replied, "and dressed him. By myself!"

"Yeah," chimed in Jack.

"You did this by yourself?" I really was amazed. He had taken it upon himself to bathe and dress his brother and, I'd later find out, brush his brother's teeth. I had no idea he could do all that! I ditched my initial urge to smell the kid to make sure soap and toothpaste had, in fact, been involved in the evening's activity; instead, I relished the budding independence and look-what-I-did delight.

Oh, how far we've come from the how-low-can-the-expectations-go limbo days of Task 1. Maybe we're graduating to legitimate hurdles. The miles we've clocked have strengthened all our muscles—theirs to be able to run alone, mine to be able to let them. I just haven't stopped long enough to enjoy the spoils. This proud display of their ability to take responsibility is a sweet experience for me as well as for them.

Of course the kids also help me keep things in perspective with reminders that we've not yet arrived in the promised land of self-discipline. On the drive home from school the very next day, my oldest shared his aspirations.

"I've decided that I'm going to live in South America," Boxster blurted from the passenger seat.

I couldn't believe my ears. Apparently he *had* been listening to my lecturesque soliloquies on the joys of charitable living. Finally, his heart was leading him to serve—and in South America, no less, embracing his missionary grandparents' legacy, living with some indigenous tribe or maybe helping orphans.

"Yeah, South America. I can take twenty thousand dollars and buy any car I want. Plus a mansion—a huge one with lots of land. And I'll have a maid *and* a butler. Yeah. That's what I'm doing."

So much for charity.

"Well, then I would take Spanish to fill your language requirement," I suggested. Mostly as an act of surrender…and an effort to not take the bait. Sometimes I think he just trolls for opportunities to get my goat.

Then I smiled. The kid makes me laugh.

OPERATION PING-PONG

Teamwork theories were in full play this weekend. One of the greatest benefits to combining efforts? Time efficiency. Projects that could easily take a month for one person working alone were completed in one weekend. The kids amazed me with their tenacity and determination not only to get that Ping-Pong table up and running but also to clear the front yard in hopes of creating a volleyball and soccer haven.

I wonder if, in their imaginations, they picture hordes of players coming to the yard armed with balls for their respective sports—a veritable field of dreams. I'm not sure they've calculated into their equation the time needed for new grass to be ready for competitive moves. But the labor this crew accomplished was commendable.

They started with the garage. Before work got underway, they asked for a little direction, a request that is always welcomed and accommodated in the Experiment. I have to constantly stop myself from stepping in and doing it all for them, but I'm happy to advise and assist when needed.

"What do we do with the stuff once we get it out of the garage?" they asked on Friday, in anticipation of the work they planned to do on Saturday.

At least they're thinking ahead. It might have been a better question to ask a few days earlier. But a day before they start is better than a day after.

"Call a few places to come pick it up."

"Really? Someone will come pick up our stuff?"

"Sure. Genesis might come if we have enough," I said, referring to a local charity organization. "Give them a call."

For years we've supported Genesis Benefit Thrift Store, a terrific organization that provides safety and counseling for women caught in an abusive environment. Not too long ago, we even had the opportunity to direct a close friend their way. We knew it was an amazing place but had no idea how significantly they touch lives. They literally gave our friend back her life—a life she had forgotten.

A flurry of team discussion yielded the conclusion that none of them wanted to call. They came back to me with the perennial kid reason: it's too embarrassing.

"Please, Mom. Pleeease call for us."

As I hesitated, Snopes sighed, "I'll call them, but I don't know what to say."

I thought about it for a moment. This really was my call to make. I wasn't sure the folks on the other end would even take a kid request seriously, and I might need to explain what we have to offer. I knew their thrift store would be able to use our stuff. I just wasn't sure we had enough for them to come retrieve it. Normally we drop off our donations.

"Listen," I said. "I'll make the call. But you guys have to look up the number and sit with me so you'll know what to do."

Apparently, a great guy named Billy, who owns a moving company, donates his Saturdays and a truck to pick up furniture and other large items people want to give to the thrift store. Happily, we fit into the schedule for Saturday afternoon. This gave the kids a huge incentive to get the garage cleared before their arrival.

The deadline whipped them into gear. I directed (pointing out what could go) and helped when needed. The kids divvied out jobs, coordinating object size with what each one could carry. Then they worked together to clear the garage. Lots of items required the lifting power of more than one kid. Fury, who had morphed into Superstud, worked like an ant. Somehow the kid moved things that weighed as much if not more than he does.

With our pile of treasure ready to go, Billy and his big truck arrived right on schedule. It was fun to see the kids working together, sticking to a schedule, achieving the desired goal. With the garage cleared, Dad put up the table. We found the Ping-Pong balls and net while cleaning. Too bad the paddles have gone missing. I guess there's a lesson in that too. Maybe the kids can start keeping track of the goods even when located in a common space like the garage.

So far, they've learned that a team operates with exponentially more efficiency than a single person going it alone. If you task a person within her skill set, it works even better. One of the girls was terrific at directing where to place things and how to take them out of the garage. Fury just wanted to carry things. My young Energizer Bunny–style workhorse could have gone on for hours, but he relied on his sister's directions. Jack desperately wanted to be a part of the action. Instead of making him sit out because he's too little (which he is), they assigned him to carry light items and bring them water...one little glass at a time. It made him feel useful. Plus, he met a need because they most certainly worked up a thirst. At the other end of the spectrum, it was fun to watch them admire their older brother who *is* bigger and stronger.

> Coming together is a beginning. Keeping together is progress. Working together is success.
>
> —HENRY FORD

They also learned that quitting simply isn't an option. If any one of them had thrown in the towel, the project wouldn't have gone as smoothly as it did. One of the kids gave much less effort than the others, which was hard for this mom to watch. But the rest worked to make up for the weaker link. I felt greatly encouraged as I watched the team stay strong. They refused to complain and moan about someone not giving her all. Instead the working kids encouraged one another to say only nice things. As they did, a zip entered their step, and I watched them work even harder. They showed compassion, rather than disdain, for the kid who chose to put forth the least amount of effort. And let's face it: every team has those players.

I was thrilled with the lessons already hitting home. I hope the kids will apply them in our daily interactions. Okay, so we all know that's unlikely to become our norm. But at least they have tasted the wonderful fruit of compassion and concern. A much sweeter flavor than indignation.

CODE NAME VOLLEYBALL

After the kids had pulled stuff out of the garage and were waiting for Billy to pick it up, Boxster's friend stopped by to grab him for a movie. As pleasantries were exchanged between families, they naturally inquired about what we were doing. The younger kids talked excitedly about our projects while our teen rolled his eyes to make sure his friend knew how weird our family is. Within minutes of pulling away, the dad phoned to ask what we planned to do with our front-yard stones.

"Would you want them?" I asked. That was one of the major hurdles still staring the kids in the face.

"Oh, we'd love them. We were just talking last night about putting a stone path by the house. I have a trailer and could come by tomorrow."

When you're on a roll, why stop? I told the kids about the trailer and the next-day time frame. You would have thought we'd won the lottery. Knuckle bumps were exchanged along with a few fist pumps. Have I mentioned we're geeks?

Sunday afternoon, Nick brought his trailer and his son. Now, not only did we have a crew of eager kids (those eleven and younger), but we also had a couple of able-bodied teens. Funny how those teen-types often complain about work while the younger troops jump right in. The young ones genuinely enjoyed watching the progress of their work, again solidifying the importance of giving our kids responsibilities at an early age. As with so many things, convincing the kids to work is easier when

Ironing Board Tip

A family is like a team where everybody either wins or everybody loses. There is no in-between. Parents must stand united, not "against" the children, but in leadership "before" the children. It is the obligation of parents to make sure children feel loved and respected. It is not the obligation of parents to ensure children feel happy.

—Dottie Jones

they're little than during adolescent and teen years. It's important either way, just easier when they're eager. On this task, though, I think the teens feigned complaining primarily for one another's benefit, lest their coolness be in question. They actually did a terrific job, as did their younger cohorts.

With a little direction from Dad on how to dislodge the stubborn stones, some jumped into the task, some staggered. Some sought ways to avoid the work, and some pretended to while actually working quite hard. But all were required to work together, which they did. Within a couple of hours, every stone had been pulled up, transported by wheelbarrow to the trailer, loaded in, and driven away. We had a lovely path of dirt covering half our yard, waiting for Raymundo to come and sod.

It was wonderful to sit on the porch and watch. The dads couldn't help but get in the mix, but I forced myself to rock in one of our freshly painted wooden chairs while sipping a nice cold glass of sweet tea garnished with lime and a sprig of mint. It was a hard job, but someone had to do it. That tea wasn't nearly as sweet as the picture being painted in front of me.

Gone were the forced teen attitudes. In their place, supernice kids were helping the younger ones dislodge and move stones. Jokes were told. Laughter filled the air. Eye rolls were exchanged. A trailer was filled not once, but twice. The recipients helped the workers, then the workers rode over to their house and reciprocated. It was a beautiful thing.

MULTIPLIED TIME

So there you have it: one impressively productive weekend.

Have you ever prayed that time could be multiplied? Well, apparently sharing responsibility is the secret. Two family projects successfully completed—at least as far as we could take them—in record time. The occasional emotional outburst (the blaming-someone-else kind, or the stating-the-obvious-injustice-as-one-kid-hauls-four-chairs-while-another-only-one-chair kind) made its way onto the scene. But on the whole, they demonstrated great teamwork.

The other day, one of my friends stopped by to drop off a wayward backpack. Not realizing I was on the other side of our gate, she talked with the kids playing in the yard.

"Did you guys do something different?" she asked.

Barton jumped to answer. "Yeah. We took out that old stone sidewalk."

"Isn't it cool?" Fury added. "Dad had the guys sod it so we can already play soccer…and it's *huge!*" (The yard did look a lot larger with the stones gone.)

"Oh. That's great. It looks so nice."

"We did it ourselves," added Snopes.

"Get out!"

"No, really. We did it all," Barton confirmed. "It was part of Mom's weird thing where we have to work."

"But we love it," Snopes piped in. "We did this, cleaned out the garage, and had everything hauled away so we can use the Ping-Pong table and play volleyball."

"Yeah. It has been *forever* since we could play Ping-Pong."

"Dad thinks he's the best," competitive Fury revealed. "Uncle Charles can beat him, though."

"Not always!" defends Barton. "Dad *always* beats Dr. Schott…and Mom."

Never doubt that a small group of thoughtful, committed citizens can change the world; indeed, it's the only thing that ever has.

—Margaret Mead

I just listened as they all started laughing. I couldn't force myself to emerge and ruin the endearing conversation. I loved listening to them and to my friend admiring their accomplishment. And I, once again, was thankful for this ridiculous "Mom's weird thing where we work." I'm fairly confident that the kids are thankful too. It's at times like these that they appreciate being different—even if they'd never admit it to me.

REAPING THE REWARDS

So much for a *month*-long task. As a reward for the kids' effort, we stayed true to our word and didn't add more to the teamwork task than was specified at the outset. That might not sound like a reward, but they received the news with relief. We're still waiting on our volleyball net. (Jon's and my procrastination disorder. It's amazing we ever get anything done!) But a yard without stones invites much play. Soccer is the game du jour. Plus, who needs a volleyball net? The girls are out almost every day bumping the ball over the lacrosse net that also serves as a soccer goal.

Karl Moore, who is "Rethinking Leadership" for *Forbes* magazine, recently interviewed Amy Edmonson, a professor at Harvard Business School, about the nature of teams in today's organizations. She said,

> I see teams disappearing, which will sound very surprising because, in fact, we hear more and more about teams. But stable, bounded, clearly defined teams are less and less in evidence. What I see more of is "teaming". So, teaming is a verb, teaming is a skill, teaming is an activity.
>
> Most of the work that is of any importance in organizations needs teaming to get it done.[4]

This month we watched hands-on "teaming" take place. In fact, we could have been a case study. The speed, the unity, the creativity, the reliance on one another, and—best of all—the self-esteem. Whenever anyone comments on our yard transformation, several very proud kids can genuinely claim credit. Not in a self-promoting kind of way, but in a "we are family" sort of way, because everyone helped. Plus it was tons of fun.

We also watched some major personality strengths appear. For example, Fury revealed his true colors during this project. That kid is one hard worker. Our challenge now is to take that passion and tenacity and steer it toward productive projects. Then help him learn how to stay positive and avoid sinking into the stubbornness that sometimes accompanies an intense personality.

I think we need to live on a farm.

WHAT THEY LEARNED THIS MONTH

- Those sometimes annoying siblings have surprising skills and strengths.
- All of us working together adds up to more than the sum of our parts...and the time needed to complete a project is more than cut in half.
- Our garage actually does have a floor.

WHAT I LEARNED THIS MONTH

- These kids have so much more maturity than I give them credit for.
- I can sit and enjoy watching from a distance rather than always needing to be smack-dab in the middle of the mix.
- There is no screen in *team*. Television, computer, and telephone screens weren't missed as the kids put their heads together to plan, strategize, and accomplish their goals.
- Jon is a competitive Ping-Pong player. Our neighbors might be reporting some late-night hollering. Okay, so maybe I'm the competitive one!

Runner's World

Equipping Kids for Life's Little Errands

> Any kid will run any errand for you, if you
> ask at bedtime.
>
> —RED SKELTON

Don't close the door!" I yelled. Boxster gave me the classic "Huh?" stare as the door closed behind him.

I choked back a few choice words and ran to the door, hoping by some chance I had pushed the unlock button. Nope. Of course it was locked.

There I stood, clothed in my unattractive yet incredibly comfortable ten-year-old flannel pajama pants topped off with a thin, slightly revealing undershirt. No shoes, but I was, thankfully, wearing proper undergarments.

The time was 7:38 a.m. I had run out the door to tell Jon to go ahead and take the carload of on-time kids to school since Boxster was running a little late thanks to a "discussion" he and I were having about some schoolwork. To be precise, about the lack of said schoolwork. Jon had driven off, and now, not only was I inconvenienced and not just a little frustrated at having to take the wayward child to school, we were locked out. We had twenty-five minutes until the tardy bell, fifteen of which would be expended on the drive to school.

I peeked through the mail slot. "Jack? Jack, come to the door," I wheedled to the child inadvertently locked inside—alone. "It's Mommy. Buddy, can you help me?"

In the house whooping it up to *Mickey Mouse Clubhouse,* Jack had no interest in the voice calling from outside.

"Why did you close the door?" I barked at the culprit on the porch. He really hadn't done anything wrong by closing the door. He was actually being responsible. Especially considering the countless times I've yelled at the kids to close the door behind themselves. But I wasn't in the right frame of mind, or wardrobe, to give serious consideration to his intentions.

My thoughts turned to our trusted neighbors who have copies of our house key. I just couldn't imagine going door to door dressed like this. So I threw all my hopes into the spare key we keep hidden for just such occasions. As you can imagine, we access it often and forget to put it back—something about a procrastination disorder. Why make things easy by putting it away after use? Waiting always makes life a bit more interesting. But on this day, a day with no time to wait, I was in luck. The key was right where it was supposed to be.

I quickly slipped into the house, grabbed the toddler and the car keys, then yelled at the teenager to get in the car. I launched back into our "discussion," at which point I bumped up against the stone wall. The one he erects when he enters the zone of minimum tolerance, hearing my words but definitely not listening.

Then I noticed the orange light blaring at me from my dashboard and remembered why I had asked Jon to drive the kids to school. I had no gas. Not only that, I had no cash. My wallet had been hiding for several days. The "discussion" turned just a notch warmer.

"I just want you to know, not only are you going to be late to school, we are going to *run out of gas*. And I'm *in my pajamas!* All because you blah-de-blah, blah, blah, blah." I wasn't even listening to myself. What difference did it make? We had reached the point of diminishing returns about fifteen minutes ago.

I pulled into a gas station, one conveniently located on our route to school but embarrassingly located at the intersection of two superbusy streets. Lots of other people stopping to fuel up. People who were dressed. Which is how I decided that Boxster would be pumping his first tank of gas. A fitting opportunity since it just happened to be Errand Month.

We haven't had our family meeting yet, but the goal for this month is proficiency in and knowledge about the many, many errands required every week to keep a household running. I want the kids to be able to head into the grocery store, the cleaners, pet store—wherever—and pick up and pay for needed items. It's important for them to learn how to find the goods (which just might involve asking for help) and to pay for them (again, an activity involving human interaction). I want them to be polite to cashiers, look them in the eye, and get over any anxieties associated with venturing beyond the familiar. Plus, it's good for the kids too, once again, to learn that things don't just appear out of nowhere.

The morning's abrupt departure from the routine was about to provide our first such opportunity, a sort of trial by fire for Boxster.

Barreling into the gas station, I underscored my irritation by a screeching and abrupt halt alongside the pump. Oh yeah. I'm mature. I dramatically removed from his pocket the four dollars I had earlier given him for lunch and, shoving the bills at him, I said, "Take this inside and tell them four dollars on seven."

"Huh?" His wide-eyed stare suggested I had lapsed into speaking a foreign language.

"We have to pay. Take it in and tell them four dollars on seven."

"Me?"

"Yes, you. Get. Out. Of. The. Car. Go. Inside"—I'd cratered to the point of being rude to my child. Then I sped up—"and tell him four dollars on seven!"

He didn't want to, but he finally climbed out of the car and inched reluctantly toward the entrance to the store.

I rolled down the window, "Could you go faster? *Hurry!*" He didn't turn to respond, but the rest of the pumping crowd looked. How nice that despite my efforts to hide from the public eye, I'd just invited attention toward all my lovely undershirt glory. I rolled up my window.

The kid paid and lumbered back to the car. I emphatically pointed to my side of the car and the pump. He responded with the "Huh?" shrug. From inside the car, I flipped the switch to open the gas tank door. Then he realized that *he* would be pumping the gas.

"What am I supposed to do?"

"What?" continuing my own tantrum, I pretended I couldn't hear him.

"What am I supposed to do?"

I cracked my window and shouted through the tiny opening, "Take the cap off!"

"Huh?" Another shoulder shrug, accompanied by a lip snarl.

"Unscrew the *cap!"*

The man at the next pump had by this time given up on ignoring the uncomfortable interaction. He subtly motioned to the kid and indicated the location of our car's gas cap. I'm sure he relished the fun he'd have describing the scene in detail for his work buddies at the water cooler later that day.

After the kid bumbled through removing the cap, trying to hand it to me through the window (not!), then putting it on the ground, he pleaded, "Can I get in the car now?"

"No! Take the handle and put it in the car!" I screeched through my cracked window.

"Huh?"

"Oh my word. Take the *handle* and *put* it *in* the *car!"*

He finally inserted the pump nozzle into the gas tank.

"Now push the Regular button."

"Huh?"

"Aaaaggghhhhh! *Push* the *Regular* button!"

Eventually he pushed the button. Then he took his own sweet time to realize you have to squeeze the handle to get the gas going. He put gas in the tank. Then he replaced the pump and the gas cap. At least I hope he put the gas cap back on. I might need to go check that soon.

We didn't talk much on the way to school. I did offer a lame "I love you" when he got out of the car. I deserved the grunt I received in reply.

I'm sure he will never forget his introduction to pumping gas. It wasn't exactly how I envisioned teaching him about the gas station. Yet again I realize that if I wasn't such an enabler, he might have learned a few years ago how to pump gas. I guess I can do that with the other kids.

Poor guy. It's not easy forging the way for the rest of the family.

Endless Errands

Errands. We all have them. We all do them. Well, all of us except kids who think that household necessities just appear as needed. Consider a few scenes at the Wyma household:

"Hey! I need some toilet paper!" A voice rises from the downstairs bathroom. "Who was last and didn't put a new roll on?... Hey!... Can anyone hear me?"

Of course, to the one who used the last square, the toilet-paper holder is like a magic PEZ dispenser that never runs out. There's always another roll, right?

"Uh, while you're up, can you get me the ketchup?" asks a diner eager to cover the taste of a meal she considers lacking in the flavor department. When no one responds, she gets up and opens the fridge. "What! There's no ketchup?" It's unthinkable that a refrigerator might be without the red flavor saver.

"What am I supposed to do? There's no detergent for the clothes that *you're* making me wash."

Hmm. "First of all, they're *your* clothes. And second, you have to tell me when you've used the last scoop. I can't patrol every item in this house to know when it runs out."

Which leads to this mind-boggling conversation:

"Have you washed your hair recently?"

"Maybe. I don't know."

"How can you not know if you've washed your hair?"

"Well, I don't have a calendar in my shower to mark off the days."

"Have you washed it in the last few days?"

No response.

"The last few weeks?" Pause. "Please tell me you've washed it in the last few weeks," I beg.

"I don't know. Maybe. My shampoo is out."

"How long have you not had shampoo?"

"Well. At least a week."

Ugh. "Why didn't you tell me?" I groan.

The chorus of "serve me" expectations crescendoed one afternoon at an AMC theater.

As a treat for the kids, I had decided not only was it the perfect day to catch a flick but also to go against my frugal grain and let each kid splurge on popcorn, drinks, *and* candy. What was I thinking?

The shift from fun outing to fiasco started when nice AMC-guy Zach asked the ten-year-old, "What would you like to drink?"

Instead of answering him, she looked at me. "Um…"

"What kind of Slurpee do you want?" I asked, pointing out there are only two flavors. And only one that any of the kids like.

"Um…"

"Come on. What do you want?" I implored.

Again, looking at me, "I guess I'll have a cherry Slurpee."

Okay. The fact that's she's telling *me* demonstrates again my kids' apparent inability to do anything themselves. She wanted to tell me so I could tell him. Forget the fact that he was standing directly in front of her on the other side of the counter.

"Tell *him*." I pointed and tilted my head at Zach.

She reluctantly turned to him, "I guess…um…well…I…well…I'll (tee-hee) get a cherry Slurpee."

Impatient me: "Okay! What kind of *candy* do you want?"

"I don't know."

"Well, go look at the shelf and figure it out," I said, muttering under my breath, "or do I need to do *that* for you too?"

This is not good. With six of us, it is going to take *forever*!

Eight-year-old Fury, next in line, has morphed into Mumble Man.

"What kind of drink do you want?" I asked.

"mmbbllmmmb…mfllmsmflll…mmmbmmg."

"What?"

"mmmbmmmnn…mmnllmbbll."

I couldn't believe this. Not only was my ten-year-old expecting me to order for her, the eight-year-old apparently decided I should talk for him, somehow interpreting the mumbles into an answer for Zach.

Rather forcefully, I said, "Please speak so we can hear you! What. Kind. Of. Slurpee. Do. You. Want?"

"mbllmmmll…blah-blah-blah-blah."

I fought the urge to strangle him right then and there as poor Zach patiently watched.

"Do you want a Dr Pepper?"

"Yes…Dr mbllmmml."

"What? Did he say Dr Pepper?" I asked the next sibling in line. After a confirming nod, I told Zach, "He'll have a Dr Pepper."

"I WANT A DR PEPPER SLURPEE!" Fury yelled.

(*Now* he decides to be heard.)

"They don't *have* a Dr Pepper Slurpee." I was clinging to my last shreds of sanity. "All they have is cherry or blue. And you don't like the blue!"

Determining his candy selection proved equally frustrating. I finally banned the child to a makeshift time-out as Zach nicely tried to calm the situation. "It's okay. No worries. It's all right."

When it was his turn, Boxster tried to slip in an order of Milk Duds and popcorn, both absolute no-nos with his braces. Now I'm not only the interpreter and ordering lady, but I'm also the teeth police. Why monitor yourself when your mother is there to take care of every need?

The eight-year-old was now crying. The others were pelting me with their drink and candy requests. I officially needed a day off from our day out.

Then came the pièce de résistance. When I had finally paid and we'd made our way to the seats, I heard muffled dissatisfaction down the row. I didn't want to ask, but the persistent mutterings compelled an inquiry.

"What's wrong?" I whispered loudly.

Shrugging his shoulders, hands raised palm-up in the standard pose of the exasperated teen, Boxster mouthed, "Where are the straws?"

Not only had he not grabbed himself a straw at the stand, he expected me to get up and go get it for him. I was beginning to wonder if we had made *any* progress in our family's new redistribution of labor and responsibilities program. Now that my eyes have been opened, I'm more and more aware of not only my tendencies to enable but also the kids' reflex to rely on me rather than act on their own behalf.

The situation was slightly redeemed when a sister quickly jumped from her seat and offered, "I'll go get it." Which she did, grabbing napkins while she was there.

I sighed, grateful that we've made some progress. Grateful that we're at least on the road to recovery. Grateful that we aren't the only ones. Since AMC Zach went with the flow, I'm guessing I'm not the first enabling mother on the other side of his counter.

After getting home and relating our AMC fiasco to Jon, I realized it was chock-full of lessons. Staring me in the face were several confidence-infusing opportunities that I missed:

- I could have given money to my oldest and let him step up to the box office to buy our tickets. I could have encouraged him to stretch his wings by talking to someone he didn't know. Maybe even pushed him to embrace his role as the oldest child. I could have capitalized on an opportunity to make this teenager feel needed in a time of life when questions of self-worth capture his thoughts at every turn of most every day.

- I could have let the kids figure out the movie time and number of tickets we needed rather than handling it all myself.

- They could have practiced their new teamwork skills and divided up the responsibilities according to each of their natural abilities. One is great at finding things; let him scout out the movie location. One loves people; let her converse with AMC Zach. One is incredibly nurturing but doesn't like talking to people she doesn't know; let her organize the order and distribute the snacks.

- Conversely, I could have assigned each of them a task they *don't* like, encouraging them to test their wings in a safe

environment so they could learn to embrace difficult
situations.

- They could have paid for the movie and concessions
  themselves, with their own money! And maybe grasped a
  few concepts like cost versus benefit.
- I could have seized the opportunity to teach so many skills,
  such as manners, hospitality, serving, organization... The
  list really could go on.

A huge chance to make my kids feel productive, successful, helpful,
and needed fell by the wayside because, once again, I stepped in and did
everything for them rather than putting responsibility on their shoulders.
(I'm pretty sure I *thought* for them too.) My role could have been limited
to chauffeur. I just needed to get us there in time for it all to happen.
Wait. No, I didn't. They can manage the time too. Why do I always assume clock duty? They can tell time and calculate when we need to leave
to arrive on time. Oh my word. Apparently, I can't stop myself! Rather
than let them think through a situation, solve problems, capitalize on
opportunities, serve one another, I kept all the responsibility—and frustration—for myself.

These things seem so small, especially in the moment. We tend to
dismiss such opportunities as meaningless. But they aren't. And neither
are all the tasks we do for them around our homes. Next time you go to
a family matinée, take a peek around. Who's juggling the popcorn and
sodas as if destined for Barnum & Bailey, presiding over her brood like a
ringmaster and calling out orders while trying not to spill? That would
most likely be me...and possibly a few other parents caught up in catering
to their serve-me kids.

THEY CAN. THEY SHOULD. THEY WILL.

Clearly, the first point of action in the errand department is to open the
kids' eyes and help them realize that items they use day in and day out

don't magically appear as soon as the thought pops into their heads. If I was one of those organized people, I would probably have a running list on our refrigerator or some public access point in order to track household needs. But I don't. Truth is, if I did have a list like that, I would likely forget to take it with me to the store. If by some chance I did remember to take it with me, I almost certainly would lose it along the way. That admitted, I should help myself and the kids by teaching the value of lists and using them. Maybe it will stick with one of them, and that child can organize our family!

The second point is to show the kids where and how to do errands. They now know where most food items reside in a grocery store. It's time they learn the ins and outs of Target, Wal-Mart, and other full-service shopping establishments.

The third objective this month is to let them do it alone. Well, at least without me. Taking along a sibling or friend is fine.

For years, I've done the errand running. When they were little, I piled my kids in a cart, then I raced through the store, filling every available nook in the basket as fast as I could before we caused a scene. Sometimes I would recruit our sweet neighbor/baby-sitter to go with me. She loved being with the kids and was thrilled to wait with them in the car while I ran in. Now that mine are older, I can safely leave my older ones at home with the younger kids or, if needed, in the car while I dash in for quick necessities.

I've realized since starting our Experiment that this approach is a major disservice to the kids. I am solidifying their tendency to assume the world is here to serve them. (Ugh. The thought of them sitting in the car watching me run and serve them is almost too much to bear at this point!) Each time I do something they could do for themselves, I reinforce their sense that they are owed certain things. That "I deserve it" mentality irks me more than any other aspect of youth entitlement.

The "you're a mom; you're supposed to cook for me, shop for me, drive me, and take care of everything for me" ideology might be a societal norm these days. It shouldn't be. I can appreciate such needs for a baby or toddler. But these older kids are more than capable of doing a lot for themselves…and for others!

Consider the confidence boosters waiting to be grabbed when we drive into a grocery store parking lot or gas station. My kid is right, to a certain extent, in his moanings that none of his friends have to do many of these things. But we've already seen what happens when kids step out and do tasks that initially seem beyond their ability. Which, by the way, we know is quite an overstatement. They (and we) have no real idea about the boundaries of their abilities because we rarely test them. So I'm eager to watch them discover how proficient they can be at this month's task.

This could even morph into a summer job! I have a friend who's built a business of running errands for people. Most of her clients are elderly, but some are busy moms who would rather pay someone to run their errands. Before I get ahead of myself, we'll stick to the errands at hand.

"Just so you know, November is our month for errands," I informed the kids—once again captives in a moving car.

"What!"

"No fair!"

"Mommm. Please. No."

As has become my custom these past few months, I completely ignored the pathetic pleadings. Then I turned into the gas station. Boxster, in a hurry to pick up his friend for a movie scheduled to begin within minutes, groaned in anticipation of the next words to come out of my mouth.

Glad I was more suitably clothed than at his inaugural experience with the gas station, I stopped the car and said, "Okay. Jump out and start pumping."

"Mom! We're going to be late."

"Well, then, you'd better get going. Because we have no gas, and I'm not pumping."

"Mom. I just did this the other day." He tried to balk, but the kid knew his near future involved interaction with the gas pump. Plus, I think he secretly likes doing it. This is my "love to learn" kid. I'm fairly certain that while he's pumping, his mind is racing to figure out how it all works, then where the gas comes from, then the countries involved, then the historical conflicts in those regions, then… I'm not joking. His mind moves so fast, he leaves me in the dust—often.

"Tick tock. The faster you get started, the quicker we pick up your friend. Plus, welcome to errands. Lesson Number One: Errands are never over. They're like laundry. You do one load and there's another. Or like dishes. You clean the entire sinkful, and a dirty dish appears. Or like—"

"All right! I get it." Even the surrender was less dramatic than last week's pumping episode.

In the usual way, he lumbered to the pump. I rolled down the window and handed him my credit card, explaining, for the world to hear, how to use the thing.

Somehow, I hear the hushed voice of sportscaster Jim Nantz describing the scene for a nonexistent crowd. "Note the young man's posture as he introduces himself to the pump. Eyes forward, ignoring the incessant chatter from the mother leaning out her window. Does she not realize that young men do not appreciate their mothers barking orders at them, especially in public, about things with which they might not be familiar? Has she shattered his 'with-it' facade? We'll have to watch and see. But as his body language clearly demonstrates, the offspring's only desire at this moment is to disappear, somewhere far, far away from the direction-laden parent broadcasting to the world the kid's lack of knowledge on the subject at hand."

"Mom. I know." He jerked the card in and out of the pump.

"Are you doing it right? You know there's a picture that shows you how to do—"

"Mom. I *know* how to *do* it!"

In and out. In and out. Something wasn't working, and I was beginning to worry that my card would be rejected due to the many failed attempts. And yes, yet again, I had no cash.

He put the nozzle in the car and pushed Regular without my direction. (At least he remembered *that*.) Still no action.

"I'm not sure you did the card right."

"I did it *right*!" he whisper-yelled back.

At this point I got out of the car. "Uh, I don't think so. ("Transaction Rejected" on the screen was my first hint.) "See, the magnetic strip needs to face this way. It's right there on the picture." I pointed at the clear image showing exactly how the card should be inserted into the machine.

"Oh."

"You're doing a great job," I added in a sunshiny voice. He didn't buy it.

He pumped. I got back in the car.

Fast-forward to day four of Errand month, which found Snopes and me headed to the grocery store. "You know this is Errand month," I reminded her.

"Mom! I'm *not* going in the grocery store by myself."

I was surprised by her reaction. As scheduled chef for the night, she was planning to whip up her famous butter and parmesan pasta. All she needed to do was run in and grab a box of noodles. If she had never done it before, that would be one thing. But when the potential purchase item holds a place of importance to her (like new mascara or office supplies—she likes officy things), she's happy to brave the aisles alone. So playing the "I don't know how to do it" card just wasn't going to cut it.

"I'm *not* going in there alone!"

"Listen. You can do it. I know you can."

"No! I don't like going into the grocery store."

"Well, neither do I. But I don't much have a choice, do I?"

"Neither do the other moms. And that's who's in there. Moms! And maybe sixteen-year-olds. But not *my* friends."

I couldn't argue with her; there really aren't many kids running these errands. So I got out and went in *with* her. It gave me the opportunity to remind her how to find an item and show her how to input our savings card information in order to receive any discounts. It reminded me that I don't have to always take the hard line. It reminded me that throwing them out of the boat to learn how to swim isn't always the best approach. Swimming with them can be just as educational—even better at times.

Of course, I couldn't stop myself from slipping in a lecture. "You just might be the only twelve-year-old checking out alone, but this isn't a big task. Not only can you do it, you can do it well. And it would make you feel great about yourself, just like all the other things we've been

We're All in This Together

Part of us paying for our son's gas means that he will run an errand for us if asked. That errand could be picking a sibling up at school or going to the grocery store. The first time I sent our son to the grocery store, I asked him to bring me chicken thighs so I could cook them in the Crockpot overnight. He brought me an entire chicken, already cooked—fried as a matter of fact. When I asked how I was going to cook the already-cooked chicken, he replied that he'd thought of that on his drive home and did not know what to do about it. Since that time I've found that it's better for a pair of siblings to go the store together; they help each other find things. When they work together, they bring home more correct items from the list than when they work independently.

—Lisa

doing. It's not and never will be about what 'everyone else' is doing. You're capable, kid."

Did she listen? Who knows. At least she didn't "Mommm!" me.

LIMITED DOWNSIDE, GREAT POTENTIAL

Like it or not, errands are an integral part of life. What better way to teach our kids about the world of work? It's not always glamorous. It isn't meant to complete us, though at times we'll find it fulfilling. The funny thing is that work—even errands—can be rewarding. Productive activity tends to be uplifting, if we can get away from false ideas about certain kinds of work being beneath us.

Not to mention, we were created to work.

That's another underlying truth I've seen revealed through each task: work serves as the foundation to our purpose on earth. God created man and woman to work, not making exceptions for an individual's affluence, intelligence, or athletic prowess.

Work is the vehicle through which God cares for creation (see Genesis 2:15). The satisfaction that comes from accomplishment, from demonstrating responsibility, from making even a small difference in our world is written into our DNA. My role as the parent is to love these kids, nurture them, and teach them how to embrace what they were created to do.

But what sounds simple becomes more complicated when you throw in a little teen apathy and adolescent mood swings and parental worries about what others might think of our family. Add some society-induced fear—the kind that propels parents to hover, race in to save, prevent pain, finagle opportunities, arrange, and manipulate so our child won't miss out—and the path forward seems less certain.

Here are a few questions I find myself asking: Do I love them enough to let them fail? to make them work? to require them to fly on their own even if it results in some unattractive, possibly embarrassing maneuvers? Do I love them enough to step aside rather than step in?

It might seem ridiculous to place errands in the category of work, but these simple tasks act as foundational cornerstones for much greater things. They tend to be safe. They have limited repercussions. Failing on an errand can only result in a certain amount of grief. They are easy to start and complete. And, as limited as their downside might be, the upside potential is terrific. Not the least of which is that future spouses will most certainly thank us for equipping their husbands or wives in practical living skills.

Taken to the Cleaners

The question, of course, is whether I can stop myself from stepping in and doing it for them. I still catch myself enabling the kids without even realizing it, as if I'm on autopilot. Seriously, though, it is so much easier if I run into the store myself.

Today, I forced myself to encourage one of the kids to run into the dry cleaners. Okay, I kicked her out of the car. All she needed to do was take in and pick up a few things. One would have thought I was asking her to step into the spotlight onstage at Rockefeller Center. Her knuckles were practically white as she gripped the seat in protest.

"What's the big deal?" I said. "You walk in. Hand the very nice guy our stack of shirts. Give him our phone number, which, by the way, you don't have to remember to do. He'll ask you. Tell him 'no starch,' and—"

"What! 'No starch'—what is *that*? I...I can't do this!" She looked like she might need a bag in which to breathe to avoid hyperventilation.

"Honey, it's okay." I kept my voice calm, almost cooing. "You can do this. I'm right here." Literally. The car was parked less than six feet from the door, which was about ten steps from the counter where our nice Cleaners Guy waited patiently. He'd already waved twice. "Just take the shirts."

She looked at me with the most pitiful puppy-dog eyes, hoping that a silent, slow-blink plea might work.

"Just get in there," I insisted. "Oh, and wait for the shirts that are clean."

"What! I have to pick up stuff too?"

"Uh, yes." Why does this surprise her? She's come with me before and witnessed the process. "That's what we do. Kill two birds with one stone. It would be silly to come back later to pick up what we can get while we're here. Plus, you like watching that little thing the shirts ride around on. You know, the roller-coaster thing."

"Yeah. I do like that." Pause. "Do you think he'd let me push the buttons?"

No way did she just say that! I always wanted to do the same thing when I was a kid. Maybe even hook myself on and ride around for good measure.

"No. Don't even ask. Just get out of the car and get in there. We have places to be and people to see." That last part came out in a burst of song.

She scrunched her nose, feigning annoyance with my ridiculous rhyme song. Then she went in, grudgingly, but with a smile on her face. I couldn't see it, but I sure could see the huge one on Cleaner Guy's face as he nodded and encouraged. And as has been the case with almost all our little tasks, she realized that she could do something out of her comfort zone. Will she want to do it again? Maybe. Probably not.

But she will.

This task might seem like it belongs in a work for work's sake category. It doesn't. I want the kids to be able to converse confidently with the adults in their lives rather than relying on me to handle their affairs. Also, although we don't have Jerry Seinfeld's Soup Nazi in Dallas, I know I need to get the kids in front of less friendly, possibly abrasive types so they know how to be kind and courteous in all situations. Check out any school playground, kids' sporting event, notes passing between teen girls (okay, so they don't pass notes; they text), and you're likely to encounter someone who hurts your kid's feelings. Is my kid going to crumble? Will she reflexively dish dirt back? Or might she treat the difficult person with respect and hold her tongue, keeping dignity intact? I want them to be free from insecurity and inhibitions, so they can rise above the fray, no matter what ugliness they encounter.

Barton's errand, however, didn't require quite that level of bravery. I've known Cleaners Guy for years. He's a kind, gentle soul who has gone out of his way numerous times to help me get clothes in and out of my car. I knew he would be perfect for our errand test. His demeanor welcomed my shy child's hesitation and most likely quiet request. It's like starter food for a puppy. Moving her from milk to steak might have been too much for this kid, so I'm thankful for personalities like Cleaners Guy who offer a smooth transition.

We're All in This Together

Grocery shopping is a chore with a large family, so we have had to do some thinking on how to make it a fun outing for all. Believe it or not, for the big Costco runs, it is easier to have everyone along: lots of hands and arms to help load and unload.

We came up with the idea of organizing the list according to how things are found in the store. Then my husband takes some kids, half the list, and one side of Costco, while I take some kids, the list, and the other side of the store. Then the race is on to see who gets their list loaded the fastest. With some competitive boys, this has been quite fun. (Attention shoppers! Race in progress...look out!)

Now that they are getting older, we also have a contest to see who can come the closest to guessing the final cost. Great for math skills.

—Chris

Barton shot me a "Mommm" look as she walked out of the store, accompanied by a smiling Cleaners Guy. He carried the load of clothes to the car since there were way too many for her little arms to hold.

She opened the door. "I did it."

"You did great," I replied, hopping out to help our friend find a spot to hang Jon's shirts.

I truly was proud of her. She's the type that admits when she's wrong and when she's learned something, which she certainly did. Her wings look a bit stronger already. The saddest and happiest part is that I know she will use them one day to fly away.

From Spectators to Participants

Errand running, like many of our other tasks, ushered the kids into a world they had previously enjoyed viewing from a window. In this case, the car window. Though drawn out of their comfort zones and, on occasion, out of their age bracket, the kids discovered how much of our daily life they take for granted.

I saw their confidence grow each time they pushed through their initial reluctance to complete a so-called unreasonable, potentially embarrassing errand—like go into Paradise Bakery & Café and grab a loaf of their favorite bread, call and order pizza delivery themselves, navigate Target, pump gas, or run in the pet store for crickets to feed Boxster's pet scorpions. (Yes, big, huge, creepy to some, cool to others, black scorpions. We've been begging for a dog. Instead, we get not-so-cuddly creatures.) Self-esteem is definitely on the rise at our house. Not the "look-at-me" kind but an inner assurance that they really are capable. A self-respect that will keep them grounded when storms threaten to blow them off course. The kind that I hope will someday help them achieve all that they want to achieve based on their God-given, and hopefully God-directed, talents.

Beyond confidence, we're also watching perseverance take root. So much of life is doing things you might not necessarily feel like doing, simply because you have to. That truth was definitely on stage this month.

WHAT THEY LEARNED THIS MONTH

- Household necessities don't magically appear the moment a need arises.
- The needs never stop. Even the jumbo pack of paper towels will eventually run out and need to be replaced.
- Getting the goods the first time is much more pleasant than needing to go back for Tilex, and then back again for the forgotten waffles, and later again for the butter we thought we had but can't make cookies without.

WHAT I LEARNED THIS MONTH

- As much as I despise them, lists can be a helpful thing.
- Completing a task *with* the kids is sometimes better than forcing them to do it alone.
- Pushing kids outside a comfort zone (sitting in the car watching mom) actually leads to an expanded comfort zone and increased confidence.

It's About Others

Service with a Smile

> Prayer in action is love, and love in action is
> service. Try to give unconditionally whatever
> a person needs in the moment. The point is
> to do something, however small, and show
> you care through your actions by giving your
> time.... We feel what we are doing is just a
> drop in the ocean, but that ocean would be
> less without that drop.
>
> —MOTHER TERESA

This month we embark upon what I consider to be our most important exercise of the Experiment: serving others. Why do I place such high value on this task? It starts with the answer Jesus gave to the question, "Which is the greatest commandment?" His response came without hesitation: "Love the Lord your God with all your heart and with all your soul and with all your mind." Then he continued, pointing out that hard on its heels follows the second greatest commandment: "'Love your neighbor as yourself.' All the Law and the Prophets hang on these two commandments" (Matthew 22:36–40).

Even before the Experiment, I tried to involve the kids in service-oriented opportunities as often as possible—not just because it's the right thing to do but also because it nurtures their emotional and spiritual health. So much of our children's world is focused on them—their desires and activities, their petty hang-ups and significant dreams. They can't stop thinking about themselves—in part due to hormones, in part due to the fact they're human. At school, it's about how they measure up to a standard or to everyone else. On the field or court, it's how well they play or contribute to the team.

Anytime I can get the kids' minds off themselves provides a much-needed reality check about the things that matter most—an imperative during the drama-infused tween and teen years.

It may be years before they realize for themselves how service to others feeds their souls. Until then, I want them frequently to breathe in the sweet satisfaction of generosity and compassion so they'll learn to recognize the comparatively bitter fragrance of self-absorbed living. When they inhale the fresh air of service, self-centeredness is exhaled out. The two can't occupy the same space.

Whether or not they grasp the deeper meaning in this task, this month I want the kids to consciously and deliberately put into action the simple principle of "others ahead of self."

We had our family meeting to talk about what our month might look like and came up with several ways we can serve not only those outside our family but also one another. We were all downright excited about this task. I think part of it had to do with the fact that, with Christmas just around the corner, everyone is in a serving kind of mood—which gives me mixed feelings about the timing. It means that for once we won't feel as if we're swimming against the tide of culture with our efforts, but I don't want our family to equate giving with only a certain time of year.

A definite positive is that our kids generally enjoy serving. We've purposefully trained in this area, so they know how good it feels. But in the weeks ahead, they will be going a bit above and beyond even our normal level of service.

We agreed on one major ground rule: an action doesn't have to be big or grand to qualify as putting others first. Sometimes I think we get discouraged by the immensity of people's needs, thinking we don't have enough time or money. Or we get lost wondering if our service is big enough. Will it really have an impact? So we postpone our efforts until we can do something big. The fact is, we can't meet all the needs around

We're All in This Together

Here are some ideas for how kids can serve outside of the holiday season:

- Baby-sit for the coaches.
- Put together care packages during finals week.
- Attend a lesser-followed sports game.
- Meet freshmen for a Coke (or any younger classmen) especially at the beginning of the year.
- If a friend is moving, offer to help. At a minimum, take pizza.
- Take steaks or salmon to the fire station for the firefighters.
- Pay for the person in line behind you at Starbucks—without letting on that you're doing it.
- Keep an eye out for whose groceries you can help load into a car when walking into or out of a store.

Nothing earth shattering, but at least they're thinking of someone other than themselves for a moment!

—Laura

us, but each of us can do something to shine the light of God's love into someone else's life.

We've decided that since we're doing something every day, sometimes the deed will be small. Basically anything qualifies as long as it's about encouraging someone else rather than focusing on ourselves!

Not-So-Random Acts of Kindness

Our series of other-centered acts started with something as simple as sympathy cards. The kids wrote a couple of thoughtful notes to encourage individuals who had been hurting, sick, or just blue. Snopes wrote one to my dad, whose best friend and business partner for over thirty years had died unexpectedly. This provided a great opportunity for me to talk about how to let someone know you're thinking about them during a difficult time. No need to try to explain away the difficulty; just sending a note of sympathy might ease the pain a bit.

On Sunday, I found out from my dad how special it was for him to get this card. I knew he would be soothed by her sweet words, but I had no idea how much it would mean to him.

Small efforts pack quite a punch. We all have friends who are suffering from grief or sickness. Sometimes it's the small acts that are remembered as the most meaningful. A former neighbor told me that when she was going through chemotherapy while battling cancer, the highlight of her week was opening the front door every Friday to find a single rose on her porch mat. With that simple gesture, an anonymous well-wisher was reminding my friend that she wasn't alone. Another friend whose child was diagnosed with leukemia found comfort in a similar act of kindness. Each week, the family opened their door to find a backpack filled with a new assortment of goodies. Maze books, word-search games, crafts—anything fun to provide some sort of mental diversion from the needles and medicine that were fighting the cancer but also making this sweet kid miserably sick.

The exhortation to love our neighbors is so broad, it often seems daunting. But these well-wishers demonstrated love in simple, hands-on ways. Like our notes of encouragement, seemingly small acts offer the recipients a lasting reminder that they are not alone, that they matter, that someone cares. Similar opportunities are all around us, if we slow down long enough to see them or to think outside the box…and then follow through.

That's the toughest part for this procrastinating family—the following through thing—but we're working on it.

Color Me Considerate

One day we made a trip to Dollar Tree, where the kids pooled their money (and I added to the pot) to buy coloring books requested by Brother Bill's Helping Hand, a local organization intent on providing patrons' kids with wrapped gifts. Each Christmas, this food pantry/clinic/preschool transforms into Santa's workshop so that kids who otherwise would receive nothing will have a few Christmas gifts.

My kids love Dollar Tree. They like to save their money to buy craft items, school stuff, barrettes, candy. While I was grabbing the cart, one of the kids shouted back, "Mom, Barton and I are going to look at brushes."

"No, we're not here for you guys," I reminded them. "We're here to get stuff for Brother Bill's."

"Ugh. Mom! I brought my money."

"I know. Maybe another day." Though I understood the temptation, I held my ground on the others-focused nature of our mission. "We signed up to bring coloring books. You can help find them. Pick whatever you want to get them."

The kids were actually happy to ditch the cosmetic aisle, racing to the back of the store where the books reside. They proceeded to carefully peruse all the options and make sure their final selection included a wide variety of books for girls and a separate collection for boys. "No boy wants that Powerpuff Girls book, Mommm," came the exasperated explanation, as if I wouldn't know that. They loaded the carts with over a hundred coloring books. As they worked, it hit them that each of these books would be some child's Christmas gift.

"Is this all these kids are getting for Christmas?" Snopes stopped to consider.

"Sweetheart, I don't know. I do know that through Brother Bill's each kid will at least get to open something."

The others pondered the reality. Then someone spoke up, "We have to get them markers too."

I watched and soaked in the moment, praying for all the hearts involved. With two carts loaded to the brim, we turned toward the checkout. Jack, who apparently had been unattended for a few moments during our frantic shopping spree, met us midaisle with his own cart. Future Hoarder of America had capitalized on the opportunity and grabbed an empty shopping cart on the way into the store. Though he couldn't see over the top of the cart, he had managed to fill the entire thing. From marshmallow Christmas ornaments to balls to shaving cream to spicy pork rinds, he had sought and found lots of treasure. Dollar Tree: a hoarder's paradise. Two of the kids took on reshelving duty while the others helped me check out.

As we drove away, my passenger-seat child, after mulling over our latest effort, floated some music my way: "You know, Mom. I really don't need anything for Christmas."

"What do you mean?" I asked.

"Well...it's just...I don't need anything."

That's as far as he wanted to go. And I wasn't going to push him to say it out loud. We both understood. He was hit by the fact that lots of kids would be thrilled to get a coloring book and markers. It made the hoped-for iPad a bit less desirable.

Yes. This is a good task. An eye-opening glimpse into the reality of how privileged they are and what a difference a simple gift can make to others. In this case, a child just like them was about to be incredibly excited to unwrap something my kids might consider peripheral.

Sister Act

"Remember, December is our month to put others first. What do y'all feel like doing today?" I asked.

The girls looked at each other blankly, then started to smile.

"It doesn't have to be huge, right?" one of them asked.

"No, as long as you're serving someone. I think it's really great if you serve each other."

"Yeah!" the other one chirped. "I'm going to make your bed," she yelled at her sister while racing up the stairs.

"I'm going to make yours too."

Clomp, clomp, clomp.

"Please make my bed nice," the first girl asked.

They have different styles of bed making. But in the end, both beds looked neat. A major gift from my slightly sloppy laid-back chick to the slightly OCD, if-you're-going-to-do-a-job-do-it-well girl.

As small as that effort appeared, they genuinely served each other. It's amazing to watch the power of even the smallest act. From that point on, they laughed and played together for the rest of the day. I caught them doing other little things for each other, like putting some clothes in the hamper, picking up a wet towel, even clearing a table and washing some dishes.

I've noticed that working hard breeds working hard. The positive

We're All in This Together

One of our favorite activities is loading up the family, and any friends that want to join, then heading to the airport to greet arriving soldiers. It's good for them to see that actual people are putting their lives on the line for freedom.

—Brett

results—such as increased confidence and a sense of accomplishment—stimulate more work. I've observed a similar effect when Boxster fully applies himself at school. Earning an A in a challenging subject inspires even greater effort. Apparently serving accomplishes the same thing.

SERVING IS CONTAGIOUS

Driving home from a movie, we heard a news story about unemployment benefits not being extended.

"What's unemployment?" the kids asked almost in unison.

I explained.

"That's terrible," one of them said.

"Yes, it's very sad," I replied.

"Why don't they just get a job?" observed another, verbalizing what so many listening to that broadcast probably thought. His matter-of-fact response assumed a job is like a Slurpee: you just go get one when you want it. We're learning that's simply not true.

Then the newscaster said that the North Texas Food Bank was concerned that the rise in need couldn't be met with current inventories.

"Hey, guys," I said. "Let's take the wagon today to our neighbors and pick up some cans of food. We can take them to NorthPark Center"—a shopping mall in our area—"and drop them off at that big red box by the valet parking."

The car was quiet for a moment while they considered whether resistance would accomplish anything; they're learning that once an idea has been presented, the outcome of any discussion is pretty much inevitable.

"Okay," surrendered Snopes. "Can I call Claire?"

"Sure." Always good to bring a friend.

As soon as we arrived home, off the girls went to get Claire, with Fury close on their heels, not wanting to miss what had now been deemed fun. Then they got the wagon and dutifully set out. Their stop at house number one immediately paid off, with enough goodies to fill the wagon halfway. Within thirty minutes, the wagon was overflowing, and they headed back home.

"Mom! That was *great!*"

"I can't believe how good I feel."

"Think of all the people who will have something to eat!"

Yep. That's what they said when bounding through the door. Clearly it was worth the risk I took in impulsively suggesting what could have been received as a goofy idea. I've got as much to learn as they do about following through on those random whims of kindness. Plus, it's hard to ignore the crazy power boost provided by their effort. My prewagon-filling crew was mopey, borderline whiny, complaining among themselves about the lack of fun things to do at home (after seeing a movie, no less). My postwagon-filling crew was ready for more. The service-oriented activity proved better than any energy drink, as evidenced by the comments when they returned with their wagonful of bounty.

The kids grabbed a quick drink, then I offered to take them over to the mall to unload the goods. Yes, this recovering procrastinator actually chose to act immediately rather than wait for a more opportune time. Maybe even I am making progress. Dad helped us load up the loot, which we then hauled to the big red donation box. When they opened the lid to put our stuff inside, the kids saw that the box was completely bare. They looked at one another and traded comments about how glad they were to have spent their afternoon gathering cans.

The positive results didn't stop with the kids' warm feelings about their service. As they put in their stash, they drew the attention of a couple of ladies standing close by, waiting for the valet to bring their car around. After I responded to their questions about what the kids were doing, one of them actually said to her friend, "Hey, we should do that."

Apparently serving is contagious.

SERVICE WITH A SMILE

I concluded this morning that the dangers of driving while texting may also apply to driving while mothering. Given how we moms love to multitask, driving can be a dicey endeavor. While keeping one eye on the road, we may also be conducting a quick tutoring session, lecturing, handing a Happy Meal to the backseat, lecturing, dealing with a whining child, lecturing, answering multiple questions about the vehicles on the road, and did I mention lecturing? Oh, the things we do for our families!

As I arrived at Boxster's school (stop number one), I realized I must have driven there on autopilot. I had been quizzing the kid the entire ride. I might not be able to remember the streets onto which we turned, the cars we passed, the police officer waving us through one of our many school zones, but I could tell you which countries sport flags with red, black, and yellow stripes.

After dropping off my well-prepared quiz boy, I said to the rest of my brood, "Remember, it's our Serve Others month."

Blank stares. Silence.

"So today let's try to serve someone at school. Quietly, without letting anyone know."

More silence.

"Okay, if you can't think of anything to do, at least you can throw away someone's trash for them after lunch."

Deeper silence.

"Doesn't that sound good?"

From the rear of the car, Snopes looked at her sister, then at me. "I'm not even going to answer that question."

After a silent chuckle, I offered an undefined reward to anyone who could silently serve at least five people today at school, no matter how small the effort.

Later, when the kids arrived home, I asked them each if they did anything for someone else.

Fury: "Uh, I forgot."

Snopes: "No."

Boxster: "Huh?" (Oh yeah, he wasn't in the car at that point.)

Barton: "I served four people. I didn't really want to, but it actually felt great. I think I'm going to try again tomorrow." Of course she is. What did she do? Nothing much. She quietly threw away lunch trash. That was it. The greatest part for her was watching her friends run to the field for a few extra minutes of play before classes resumed. She also went out of her way to talk to a girl who had been left sitting by herself. "I wouldn't have noticed if I hadn't been throwing away the others' trash," she told me.

And so went our month of service. We made manna packs (brown paper lunch sacks that the kids decorated, then filled with a bottle of water, cheese crackers, peanuts, and Hershey's Kisses) to keep in our car so we can hand them to the homeless. We baked for the neighbors, cleaned yards, were secret Santas, and so much more. One of the things we most appreciated about this month is that, unlike many of our other tasks, we're not alone in this. Plenty of other parents have picked up on the value of teaching their kids to serve others.

The neat thing about people who incorporate service into their daily lives is that either they don't talk about it or they do it without even realizing they are. I was chatting with a couple of friends about effective ways to serve the homeless on a day-to-day basis. One of them confessed she really doesn't do anything in this area. Then she said, "I tell the kids that no matter what we think, we just can't drive by someone without helping. So I keep envelopes in the car with directions to Union Gospel Mission, a McDonald's gift card, and a five-dollar bill. We give one to anyone asking for help at a street corner." Clearly, she's serving to the point where it's second nature. Keeping a stash on hand is just one of the many quiet ways this incredibly generous, humble woman serves.

Apparently, the more you serve, the more you realize it's not serving at all. It becomes a way of life—an honor rather than a sacrifice.

I turned to our other friend. "Are you doing anything with your family to serve this season?"

"No, I've just been too swamped to put anything together."

"Really? You guys always seem to have something up your sleeve."

"I know. I've got to get on it."

We continued chatting. Blah-de-blah-blah. Yada-yada-yada.

"And then I need to drop by Starbucks for Sophie," she said.

"What's at Starbucks?"

"She put together a box for people to donate stuffed animals that can be sent to kids in Haiti."

"Um, I'd say that's serving."

"Oh! You're right. She's been working on it for so long, I really didn't think about it."

See? Serving is so deeply woven into their family values, this act of generosity didn't even stand out to her.

Sophie's dad is an orthopedic surgeon, one of the first on the scene after Haiti's catastrophic earthquake. He worked with others to set up a medical center of sorts and care for those who had lost limbs or had been crushed or needed medical attention for other reasons. When he told his kids where he was going and how the team planned on helping, sweet Sophie's heart went out to all the hurting kids. So she went to her room and pulled together a bag of stuffed animals for her dad to take along to help give comfort to those children.

Although it had been months since her dad traveled to help, this twelve-year-old hadn't forgotten the impact such a small contribution can have on those in need. She went to our neighborhood Starbucks. Asked permission. Then put up a big box. Another box parked on the other side of the register solicited donations for a seventeen-year-old's similar idea. Both boxes were filled with stuffed animals and bears!

The message? People want to give. Those girls not only served but provided a tangible vehicle for others to serve.

Another humble servant is my friend Cynthia. She's a maniac for service, always quietly taking care of people. I asked her what their family was doing to serve this season. "We've had a superhard week," she said, "and I just don't think I'm going to get around to serving."

Later I learned that Cynthia, who "isn't serving," had arranged for a group of at least twenty to meet on Saturday morning to wrap gifts for Brother Bill's, the same organization we'd donated the coloring books and markers to—a fabulous agency that has served the poorest zip code in Dallas for the last seventy years.

Serving is so engrained in Cynthia's life, she had no idea all she had done or does. To our delight, she let us in on the gig. We were as blessed as those kids will be when they open gifts on Christmas Eve. The greatest part? It was all behind the scenes.

I especially like to include the kids in opportunities like this because, as much as possible, I'd like to see them serving anonymously. Behind-the-scenes generosity helps us avoid the temptation to focus on and celebrate our own efforts. When we allow the spotlight to turn toward us, it diminishes the sweet flavor of serving.

The first question which the priest and the Levite asked was: "If I stop to help this man, what will happen to me?" But the good Samaritan reversed the question: "If I do not stop to help this man, what will happen to him?"

—MARTIN LUTHER KING JR.

This truth is affirmed by yet another tip found in Scripture. Jesus said, "But when you give to the needy, do not let your left hand know what your right hand is doing, so that your giving may be in secret. Then your Father, who sees what is done in secret, will reward you" (Matthew 6:3–4). Though the passage doesn't specify the promised reward, from my perspective it's deeper intimacy with the Lord—a much greater treat than any praise this world has to offer. It's so nice that he knows how tempted we are to think we're pretty great. So many of our problems go back to that pride issue, that "it's all about me" perspective we're so purposefully working against in our Experiment.

Washed in Humility

Today's act of service left me humbled. And a bit breathless.

I wasn't quite sure what to expect when we entered the tiny apartment, in which an air mattress served many purposes as the only piece of furniture. But nothing in the warm welcome we received hinted at the fact that Rocky had lost his job and that his family had been kicked out of their temporary-living-situation hotel room.

We stood in awe of this sweet family. Living day to day, not knowing what's around the corner, or where they will live. We were inspired by their determination to make it through this difficult season. And we were grateful to our friend Vincent, who not only runs the vibrant YBC after-school program for kids in the neighborhood (the one where Boxster found summer employment) but has started a church to minister to families whose lives have been touched by the center.

Vincent's own story of redemption is incredible. Several years ago, after having been targeted by a group of drug dealers looking for their next top salesman, he stood in front of a judge who, by the grace of God alone, gave Vincent one last chance. Knowing exactly who was behind that free ride, Vince dedicated his life to learning, serving, sharing, and teaching others about Christ.

He went to live with his aunt, finished school, and came to Dallas to attend Dallas Theological Seminary. Now he tends his corner of the world on Stults Road, ever ready to aid those who find themselves in need of some serious help. People like Rocky and his family.

Rocky needed sixty dollars to cover the past-due bill at the hotel where his family had been living until they were evicted for nonpayment. Plus, they hoped to find financial help with the deposit for an apartment in the area. He went to the church next door. No go. Then to the church on the other side of Vince. No go. He ended up at Vincent's center, having no idea this after-school program was connected to a church.

Vince, who wasn't there, asked his assistant Jessica, when she called him, how much the family needed to finish out the week.

"One hundred thirty dollars," she replied.

"Pay it all," Vince responded. "And ask him to fill out a wish list. We want that family to know they're loved at Christmas."

That's where our family came into play. We've helped Vince's families in the past. Even though we've been a bit service inundated this month, I had checked in with him by e-mail to see if we could help in any way.

"Vince, do you have anyone we can get gifts for this year?"

"We're not doing it like we've done before. That was too crazy. Too much focus on the stuff and not on God. But I might have someone who needs some loving. I'll get back with you."

Within a day, Vince e-mailed me Rocky's information. This family was not a member of Vince's church or enrolled in YBC's after-school program. They just needed help. And Vince, who is always looking outward, stepped up.

I called my neighborhood Bible study group. They pitched in. We divvied up the wish list. Some went to Target, some Wal-Mart, some Sam's Club. Several met at our house so the kids could wrap the gifts. Afterward, we went to the complex to deliver the goods. My kids, who might have started to grow numb to the act of serving, found their enthusiasm rejuvenated by the other families involved. For a few of the young people, this was a whole new experience, much different from dropping donations off at a church or at the food bank collection box at NorthPark mall. This meant getting personally and physically involved, going to a family's home, walking into an empty apartment, shaking hands with the recipients (two of whom were also kids), and seeing firsthand the hardship of unemployment.

This family couldn't be written off as slackers. No, they were giving it their all but had landed in a tough spot. I watched our kids, most of whom view furniture as a given, absorb the sight of a single air mattress serving as both couch and bed. I also witnessed one of our Bible study families, a crew currently in the midst of difficult circumstances, reach beyond their own hurt at home and extend love to someone in a different kind of tough situation.

The power of compassion and service extends far beyond the recipient; it always touches the one who is serving.

That day Rocky and his family were loved. We prayed with them and asked them to come enjoy a Christmas Eve service at Vince's church. They knew in whose name we were there. Maybe at the service they would hear the story in full.

As with all our service tasks, when we left that apartment, a feeling of humility descended upon Jon and me. While the kids were chatting in the backseat, we were overwhelmed by God's kindness to allow us the opportunity to serve and to be a part of the amazing way he cares for people. We stopped the car and prayed for this family. The kids participated; one even thanked God for allowing us the ability to help. They, too, were humbled. It's beautiful to be a small cog in God's great plan to love someone.

The breathless part came as we were blown away by the enormity of it all. A family with absolutely nothing. Living in an apartment complex filled with families in similar situations. All our seemingly small acts of service added together don't come close to being a drop in the bucket of satisfying the immensity of people's need. How can you fix it all? How can you provide for all those needs? How can you take care of everyone?

We can't.

But there is One who can and literally does. For whatever reason, in his infinite capacity to love, he uses us. What's *our* role, then? I think it requires several things from us. We're learning, and the kids are learning, about the importance of being available. If we're racing around and our calendars are full, it's hard to find the time to share God's love. The next requirement is keeping our eyes and hearts open. It's hard to see opportunities to serve when we're blinded by our own needs. I've loved watching the kids realize that what they tend to consider necessities really fall into the category of luxuries. In fact, their eyes see more than mine. We're all learning a lot about the third prerequisite for being used by God: being obedient to act when you feel the nudge. One time the kids saw someone who looked like he needed help. By the time they got around to telling me and we then circled back, he was gone. It was a good lesson to follow through in the moment rather than wait.

So our job is to open up, listen up, follow up, and follow through. The kids have learned that when they do, it sure feels good. Lots better than making life be about themselves.

WHAT THEY LEARNED THIS MONTH

- Serving forces our eyes off ourselves. When eyes are focused outward, inward health is cultivated.
- Forget Monster, Red Bull, or whatever energy drink is in vogue. If you're looking for a lasting buzz, let serving give you a big shot of energy.
- Serving is completely counterintuitive. It's opposite of what society heralds (competitive success, winning, striving) but results in what the world longs for (peace, contentment, happiness).

WHAT I LEARNED THIS MONTH

- Serving all but extinguished the kids' desires for "things." All of them wanted less for Christmas, without my manipulating such response.
- Available, obedient, silent serving—the kind where no credit is sought or earned—offers almost palpable intimacy with God.

Ladies and Gentlemen

Minding Our Manners

> Manners are a sensitive awareness of the
> feelings of others. If you have that awareness,
> you have good manners, no matter what fork
> you use.
>
> —EMILY POST

In his 1912 play *Pygmalion,* George Bernard Shaw offered a wonderful definition of manners: "The great secret, Eliza, is not having bad manners or good manners or any other particular sort of manners, but having the same manner for all human souls: in short, behaving as if you were in Heaven, where there are no third-class carriages, and one soul is as good as another."[1]

Our goal for this month is to introduce manners. Well, reintroduce and hopefully give meaning to topics that teach us how to live in community with and behave properly toward others. I want the kids to learn that things like holding open a door for another person, properly setting a table, politely engaging in conversation those with whom we come into contact are all important aspects of life.

Our efforts will begin at home with the meal manners (food passing, table setting, seating ladies, and such), interpersonal politeness (etiquette on the Internet, over the phone, and in person with adults and peers), and other basics such as thankfulness, looking people in the eye, and using appropriate language. Much of this we already do, but we'll be giving special attention to some things we've overlooked or become careless about.

Letitia Baldrige, White House social secretary during the Kennedy administration, wrote a terrific overview of the whys and hows of basic etiquette in her book *More Than Manners! Raising Today's Kids to Have Kind Manners and Good Hearts.* She's quick to point out that the learning of manners begins at home. And it's not so much the acts in themselves that matter but the heart attitude behind them. She begins her work by pointing out the exact concerns we've been attempting to address through the Experiment:

> With the increasing erosion of human values in our society, it's time we stopped the hand-wringing and actually started to do something about our kids. If we adopt a mind-set of paying attention to what children are seeing, doing, and saying, and match it up with how we want them to be when they step from childhood into adulthood, and talk to them about it, and show them that high moral standards are not simply material for stand-up comics to make fun of, but for real people to live their lives by, we might succeed.
>
> Never has our society seemed more inward directed and in need of real change in our relations to one another. But we can help turn that around.

How nice to know we're not the only ones frustrated with the current state of affairs. She goes on to say this about manners:

There are many rules of etiquette that have only to do with form and presentation, such as forks go to the left and knives and spoons to the right of the plate in a place setting. (It's efficient and it looks good that way.) Then there are manners and goodwill toward others, which have little to do with form and presentation and *everything to do with the heart.* I like a definition supplied by a high school junior, a young man who was also captain of the school wrestling team: "A kind heart and kind manners mean you don't hurt feelings and you make other people feel good."[2]

I couldn't agree more. We'll go through the motions when it comes to presenting good manners, but it's the kind heart I care about. Who knew this task would be such a nice complement to our month of service?

What's Behind It All?

The resistance to certain behaviors required by proper etiquette has been a bit intense.

"Open the door for your sister," I instructed Fury as we piled into the car to pick up Snopes from volleyball practice.

He stared at me in disbelief while considering how exactly he could navigate a car door while jumping in first to nab his coveted seat next to Jack and eat his bag of Goldfish all at the same time. He's talented. I knew he could do it.

"Why?" My directive was apparently putting a kink in his plan.

"Because ladies go first."

"Why?"

"Because…it's the polite, proper way to act."

"Who made *that* up?"

"I don't know… Emily Post maybe? It actually goes back to the way men should treat women, which is to cherish them, to care for them."

"That's gross."

"Well, that's what we're going to practice. And chew with your mouth closed. *That's* what's gross."

"When do I get to go first?" he asked, completely ignoring the request to keep his food noises to himself.

Isn't that at the heart of all our entitlement issues? The obsession with being first in everything? Searching for significance through achievement and self-promotion, ending up ahead and on top?

Though we've just come off an undeniable high (even the usual naysayers can't deny the power of serving), the crew doesn't seem to be ready to accept that at the heart of good manners lies the same principle they found so rewarding: putting others' interests ahead of your own. Come to think of it, putting others' interest ahead of our own just might be the hidden theme behind almost all our tasks. Even behind work itself.

Consider, for a moment, how much humility comes into play when cooking for others, pumping gas, running errands, folding your brother's laundry, or picking up the wet towel someone abandoned on the bathroom floor. As we've progressed through the Experiment, as they've allowed work to genuinely become a part of their lives, I've noticed an overall change, gradual but certain. The moaning and groaning has ceased to take center stage. It's still present but tends to be in the wings and less noisy. Well, maybe equally noisy, but definitely shorter lived.

When we started out, I didn't expect all the side benefits I've been witnessing. What was born out of frustration with my unintentionally overindulged kids has become an interesting case study in the myriad benefits associated with equipping. The biggest of these being the kids' capacity to see beyond their own immediate desires and look instead to the needs of others. Again, it takes us back to the second greatest commandment: "Love your neighbor as yourself." That's the secret behind it all. Really. *All* of it. So simple...yet such a staggering challenge.

Though we've traveled miles closer to our destination of fully equipped, self-disciplined, personal accountability, the kids are proving their need to continue trekking onward as we start our last month of tasks. Succumbing rather than embracing might best describe their approach to the task of minding their manners. For me, trying to stay on top of manners amid all our other activities is quite the challenge, mostly because of my tendency to forget my role as the Enforcer.

Until I'm pulled back into reality.

"I'm starving," announced Snopes after she grumped into the car. Apparently, it's all about food around here.

"What did you have for lunch?" I asked.

"Nothing."

"Was it gross?" I asked, referring to her effort to spice up a sack lunch.

"No. I for—"

"Hey, Mom!" This from the backseat. "Mom! Hey, Mom!"

"What happened? You forgot it?"

"Mommm! Hey, Mom! I *have* to be at school at seven fifteen tomorrow!"

"Yes," Snopes answered.

"I'm so sorry, honey. How about if we—"

"Hey, Mom! Mommm!"

"Okay. Who's doing that—the completely interrupting me thing?"

"It was me," Barton confessed.

"Well, stop. Did you hear me having a conversation? I'm a person, you know. When I'm talking, I might like to finish a sentence before changing track. I'll answer you when I'm done."

"Okay."

New to our growing list of manners to master: don't interrupt people when they're talking.

I think I forget to enforce common courtesies like "don't interrupt" because they happen day in and day out. I remember correcting the kids when they were younger. But somewhere along the way, they've drifted into some bad habits, and I've forgotten to remind them. I realize it's not deliberate rudeness; the kids just get caught up in their own thoughts and forget that someone might be thinking about something other than them.

Yet again, I was hit squarely in the eyes with the principle behind most manners: considering others ahead of yourself. I decided to drive home that point. "When you interrupt someone, you're basically implying that what you have to say is more important than what they do."

"I didn't mean to."

"Well, I'm sure you didn't. But we're all going to try to wait for people to finish talking before we jump in."

Silence.

Apparently, I'd shut her down. Yes, she's moving into full tweendom, the place where a few constructive words lead to silence. Any potential learning opportunity obliterated by hurt feelings. My best solution is to insulate my own feelings, act like an adult, and keep on keepin' on.

Later, during family dinner at a restaurant, Boxster rocked. He and

Expert Advice: The Basics of Etiquette

Former managing editor of *Today's Parent,* Dan Bortolotti, identifies manners as one of the "10 Things Your Teen Needs to Know":

> While etiquette standards constantly change, basic politeness and courtesy are never old-fashioned. Teach your teen to take off his baseball cap in a restaurant. Get him to phone his grandparents to thank them for the birthday gift. Make sure he understands that the language he uses around his friends may not be appropriate at work.[3]

Barton agreed to share a Dr Pepper (one can, two glasses of ice). Instead of hogging it all, he took her glass and filled it to the brim (who is this kid!) and even gave Jack a few sips. When his sister didn't like what was on her plate, he shared some of his coveted chicken quesadillas. He even let her sit in the front seat on the way home. I couldn't believe it.

Who knows where good manners will show up next? But you can rest assured, they are always about putting others first.

COTILLION

If I wasn't already convinced of my enabling issues, last night clinched my good-standing status in the Let Me Do It for You Club—all thanks to Cotillion.

Cotillion: The rite of passage for many young people who grudgingly submit themselves to etiquette coaches who do Emily Post proud. From learning how to dance to considering proper cell phone use and knowing the positioning and use of tableware, all facets of foundational social graces are addressed in Jon D. Williams's six-week session, which Boxster was forced to attend.

Believe it or not (and certainly said child would fall into the "not" camp), it has been great. Worth every penny. As is usually the case, kids tend to appreciate direction given by someone other than their parents. Add to the mix a room full of other kids gleaning the same etiquette tips, and the stage is set for learning lifelong lessons. But each Wednesday night, we hit a bit of a high-stress level when the doorbell announces the arrival of the Cotillion carpool. With the ride at the door last night, my son and I stared at each other without a clue how to knot the necktie that's supposed to adorn his proper attire. Considering we're five weeks into the program, you'd think one of us would have learned by now.

Here's where enabling enters the picture. And let's not forget my procrastination issues, which led to the "we'll remember to get Dad to teach us next week" excuse. Next week has come and gone *five* times. Thank

goodness for the kid in the carpool who has been doing it for us. But tonight, no such luck. Superknot Kid has hopped a different carpool.

"Where's Dad?" (Typical question. Teens think everyone should be
at their beck and call.)

"Well, he's not here."

"Mom! My tie!"

We both eyed the J.Crew strands draped around his neck.

"I don't know *how* to tie a tie," I reminded him.

"What am I going to do? I can't go without my tie done. Everyone
will make fun of me."

He's right. Kids can be mean, especially teenagers eager to distract
attention from their own imperfections.

"Let's YouTube it. There's got to be a video." The mom driving carpool felt our pain. Relieved that her husband had made it home from
work in time to handle her own kid's tie issues, she was happy to wait.

And there it was. "How to Tie a Windsor Knot." We watched it together. Then proceeded to follow each step, just like the guy demonstrated. Right side longer than the left, loop over, then under, a little twist.

Umm—no go.

I don't get it. How can the guy on the video make it look so easy, yet
when I do *exactly* what he shows, there is no knot. Just a clump. And why
am *I* flipping one side of the tie over the other? Why isn't the kid doing
it? Why didn't he ask his dad to teach him how to tie a tie? *Why didn't
Dad initiate teaching his kid to tie a tie?*

I composed myself.

Learning how to tie a tie may be an art passé—not on the front
burner in these days of casual wear—but that's not the issue. The issue is,
my child had settled into "how can you serve me" mode. Instead of learning how to do it himself, he's been content to let his friend knot his tie. In
fairness, I should mention that Superknot Kid was taking care of everyone's tie, not just my boy's.

Here's a shout-out to the dad who equipped the now-popular tie-knotting boy, whose self-esteem has been supersized by getting to display his vast knowledge of stylish dressing. And here's a note to self: especially in situations of the social type, equip your kid.

I hope that someday soon Boxster will be empowered to figure out even the small things like fixing his tie. But I also hope that his dad and I realize that what seem like small, insignificant, easy-to-postpone, even unimportant tasks still pack quite a punch in the lesson arena. Yet again we've communicated the wrong message to our kid: "Rely on someone else to get you through rather than do it yourself."

This particular equipping opportunity fell flat. The kid's tie resembled a wad rather than a knot. But he went and he survived. I relayed the events to Jon when he arrived home later. His solution? Get a clip-on.

I think we know who needs Cotillion!

Manners on the Move

My friend Lynne has her kids doing three simple activities this month, all of which happen to be based on manners. I saw their work in action in carpool today:

1. *Address adults by name and look them in the eye.* "Hi, Mrs. Wyma," said a normally silent young man as he got in the car after school. I missed the looking in the eye part since I was trying to drive.

2. *Thank people by name.* "Thanks for the ride, Mrs. Wyma." I've been driving the kid for years and have never heard much more than a peep from him. I was more than a little surprised by the cheerful and sincere gratitude. So much so, I placed an inquiring phone call to his mother, which is how I learned about her activity of the month and the third requirement...

3. *Answer a question with a question.* Adult: "Hi, Bobby. How are you today?" Kid: "Hello, Mrs. Wyma. I'm doing well. How are you?"

Such a great idea! As a mom, I love this plan. Three simple things to get her kids focused on someone besides themselves through manners. As a recipient, I was pleasantly surprised and touched.

I've seen noticeable results from this month's focus on good manners in our family as well.

When the family piled into the car on Sunday, Boxster graciously opened the door and again let his sister sit in the front seat—all without a single word from me. I could barely believe it! I guess my manner talks haven't all fallen on deaf ears. Boy, did I gush—on the inside. He doesn't like too much attention. But on the sly, I caught his eye and gave him a thank-you wink.

Later when we arrived at the mall and needed to hop on an elevator, once again the kid let the others go in ahead of himself. A conspicuous change from the usual mad dash, like the rest of the crew, to see who could press the button first. Granted he's a bit older and really couldn't care less about punching the button, but it sure was nice to see him at least considering the idea of manners.

With an audience captive inside the elevator, I seized the opportunity for another minilecture on manners. "Now it's always nice to let the ladies in the elevator get out first."

"Why?"

"Well...because."

"What if the elevator is on fire?" asked Fury. "Am I supposed to just burn up while the girls go first?"

"No. And I highly doubt the elevator will be on fire."

"If it is," piped in Boxster, "you have to crawl out the top because there's no way you're getting out the door."

Everyone looks up.

"Where's the door for the top?" Snopes was sounding nervous. "I don't see a door. What's out there? Will someone come help us? *Are we going to burn?*"

"We're *not* going to burn," I assure them.

"I'm scared," said Barton.

"Me too!" By this point Snopes was yelling.

The bell for our floor dinged and the door opened. So much for letting others out first. Waiting riders quickly edged away to avoid being trampled by the kids as they raced to exit the box of certain death.

Oh well. At least we saw *some* manner action.

The *whys* are interesting, though. Why do the ladies get to go first? Why should a man give a woman his seat on the bus or train? Why are the women served first at a swanky restaurant? Why is the fork on the left and knife on the right? Why do you have to write thank-you notes? Why? Why? Why? Why? Why? I'm being peppered like never before with inquiries.

And most of the time, I don't have answers. But at the core of it all still lies the principle of putting other's concerns ahead of our own.

Whether it's racing to the car and staking claim on the front seat (though I'm not sure why any of them would want to be in such close

Expert Advice: Emotional Intelligence

In her article "Whatever Happened to Manners," parent Jane St. Clair observes,

> "Emotional intelligence" or the ability to put yourself in another person's place is being studied as a measure for success every bit as important as academic intelligence. What parents need to do is teach teens to control their reactions to rudeness as a matter of survival: especially when driving or in public places with strangers. But teens should also learn to treat friends, family and co-workers with kindness, decency and forgiveness.[4]

range to the driver and her ever-present lectures) or grabbing the best roll off the plate before someone else can get it, most etiquette-related gaffes center on selfishness.

Our progress toward others-centered living continues in fits and starts, as evidenced by the conversation that took place when it was time to get in the car and head home from the mall.

"You go first."

"No, *you* go first."

"No! You go first."

"That's not fair. *You go first!*"

"Mommm!"

Hmm. Is there such a thing as being too polite?

LIFE SECRET

Our back-to-back tasks of serving and manners have proven to be two critically important activities. Not only have they taught the kids life-enhancing truth based on putting others ahead of self, but they have also helped smooth the bumpy teen road of self-obsession. During a phase of life when kids can hardly help but be consumed with themselves, these two activities just might provide the secret to sanity.

At the core of today's youth entitlement problem is a generation of kids and young adults convinced—dare we admit, trained to believe—that the world does, in fact, revolve around them. The simple remedy: teach them to consider others ahead of themselves. Start young, on the playground. Find the kid no one will talk to and send yours over to chat. Why fight to be in the popular crowd when all it leads to is self-absorption? A little time with the "left out" gang does wonders for the soul.

I've been amazed to see that consideration toward others forms the basis of almost all the tasks we've implemented in the Experiment. Each assignment redirected the kids' attention off themselves and onto the world around them. Whether it was making their beds ("My friends really do like playing in a clean room better"), cooking dinner, washing and putting away clothes, cleaning the bathrooms, vacuuming, or the 100 percent others-oriented tasks of hospitality, serving, and manners, the kids learned to get outside themselves and consider for a moment the people with whom they share life. Even though they moaned and groaned and protested the unfairness of their plight, by the end of each project, they were less self-absorbed, more fully dimensional people.

Worth considering as we close out our twelfth month.

WHAT THEY LEARNED THIS MONTH

- Letting your sister go first won't kill you.
- Manners are more than "please" and "thank you."
- Practicing good etiquette prompts respectful attention and admiration from adults.

WHAT I LEARNED THIS MONTH

- YouTube can be extremely helpful in a pinch—if, of course, you actually have time to incorporate what you learn while siblings are screaming and the carpool is waiting.
- Only so many "whys" can be answered with "because."
- Though society has become increasingly casual, it's important to teach our kids that kindness and good manners never go out of style.

A Clean Sweep

Tossing Out Entitlement for Good

> I took the one less traveled by,
> And that has made all the difference.
>
> —ROBERT FROST

As Jack and I were on the way to school, fulfilling my role as that day's designated carpool driver, my car was hit. Our little line of vehicles had been waiting behind a car trying to turn left when— *Wham!*—out of the blue the vehicle behind me plowed into mine, which in turn bumped the car in front of me. I was the meat in a wreck sandwich. Knowing that I'd never arrive on time, I called in a sister favor to my friend Lynne, who grabbed the crew from school while I was stuck waiting for the police.

While passing the time, I got acquainted with my fellow crashers: Sam, the kid who had caused our wreck, and Phil, a pest-control specialist whose company vehicle, full of all his pest-killing stuff, had been at the front of our little pileup.

Sam, a supersharp young man, felt terrible. Within minutes of the crash, he was out of his car, insurance card in hand, eager to take responsibility, not make excuses or dish out blame. He was so worried that Jack or I might have been hurt. Thankfully, the jolt did nothing more than hurl the Future Hoarder of America's treasures (today a set of jacks, a stuffed penguin, and some golf balls) from their safe spot in his car seat. Sam's next action, which I especially loved, was to call his folks.

As we stood on the curb waiting for the police to finish with Sam, the pest-control guy and I talked quietly.

"Do you have kids?" I asked as we peeked in the car to check on Jack.

"Yes ma'am. I've got two." While I appreciated his politeness, especially after our month of manners, he wasn't *that* much younger than me and could have left off the "ma'am."

"How old are they?"

"Twelve and thirteen."

"Oh…" I raised my eyebrows in empathy.

"Yes ma'am. It's a bit more work than I ever would have imagined."

He went on to tell me that his kids, especially his son, have been a challenge. Not just their laziness and lack of effort, but also their incessant asking for things, like games, shoes, clothes. Even though his kid apparently has every gaming system and every game for every gaming system, he wants the new Xbox latest and greatest thing. Forget about the cost.

"He thinks I can go in the backyard and take the money off trees," Phil lamented. "When I was his age, I had a job at Minyards bagging groceries. I didn't ask my parents for money all the time or spend like crazy. I liked making money and having my own things."

I couldn't believe it; he was saying exactly what I've been thinking.

He continued, "I don't know what's going on with kids these days. They lie around and expect us to buy them everything. I don't know what it will be like in a few years, but if they keep it up, it's not going to be good."

He paused for a moment, then went on, "I think a lot of it is my fault. I don't push him. It's just…well, I'm a divorced dad. I only get to see them on the weekends, and all I want to do is say yes. Saying no is better, but it sure is hard."

I can't tell you how comforting it was to hear this pest-control guy share his story. Yet again I was reminded that we are all in this together. Saying no, requiring our kids to work hard is difficult for a lot of us. It's not a socioeconomic issue, confined to only certain groups; it's rampant across a generation.

I know some families have this stuff under control. They have kids who work hard, maybe even have paycheck-earning jobs. But for us recovering enablers, it's nice to know we aren't alone in the trenches. "No" and "work for it yourself" will absolutely pay off, though it may take a while for the new reality to penetrate into the psyche of apathetic, entitled kids.

The truth is, that seemingly disinterested kid is actually very interested. He's just mastered the skill of hiding it. He has even fooled himself into believing he doesn't care, but it's not true. I've watched my kids move from disinterest to engagement, performance, and genuine interest. They like the rewards of independence, and as they (and I) recognize their vast capacity for responsibility, it nurtures a desire to accomplish more. If we can start saying no, equip them for accountability, then get out of the way—I can't wait to watch them soar.

OUR NEW NORMAL

We've now completed our one-year Experiment in conquering entitlement and nurturing personal responsibility. Sadly, I need a few more months—probably more like years—to finish the job. Okay, so it never ends. At least around here, with our youngest now four, we've got lots more equipping years ahead of us. I'd add them up, but that would involve too much effort and too many of my precious remaining brain cells. Plus, according to my kids, I don't do math.

Bottom line: we'll be staying the course and requiring our kids to live up to their capabilities.

Yesterday, I told the kids that we'll end the Experiment with a day or two of them doing *everything*. I think I will put tasks in a jar and let them draw out a job, then prove they can do it. This could be challenging for a few of them, especially the ones who would rather pay someone else to do it for them. As I mentioned earlier, my sister jokes that all problems in life are a staffing issue. I have a few kids who would agree.

Amid a chorus of moans, I said, "Hey! We've almost made it a year. Think of all the tasks we've done—that *you* have done!"

"Great. Now it's over. We can go back to normal," Boxster replied, relieved.

"Oh no, honey. We have a new normal."

The barrage of groans, eye rolls, and an obligatory "Mommm!" left me unmoved.

"Moan and groan all you want. I've talked with your dad about doing a little something special to celebrate all we've accomplished." (I had told Jon I thought a trip to Disney World was in order; we've never taken the kids there. His response? A gasp and, "I was thinking more along the lines of Sonic.")

"Yes!" said an excited Barton. "I know exactly what our reward can be! We can get one of those Slurpee coupons you got us a few years ago." Little did she know those coupons weren't from me but were an incentive from the Dallas Public Library summer reading program. Apparently her dad's frugality has rubbed off on her.

Looking back on our year, I wonder, *Have we accomplished anything?* Oh, I hope so. In fact, I know we have, but I also know we have a long way to go. It's a work in progress—kind of like me.

Well Worth the Effort

I launched the Experiment with the goal of clearing out entitlement attitudes by helping my kids become familiar with and proficient at basic household duties. It grew into so much more. Two glaring lessons stare me in the face as I consider our yearlong battle against entitlement: (1) less of self and (2) doing for others. These are the tactics that lead to lasting victory. The self-centered perspective of entitlement can't flourish in a person who values and is considerate of others.

I also gained a deeper understanding of why work matters, for all of us. Initially, I required the kids to do the work simply for the sake of accomplishing a task and broadening their capabilities. Well, that and I was sick of the clutter. But rather quickly I recognized the deeper meaning behind work, the essence of why work is and needs to be an integral part of all our lives.

Dorothy Sayers explored the sacramental nature of work in her essay "Why Work":

> I have already, on a previous occasion, spoken at some length on the subject of Work and Vocation. What I urged then was a thoroughgoing revolution in our whole attitude to work. I asked that it should be looked upon, not as a necessary drudgery to be undergone for the purpose of making money, but as a way of life in which the nature of man should find its proper exercise and delight and so fulfill itself to the glory of God. That it should, in fact, be thought of as a creative activity under taken for the love of the work itself; and that man, made in God's image, should make things, as God makes them, for the sake of doing well a thing that is well worth doing.[1]

I couldn't agree more. Rather than moan and groan about how entitled kids are these days, let's equip them to work hard and let's seek out creative ways to help them embrace the value of meaningful work. Then at the end of what most certainly will be a long road, most likely a countercultural road, we can sit on our front porches (sweet tea in hand) and watch them soar. I'm convinced, because I've watched it work, that when you teach your kids how to do things, then sit back and let them go, they will reach for and achieve goals much higher than any parent would have set.

So I saw that there is nothing better for a man than to enjoy his work, because that is his lot. For who can bring him to see what will happen after him?

—ECCLESIASTES 3:22

So often we look to world, civic, and political leaders to solve societal challenges. The future world shapers are sitting at our dinner tables, able and ready (though likely hesitant) to fulfill their role. These kids—our kids—will be the ones who take all the technological advances, pair them with confidence gained through years of pushing boundaries, and change the world for good. Simple daily work and other-centered tasks pave the way for just such achievements.

Culture doesn't determine who people become. People determine what the culture will be. Might our equipped, empowered, unentitled kids be the ones who set the course for the future.

Author's Note:
How the Experiment Began

Sitting at my dining room table across from a friend, I bemoaned my lack of experience, skill, and knowledge of how to parent my budding teens. As with most parents I know, this gig ranks high on my "What's Important in Life" list. Few goals hold a higher priority for me than loving and training my kids well.

So as I considered the myriad challenges of this daunting endeavor (complicated emotions, frequent arguments, dating, not dating, appropriate clothing, music, movies, friends), I told my friend how badly I needed a MOTS (Mothers of Teens) group. In earlier years when I was stuck at home with a load of toddlers, a wonderful ministry called MOPS (Mothers of Preschoolers) provided so much encouragement and helpful direction. I longed for similar support in parenting my teens, for counselors and companions to travel the road with me. I craved the sage voices of experience, speaking wisdom into my busy day so I can gauge situations and prioritize according to their actual significance, not what I fear them to be. I needed someone to assure me that frequent bursts of tears are normal for a preteen girl. That a high percentage of teen boys have hair fetishes. That constant and inane arguments are standard operating procedure for a kid figuring out who he is and what he thinks. I wanted someone to point out the red-flag concerns, the danger zones and lies that trick kids into thinking the world would be a better place without them in it.

The problem with all this? There is no MOTS. And if there was, who has time to go to a meeting? As I described to my friend the sense of frustration and isolation, the solution hit me. "Hey, all the thirtysomethings and younger people do life through blogs. Why don't we? I'd be happy to get guest bloggers to post about some pertinent parenting-teens topic if we can get the word out for people to read." She agreed it was a good idea, and the TheMOATblog.com was born.

I figured we needed a little spice to attract an audience. And since we'd also been talking about the ongoing challenge of getting our kids to pick up their stuff, I thought it might be fun to come up with a strategy to teach my kids some basic life skills and document it along the way. From that initial idea grew the Experiment—and eventually, this book.

I quickly learned I wasn't alone in my parenting predicaments because thousands of people have tuned in to read the blog. People also tuned in to hear from the fabulous guest bloggers who countered my off-the-cuff ideas with hard-won wisdom about meeting the challenges of parenting with grace and humor.

Our family is a work in progress, that's for sure. If nothing else, we provide comic relief. Jon has teased me that people tune into the blog partly for the guest posts but mostly for the same reason some people watch NASCAR: the wrecks. We've got plenty of those. But now we also have several hands to help pick up the pieces—several capable and equipped young hands. I hope to see you over at TheMOATblog.com, where we can encourage one another through the difficult times and rejoice over our breakthroughs.

Meanwhile, thanks for walking the road with me.

Kay

ACKNOWLEDGMENTS

Sitting at my dining room table two years ago, my mother-of-teens, commiserating friend Lauren Greer encouraged me to start a blog. My thirty-something friend Chrys Mundy helped with the nuts and bolts and got it launched. Who knew it would lead to a book? I'm grateful to those who thought it might and encouraged me to try.

Thanks to my sister Kathy for introducing me to her friends the Wolgemuths, who took a chance on representing an often flakey mom and accidental author. Thanks to Erik Wolgemuth for the countless hours logged on this one, for listening to me ramble and for endlessly encouraging.

Thanks to sweet Laura Barker for taking my words and making them sound better, because along with being a recovering enabler, procrastinator, manipulator, controller, forgetter (sorry for those I'll forget to thank!), and so much more, I'm a grammar hacker.

Thanks to friends like Jane Jarrell, Chuck and Ann Bentley, Ann and Bob Silva, Nancy Brown, Alex Wagner, Marcy Sosnowski, Chris Wills, Elizabeth Stewart, Tanya McCullough, Lynn Campbell, Jennifer Royall, Leslie Merrick, Melissa McDonald, Lynne Schott, Julie Fairchild, Christine Sitton, Bronson Stocker, and Nancy Lovell—all of whom I've tapped more often than they would like to admit.

Thanks to all my MOAT friends who have walked the road with me (it sure would be lonely alone!) and to the terrific guest bloggers and advisors who have shared their wisdom.

Thanks to my family. My mom and dad, Sue and Don Wills, for setting the bar high, for helping me clear the heights, for catching me when I fell. To my brothers, Charles and David, and their spouses, Paula and Chris (you get two mentions, girl!), who are there for me when I call. Thanks to Dick Wyma, a steady source of inspiration and encouragement.

A special word of thanks to my husband, Jon, the most trustworthy person I know, and to my amazing children. Words can't begin to describe the amount of love and admiration I feel for these people. I am honored to know them, let alone to live life with them.

If there is any truth or wisdom in this book, it isn't mine. I'm just along for the ride. All wisdom within is supplied by the Author of truth. He has so much more to share and gives generously without finding fault (see James 1). Check it out sometime. We read the New International Version (1984) around our house.

NOTES

Introduction: The Epiphany

1. Theodore Roosevelt, "The Strenuous Life" (speech, Hamilton Club, Chicago, April 10, 1899), Theodore Roosevelt Association: Speeches, www.theodoreroosevelt.org/research/speech%20strenuous.htm.
2. Emily Flynn Vencat, "Narcissists in Neverland," *Newsweek*, as posted on The Daily Beast, October 15, 2007, www.thedailybeast.com/news week/2007/10/15/narcissists-in-neverland.html.
3. Larry Gordon and Louis Sahagun, "Gen Y's Ego Trip Takes a Bad Turn," *Los Angeles Times,* February 27, 2007, http://articles.latimes .com/2007/feb/27/local/me-esteem27.
4. Emily Bennington, "Let Your Kids Fail," HuffingtonPost.com, August 7, 2011, www.huffingtonpost.com/mobileweb/1969/12/31 /helicopter-parents_n_873368.html.

Task 1: Operation Clutter Control

1. Definitions are from Dictionary.com; explanatory sentences are the author's.
2. This theory was introduced by Maxwell Maltz, *Psycho-Cybernetics: A New Way to Get More Living Out of Life* (Englewood Cliffs, NJ: Prentice-Hall, 1960), xiii–xiv.
3. Adapted from "How to Form a Good Habit," wikiHow, www.wikihow .com/Form-a-Good-Habit.
4. Adapted with permission from Chuck Bentley, "Table Talk—Kids & Money, Part 1," www.themoatblog.com, March 3, 2010.
5. Lori Gottlieb, "How to Land Your Kid in Therapy," *The Atlantic,* July/August 2011, www.theatlantic.com/magazine/archive/2011/07 /how-to-land-your-kid-in-therapy/8555.

Task 2: Kitchen Patrol

1. Barack Obama (speech, George Mason University, March 19, 2010), The White House, www.whitehouse.gov/the-press-office /remarks-president-health-insurance-reform-fairfax-virginia.

Task 4: Working for a Living

1. Paul Scott, "The Science Behind Bonking," *Runner's World,* March 1, 2004, www.runnersworld.com/article/0,7120,s6-242-301--6263-0,00 .html.

2. Ann Burnworth, "Entitlement Culture Gives Youth Unrealistic Expectations," *Evansville Courier & Press* (Indiana), February 9, 2010, www.courierpress.com/news/2010/feb/09/entitlement-culture-gives -youth-unrealistic.

3. Fair Labor Standards Act Advisor. United States Department of Labor, www.dol.gov/elaws/faq/esa/flsa/026.htm.

4. Adapted with permission from Lisa Clark, "Table Talk: It's Summer!!! Time to...Work???!!," www.themoatblog.com, June 8, 2011, www.the moatblog.com/moatblog/2011/6/8/table-talk-its-summer-time-to-work -by-lisa-clark.html.

5. Norm O'Reilly and Rick Burton, "The Secrets of Leadership are Often Found at the Bottom," *Sports Business Daily,* June 6, 2011, www.sportsbusinessdaily.com/Journal/Issues/2011/06/06/Opinion /Burton-Oreilly-column.aspx.

Task 5: Domestic Dirty Jobs

1. Cynthia Townley Ewer, *Houseworks* (New York: Dorling Kindersley, 2006), 70.

2. Adapted with permission from Ron Harris, "Table Talk—Best Efforts," www.themoatblog.com, April 14, 2010, www.themoatblog.com /moatblog/2010/4/14/table-talk-best-efforts-by-ron-harris.html. Proverbs 21:5 is taken from the New Living Translation of the Bible.

Task 6: Roll Tide

1. Peter Walsh, as quoted on *Nate: The Nate Berkus Show,* www.the nateshow.com/videos/detail/1371/peter-walsh.

2. Mark Gregston, "The Family Citizen" on *Parenting Today's Teens,* May 28, 2010, podcast, www.heartlightministries.org/blogs/pttradio /2010/05.

3. Adapted with permission from Andy Kerckhoff, "Table Talk—Prepare Your Children, Protection and Provision Are Not Enough," www.the moatblog.com, July 15, 2010, www.themoatblog.com/moatblog/2010/7 /15/table-talk-prepare-your-children-protection-and-provision-ar.html.

4. Adapted with permission from Jody Capehart, "Table Talk—Technology & Teens, Part 1," www.themoatblog.com, April 21, 2010, www .themoatblog.com/2010/03/tab/

Task 7: The Handyman Can... Or Can He?

1. Dan A. Myers, MD, *Biblical Parenting: A Child Psychiatrist's View* (CreateSpace, 2010), 210–211.

2. Anushka Asthana, "They Don't Live for Work...They Work to Live," *The Guardian/The Observer,* May 24, 2008, www.guardian.co.uk /money/2008/may/25/workandcareers.worklifebalance.

Task 8: The Entertainers

1. Hilary Stout, "Antisocial Networking?" *New York Times,* April 30, 2010, www.nytimes.com/2010/05/02/fashion/02BEST.html?page wanted=all.

2. Max Beerbohm, "Hosts and Guests" essay in *And Even Now* (New York: E.P. Dutton & Company, 1921), 144.

Task 9: Team Players

1. Joseph R. Carroll and Burton Bernstein, "Teamwork," Talk of the Town, *New Yorker,* September 5, 1964, www.newyorker.com /archive/1964/09/05/1964_09_05_022_TNY_CARDS_000277047.

2. Steve Denning, "Cisco and the True Meaning of Teams," Forbes.com, May 10, 2011, www.forbes.com/sites/stevedenning/2011/05/10 /cisco-and-the-true-meaning-of-teams.

3. Pat Lencioni, "A Penalty for Discounting Teamwork," *Businessweek,* March 4, 2011, www.businessweek.com/managing/content/mar2011 /ca2011031_356616.htm.

4. Karl Moore, "HBS's Amy Edmondson on the Death of Teams," Forbes .com, July 19, 2011, www.forbes.com/sites/karlmoore/2011/07/19 /hbss-amy-edmonson-on-the-death-of-teams.

Task 12: Ladies and Gentlemen

1. George Bernard Shaw, *Pygmalion,* 1957 (Act V, Line 197), http://classiclit.about.com/library/bl-etexts/gbshaw/bl-gbshaw-pyg-5 .htm?p=1.

2. Letitia Baldrige, *More Than Manners! Raising Today's Kids to Have Kind Manners and Good Hearts* (New York: Scribner, 1997).

3. Dan Bortolotti, "10 Things Your Teen Needs to Know," *Today's Parent,* October 2008, www.todaysparent.com/tweens-teens /tween-teen-behaviour/10-things-your-teen-needs-know.

4. Jane St. Clair, "Whatever Happened to Manners," www.by parents-forparents.com/manners.html.

Conclusion: A Clean Sweep

1. Dorothy Sayers, *Creed or Chaos? Why Christians Must Choose Either Dogma or Disaster* (Manchester, NH: Sophia Institute, 1995), 89.